SEEING BY ELECTRICITY

SIGN, STORAGE, TRANSMISSION

A SERIES EDITED BY JONATHAN STERNE

AND LISA GITELMAN

SEEING BY ELECTRICITY

The Emergence of Television,
1878–1939

DORON GALILI

DUKE UNIVERSITY PRESS
Durham and London | 2020

© 2020 Duke University Press
All rights reserved
Printed in the United States of America on acid-free paper ∞
Designed by Jennifer Hill
Typeset in Minion Pro by Copperline Books

Library of Congress Cataloging-in-Publication Data
Names: Galili, Doron, author.
Title: Seeing by electricity : cinema, moving image transmission,
and the emergence of television, 1878–1939 / Doron Galili.
Description: Durham : Duke University Press, [2020] | Series:
Sign, storage, transmission | Includes bibliographical references
and index.
Identifiers: LCCN 2019024074 (print)
LCCN 2019024075 (ebook)
ISBN 9781478007722 (hardcover ; alk. paper)
ISBN 9781478008224 (paperback ; alk. paper)
ISBN 9781478009221 (ebook)
Subjects: LCSH: Television broadcasting—History—20th century. |
Television—History—20th century. | Motion pictures—History—
20th century.
Classification: LCC PN1992.2 .G35 2020 (print) |
LCC PN1992.2 (ebook) | DDC 385.4409—dc23
LC record available at https://lccn.loc.gov/2019024074
LC ebook record available at https://lccn.loc.gov/2019024075

Cover art: John Logie Baird's (1888–1946) first television
demonstration, 1926. Photograph taken from the screen
of his first Televisor. Universal Images Group/Getty.

To my family

CONTENTS

ACKNOWLEDGMENTS

Work on this book has spanned many years and quite a few locations, and along the way I have gathered a long list of people to whom I owe a great debt of gratitude. First and foremost, I would like to thank Yuri Tsivian for his enthusiasm, support, and constant attentiveness to the broadest historiographic concepts and the minutest details, which allowed for this research to come into being in the first place. Tom Gunning's matchless intellectual generosity and rigor and James Lastra's invaluable guidance have been crucial in inspiring and shaping this work. I am most grateful for the encouragement, advice, and friendship I have received from Jan Olsson, who told me to "always travel south!" but is nonetheless directly responsible for the fact that I am typing these words right now in Stockholm. It was an extraordinary honor to learn from four scholars like them.

I am also grateful for the Franke Institute for the Humanities' doctoral fellowship, the Dan David Prize scholarship in the field of Cinema and Society, and the postdoctoral fellowship in cinema studies at Stockholm University, which generously supported different stages of this project. To the Archive Center at the National Museum of American History and the Wayne County Historical Museum, I am thankful for allowing me to conduct research of primary sources, and to Steve McVoy and the Early Television Museum in Hilliard, Ohio, I am thankful for the rare pleasure of seeing some of the first televisual technologies in real life. In this day and age, it feels only appropriate to also thank the people responsible for web-based archival resources. I include a list of those I have consulted in the bibliography, but would like to note especially the Histoire de la télévision site by André Lange, a truly indispensable resource for media history research.

Courtney Berger and Sandra Korn at Duke University Press were extremely generous with their patience, support, and faith in this project, and I am thankful for having the opportunity to work with them. I also wish to thank the series editors, Lisa Gitelman and Jonathan Sterne, and the two anonymous readers, whose feedback improved this book a great deal. My good friends Yocheved Seidman and Avital Peres Rachmilevitch shared insightful comment on early drafts of this work, and the expertise and kindness of Bart van der Gaag and Daniel Schloss made it possible to include the images that illustrate it. I am indebted for their tremendous help.

My interest in the early history of television developed first during my days at UCLA, where I was fortunate to study under Jan-Christopher Horak, Steven Ricci, and Vivian Sobchack and to become acquainted with the exciting concept of media archeology from Erkki Huhtamo. I am deeply thankful to them, and likewise to the friendship and encouragement from Ross Melnick, Emily Carman, and Andrey Gordienko. I consider myself very lucky for the exceptional group of colleagues I had at the University of Chicago. Rad Borislavov, Lee Carruthers, Ken Eisenstein, Hannah Frank, Oliver Gaycken, Adam Hart, Matt Hauske, Jim Hodge, Andrew Johnston, Ian Jones, Sarah Keller, Diane Lewis, Katharina Loew, Bill Martin, Dan Morgan, Jason Paul, Inga Polman, Scott Richmond, Ariel Rogers, Ivan Ross, Charles Tepperman, Julie Turnock, Neil Verma, Artemis Willis, and Josh Yumibe were the brightest and friendliest colleagues anyone could wish for. I am also indebted to the support and many hours of stimulating conversations with Robert Bird, Patrick Jagoda, Françoise Meltzer, Noa Steimatsky, and Jennifer Wild, and for the encouragement and ongoing influence of Miriam Hansen. In particular, my appreciation goes out to Christina Petersen, who was literally by my side at the moment the idea of this research came into being and at the moment it finally got out of my hands. This book—and the experience of writing it—would be far poorer without her.

During my time at Oberlin College, I was lucky to teach alongside a stellar group of colleagues and friends, and to this day I remain grateful to have worked with Grace An, Rian Brown, Pat Day, Burke Hilsabeck, Geoff Pingree, and Alberto Zambenedetti. I also owe a great debt of gratitude to my friends and colleagues at Stockholm University, not only for many conversations about this research but also for making me feel at home, in the fullest sense of the word. Thank you, Marina Dahlquist, John Fullerton, Gert Jan Harkema, Trond Lundemo, Jonathan Rozenkrantz, John Sundholm, Tove Thorslund, and Patrick Vonderau. And in particular, thank you, Kim Khavar Fahlstedt, Joel Frykholm, Kristoffer Noheden, Ashley Smith, and Nadi Tofighian, for the countless pleasant hours spent together since I moved to Stockholm. I can only hope I deserve to have such good colleagues and friends as you have been.

It was a sincere pleasure to get to know and make friends with my fellow travelers in early television history. Anne-Katrin Weber has been a gracious colleague, and I benefited a great deal from her admirable research and her always-sharp criticism. Philip Sewell was extraordinarily generous with his time and insights from the second I met him, and his own work provided a model for how to study television today. I am thankful for the opportunity to have a long ongoing dialogue with William Boddy, Max Dawson, André Gaudreault, Hollis Griffin, Johannes von Moltke, Lynn Spigel, Luke Stadel, William Uricchio, and Mark Williams, who offered invaluable feedback and advice in various conferences and symposia along the years. Collaborating with Richard Koszarski on an offshoot study of television in pre-1939 films has been not only an honor and a privilege but also a priceless lesson in the art of meticulous historiographic research. That said, however, all mistakes and omissions in this book are strictly mine.

Throughout the years of writing, my colleagues Maggie Hennefeld, Laura Horak, Kristina Köhler, and Daniel Wiegand have provided a great deal of support, ideas, and fun times. As a friend, a neighbor, and a fellow scholar, Ronen Steinberg has been a role model to me for over a decade and a half now, and I still am trying my best to follow his example. David Robinson has been an infinite source of inspiration and generosity. Even if he is unlikely to agree with many of the ideas I present here, the truth remains that it is because of him that I started writing about cinema history in the first place. I owe a very special thanks also to Nick Baer. While working on this book, I had the honor of sharing with him ideas, sources, running tracks, hotel rooms, and a footnote—and it always felt like being among family. Finally, I am thankful to Boaz Hagin. Though he was formally my teacher for only one semester back in 1998, he has continued to inspire, challenge, and instruct me through the years and provided priceless comments on every single section of this research. I can only say that I have no clue how I'd have done it without him.

I dedicate this book to my family: to Lily, Danny, and Amir Galili, without whom nothing that I ever do would be even imaginable; to Anna Jörngården, whom I met while working on this project and is the best thing that ever happened or will happen to me; and to Mira Jörngården Galili, my *lilla älskling* and the real book lover of the family.

An earlier version of chapter 6 was published as "Television from Afar: Arnheim's Understanding of Media" in the anthology *Arnheim for Film and Media Studies*, edited by Scott Higgins (New York: Routledge, 2011). Several sections of chapter 2 develop ideas that appeared in an earlier version in "L'histoire des débuts de la television et les théories modernes de la vision," in the anthology *Télévision: Le moment experimental, 1935–1955*, edited by Gilles Delavaud and Denis Maréchal (Rennes: Apogée, 2011).

INTRODUCTION

The inaugural meeting of the International Institute of Educational Cinematography's Coordinating Television Committee, which took place in Nice, France, in April 1935, provided a rare opportunity to hear cinema pioneer Louis Lumière discuss the new medium of television. An honorary guest of the newly formed Committee, Lumière delivered an opening address to an audience of broadcasters, technicians, and film industry representatives who had gathered to talk about the future of television and its relationship with cinema. Lumière spoke of television's potential in an enthusiastic manner typical of the 1930s. He spoke of television as one of the technologies "which have so profoundly changed our social life in all its forms" and anticipated that it would assist in broadening humanity's knowledge. In addition to these celebratory statements, Lumière also reflected on television's place within a long lineage of older media. He noted that television is "still a novelty, but it has an ancient affiliation. Like all novelties, it arouses both skepticism and enthusiasm. As with all the culminations of old affiliations, we try to establish its origin and also its connection with the inventions and applications which preceded it."[1]

It is not unlikely that Lumière made this claim merely self-servingly in order to posit his own invention of the cinematograph in the lineage of the most recent celebrated technological marvel. But even if this was the case, his statement is still significant, for it is an early instance of inquiring about the origins of one medium by way of focusing on its relationships with other media, a method that has become fundamental in recent works in film and historiography. While his claim about the "culminations of old affiliations" maintains a sense of a historical trajectory of progress that is overall rejected today, the conception of television's "ancient affiliations" could be read as anticipating recent historiographic approaches to intermediality and in particular to studies in the field of media archaeology. What Lumière suggests at this moment of the very beginning of public television broadcasts is that the history of television is intertwined with the history of related media, hinting that its mid-1930s fruition is indebted in one way or another to the cinema.

By the time Lumière delivered his address, commentators and technicians writing on television had identified the origins of the new medium in a series of inventions and experiments involving the electric transmission of moving images which date back to the late 1870s and provided the foundations for the eventual realization of television apparatus. The appearance of these early ideas about the electrical transmission of image, known at the time as technologies for "seeing by electricity," coincided with crucial moments in what is often regarded as precinema history. During the same years as the first articles on the prospects of moving images transmission were published, figures such as Eadweard Muybridge and Émile Reynaud demonstrated advances in serial photography and the projection of animated pictures. Thus, readers of the June 1880 volume of *Scientific American* could read about Muybridge's demonstration of the zoopraxiscope, an animated photography projection device, on one page, and two pages later about a method for "seeing by electricity" using a selenium camera and a transmission device. No working television apparatus existed until several decades later, but as William Uricchio has noted, by the time cinema emerged in the late nineteenth century, "the basic conceptual problems of the technology had been resolved, and an imagined and technologically possible way of seeing at a distance was fully anticipated and articulated."[2]

However, while Lumière's 1935 speech on television calls for an exploration of the medium's origins and early intermedial affiliations, his own capacity as a cinema pioneer also symbolizes the principal obstacle of carrying out such a historiographic task. The prominent status that cinema had quickly gained and maintained throughout the twentieth century too easily gives the impression that film is the inevitable vanishing point of the histories of the moving image and of screen practices. Indeed, some of the canonical histories of moving image media have rendered the rich visual culture of the nineteenth century as a mere precursor of cinema. Falling out of the strictly precinema narratives, the history of early electric moving image transmission media has been marginalized in such works, in favor of a focus on themes such as projection, photography, and optical toys, which provided the more immediate context for the coming of film.[3] Although more recent works in film historiography have rejected such precinema teleologies in favor of a broader interdisciplinary view, which places the coming of cinema alongside a myriad of other modern phenomena, only very few of them engaged with the early history of television.[4] Scholarship in the younger field of television studies also largely overlooked the medium's historical origins in the nineteenth and early twentieth centuries, though for different reasons. Conceiving of television primarily as a mass medium, television scholars focus on questions of texts and interpretations, programming flow, media effects, and reception. Whereas several key works on the beginning of television broadcasts provided important context for the launching of the mass media practice, most major works on the history of television take as their starting point the post–World War II era.[5] The current rise in interest in media archaeology and sound studies has led to an expansion in scholarship about early television history.[6] Still, the richest body of information about the earliest phases in the emergence of television currently exists in technological histories of the medium, but since such works are often written by electrical engineers and for electrical engineers, they typically lack critical examination of the historical and cultural origins of the technologies.[7]

The challenges in early television historiography, however, stem not only from disciplinary oversight or marginalization but also from the very historical terms that govern discourses in media-historical scholarship. Namely, in the rich and influential corpus of scholarship on early cinema and modern visual culture, late nineteenth- and early twentieth-century modernity has become closely identified with cinema's materiality and aesthetics. By this, I do not mean only that it is filmic records of the previous turn of the century that inform our ideas about the period; much more profoundly, the vast pathbreaking body of scholarship about the relations between fin-de-siècle visual media and the social, technological, and cultural changes brought about by modernization has established a compelling understanding of the coming of cinema as "the fullest expression and combination of modernity's attributes."[8] Film historians working in this tradition have explored cinema's origins in relation to various aspects of modernization, such as transformations in sensory experience, processes of urbanization and technologization, and the rise of sensational and spectacular entertainment forms.[9] Often drawing on Charles Baudelaire's definition of modernity as "the ephemeral, the fugitive, the contingent" and on Walter Benjamin's corresponding discussion of the transformation of sensory perception in modernity, several film historians have pointed out correspondences between the dominant aesthetic mode of early cinema and the fragmented, fleeting visual experience of urban-industrial modernity; between the film camera's ability to inscribe movement in duration and modernity's cultural concerns with recording, archiving, and gaining access to the instant; and between the mass production, circulation, and appeal of the cinematic image and the formation of modern capitalist mass culture and modern forms of subjectivity.[10] Given the central role that cinema has come to play in our understanding of modernity, the very terms available for the discussion of the historical context for television's emergence are already determined by their close association with the cinema.

To be sure, no film historian that I am aware of has argued for the exclusivity of cinema's role in the culture of modernity. Yet if we consider that, as Tom Gunning has persuasively shown, early cinema "metaphorised modernity" and serves as an "emblem of modernity," how are we to establish the origins of television, a distinct moving image medium that appeared and developed during the same cultural-historical moments?[11] A history of the origins of television that wishes to remain mindful of the medium's specificity must not only excavate the technological history of moving image transmission and the media practices and discourses that surrounded its formation. It must also account for how it is that out of the social, cultural, and intermedial context of modernity, two distinct forms of moving image media emerged: one for the photographic inscription and reanimation of pictures, and one for the electric transmission of images at a distance. Such a history, in turn, ought to establish television's place in a number of alternative lineages, including ones that fall outside the realms of visual media— namely, those of the history of electrification, of signal communication systems like the telegraph and the telephone, and of networked technological configurations. In other words, a history of the origins of television must seek to portray the correspondences between the moving image and the historical process of modernization in a broader, more ambivalent manner than is typically acknowledged. This book attempts to do so.

Seeing by Electricity traces the earliest phases in the history of television in order to come to terms with what Lumière has called its ancient affiliations. My focus is on the period in television history that preceded the mass media application of television. This period spans from the initial conception of electrical technologies for moving image transmission in the 1870s to the launching of regular television broadcast services, which were first introduced in Nazi Germany in 1935 and were followed by the British Broadcasting Company (BBC) in 1936 and by the National Broadcasting Company (NBC) in the United States in 1939. As this book shall argue, the intermedial relationship between film and television did not start with their economic and institutional rivalry of the late 1940s; rather, it goes back to their very origins. The book considers how television influenced the history of cinema in many intersections during its first five decades, starting with playing a role in the initial reception of early cinema in the turn of the twentieth century, through how it signaled new opportunities and posed new threats on the Hollywood industry of the classical system, to how the first generations of film theorists speculated about the coming of a new nonphotographic apparatus of moving image, and up to how television offered a radical alternative to cinema in the view of various modernist avant-garde projects. Thus, whereas this is primarily a work of media historiography that sheds light on underexplored periods in television history, the research I present in the following chapters also holds implications for how we are to theorize the present state of moving image media. If the proliferation of digital audiovisual technologies in the twenty-first century has led many scholars to reassess the nature of cinema in light of new moving image media, this book argues that in fact cinema was "haunted" throughout its history by a looming other form of moving image media, which continuously threatened to replace it and render it obsolete.

Historiographic Frameworks and Considerations

The very notion of the origins of television could be narrated in accordance with various different frameworks. Media historians have approached television as part of the history of domestic media, of small-screen apparatus, of electronic media, of broadcasting, of moving image media technology, and most recently as part of the history of video.[12] Even the use of the word "television" appears problematic in the context of the discussion of the medium's origins. The word was coined only in the year 1900, and in the decades prior to that, moving image transmission apparatus was referred to utilizing numerous different names, such as "telectroscope," "diaphote," "telephote," "telehor," "phantoscope," "electric telescope," "distant seer," and, of course, "seeing by electricity." Furthermore, the word "television" denotes a sense of self-identity, which is foreign to the late nineteenth-century conceptions that have set the stage for the medium's emergence. In other words, "television" as we presently use it inevitably invokes a bundle of popular and theoretical conceptions, established forms of spectatorship, and affiliated cultural practices that were in no way part of the culture and the discourses that surrounded its emergence.

I therefore consider the subject of this book to be, rather, the history of *moving image transmission*. I prefer this term for two main reasons. First, the category of moving image transmission is flexible enough to encompass the characteristics of both the earliest speculations and experiments in question here, which were not yet television per se, and those of the realized manifestation television in the various forms it took throughout its history. Whether we think of television as an analog or digital technology; as broadcast, narrowcast, or point-to-point communication device; as based on cable or wireless transmission; as delivering "live" events or prerecorded material; or as a domestic or public viewing medium, we principally address a media practice that involves the transmission of moving images to a distant viewer. Second, the emphasis on the notion of transmission in the discussion of the origins of television also foregrounds important aspects in its relation to cinematic moving images. The basic operation of the cinematic apparatus involves capturing, storing, and reanimating scenes by means of displaying a rapid succession of discrete inscribed images. Conversely, the basic operation of moving image transmission technologies involves the scanning or dissecting of a captured image to discrete picture-elements, which are in turn converted to signals (either analog or digital) and conveyed at a distance (either by wire or wirelessly) to receiving devices that represent them in the form of a visual image. In this sense, the framework of history of moving image transmission proves useful not only for the study of the technological, institutional, and cultural formation of television as a particular medial formation of moving image transmission apparatus but also for the exploration of its intermedial relationship with the cinema.

The distinction between recording and transmission draws on fundamental media-theoretical ideas that could be traced back to Harold Innis's categorization of spatial and temporal techniques of communication. For Innis, "media that emphasize time are those that are durable in character, such as parchment, clay, and stone. . . . Media that emphasize space are apt to be less durable and light in character, such as papyrus and paper."[13] Applying a similar logic to modern media technologies, William Uricchio and Siegfried Zielinski—two of the most prominent contributors to the study of early television history—have emphasized the discrepancy between cinema's recording function and televisual instantaneous transmission. Uricchio has explored the "competing temporalities" of film and television in a series of articles that highlight the nineteenth-century cultural fascination with the idea of simultaneity or "liveness," as evidenced most potently in early responses to the introduction of the telephone and numerous imaginary depictions of image transmission media.[14] Uricchio hypothesizes that late nineteenth-century audiences encountered the medium of cinema with a sense of disappointment because it fell short of fulfilling the promise of simultaneity that flourished in early televisual imaginaries. Cinema, Uricchio suggests, appeared as a detour in the history of television, a partial realization of the medium that emerged only later in the twentieth century. Zielinski, similarly, argues that "the two intrinsic targets of the projects [of cinema and television] were poles apart," since "in contradistinction to the [cinematic] preservation of images for the purpose of processing and presenting them, the lineage of television is concerned essentially with overcoming spatial distance without any loss of time."[15] In his book *Audiovisions*, Zielinski narrates a wide-ranging media history that concludes in the digital-era convergence of the distinct historical trajectories of cinema and television. The stated goal of *Audiovisions* is to come to terms with the contemporary media situation by way of defining cinema and television's "historically delimited significance as specific cultural configurations."[16]

While I share Uricchio and Zielinski's historiographic concern with the dissimilar technological affordances of the cinematic and the transmitted moving image, my interest in this book is to explore historical instances of intermedial influences, technical amalgamations, and shared imaginaries that problematize the clear-cut distinction between the fundamental medial functions of recording and transmission. Media theorist John Durham Peters has offered an important critique of the tendency to distinguish between communication media based on their spatiotemporal features. Whereas transmission media overcome space and recordings overcome time, Peters has made a case for the ultimate unity and interconvertibility of these distinct traits. Transmission, however fast, takes time; recording, likewise, costs space, as it involves the inscription of temporal events onto spatial coordinates.[17] Thus, based on examples drawn from limited cases of large space- and timescales in geology and astronomy as well as from the history of media technologies, Peters has shown that "to send a message (transmission), it must be preserved from death or corruption in transit (recording)," while "to record, one must alienate the original by writing onto some surface."[18]

This important conceptual intervention does not cancel out the categories of recording and transmission altogether, but does have implications regarding how we are to frame televisual transmission in relation to other forms of moving images, for it invites further research on media process that occur across the separate categories. Yet it is not only media-philosophical notions that motivate my inquiries into the overlaps between storage and transmission, for the historical records themselves are full of instances of hybrids, amalgamations, and border crossing between cinematic and televisual properties and principles. As Anne-Katrin Weber puts it, such intermedial configurations call for historical narratives "encompassing composite and heterogeneous media forms that emerge at the intersections of henceforth inseparable paradigms and industries."[19] Concepts about storage and transmission media appeared early on in the popular imagination in their purest form, but very quickly they became intertwined, and at times they were even confused with one another. In technological designs, operative plans, pioneering theoretical projects, fictional narrative, avant-garde practices, and journalistic reports, mixes of "live" transmission and "canned" films appear throughout the late nineteenth- and early twentieth-century discourses on film and television. Therefore, rather than considering the early histories of cinema and television as distinct parallel lineages determined by their technical characteristics, this book argues that from its very beginning, the idea of the moving image was conceived in a variety of formations. Indeed, it was only against this backdrop that, in the 1920s and 1930s, distinctive medium-specific definitions of cinema and television were first articulated.

Another methodological principle that informs the history I present in this book is the notion of intermediality as a historical category. Film historian André Gaudreault has suggested that intermediality does not only designate instances in which a media form reaches out beyond its established boundaries, but is also a constitutive element in media history. In his writings on films from around the turn of the twentieth century, Gaudreault has shown how cinema did not come into being as a full-fledged autonomous medium. Rather, early films merely emulated existing practices of other media forms, and only in the following decade did cinema develop medium-specific traits and institutions.[20] Based on these observations, Gaudreault (in collaboration with Phillippe Marion) develops a model for media historiography that distinguishes between distinct moments of two "births" of a given medium.[21] The first birth is marked by the appearance of a new technology, a new tool in the service of old practices or an extension of existing media. The second birth, conversely, involves the establishment of medium-specific professional procedures and the attainment of cultural legitimacy, which provide the medium with an autonomous acknowledged identity. The model of two births thus suggests a process of distinction vis-à-vis the surrounding mediascape, in which a new medium transforms from being integrated among other media to possessing singular specific traits and institutions. Granted, no medium ever severs all of its intermedial connections. A medium's autonomy is always relative, but the nature of its intermedial relations changes radically around the formation of its distinguished features.

Gaudreault and Marion's discussion of medium specificity as a product of a historical process of cultural, aesthetic, and institutional formation is productive for the historiography of television. In light of their intermedial framing of the emergence of new media forms, my account of the period that preceded the launching of broadcasting services is intended to be read neither as a "prehistory of television" nor as a Bazinian pursuit of the medium's origins in order to "reveal something of its nature."[22] Rather than supposing a fixed or inherent essence of the medium, this book is concerned with the multiplicity of possibilities that typified the early stages of television's history. It surveys the various ways in which the early speculative conceptions of moving image transmission had borrowed and adapted attributes from other media, and the major transformations the very notion of image transmission underwent before its public launch in the form of a broadcast medium with a fairly distinctive media identity.

At the same time, the case of television poses unique challenges that necessitates making some adaptions to the cinema-inspired model of the double birth. What is unique about the case of television, and what makes it an exemplary case for intermedial historiography, is its unusually slow and drawn-out period of emergence. The initial ideas about televisual communications had existed for fifty years before the introduction of the prototypes of television apparatus. The history of moving image transmission media, therefore, starts with the numerous discursive inventions of televisual media in the nineteenth century, long before the supposed "first birth" of television technology.[23] Second, almost six decades had passed between the initial articulated speculations regarding the electrical transmission of moving images and the formation of television broadcasting stations (in the case of cinema, conversely, only six years had passed between the moment Thomas Edison first expressed interest in designing a motion picture apparatus and the commercial deployment of the kinetoscope).[24] The sixty-year period of the emergence of television marks not only radical changes in the surrounding media environment but also a new phase in the history of modernization. In this respect, the concepts of both the medium of television and the cultural context within which it emerged are, at best, moving targets. The first ideas about seeing by electricity were expressed shortly after the invention of the telephone and were considered to be a new type of telegraphic technology; as such, they were shaped by the distinct cultural imaginary of the fin-de-siècle urban industrial modernity, typified by the rapid introduction of technological communication and transportation novelties and an alteration in the notions of time and space. But the first working television prototypes appeared in the midst of the distinctive form of twentieth-century modernity, defined by Miriam Hansen as "the modernity of mass production, mass consumption, and mass annihilation, of rationalization, standardization, and media publics."[25] In that age of mass media such as broadcast radio and the Hollywood studio system, television became part of what has become known as "the culture industry," governed by big and powerful commercial conglomerates that emulated Fordist principles of standardization and rationalization. Tracing the history of this slow emergence, in sum, allows us to observe a vast array of technological and cultural changes that not only shaped television but transformed the entire modern mediascape.

Periodization and Chapter Breakdown

The six chapters of this book focus on different aspects of the relationship between cinema and moving image transmission and are organized in two distinct sections. Part I, "Archaeologies of Moving Image Transmission," deals with the speculative era in television history, which spans nearly half a century between the earliest publications on the prospects of image transmission in the late 1870s and the presentations of the first working television prototypes in the mid-1920s. Focusing on the conditions for the first imaginary formations and technological schemes for image transmission apparatus, the chapters in this section demonstrate how—much like Wolfgang Ernst has observed regarding the electronic tube—television "has no linear discursive history but instead, especially in the beginning, followed more of a zigzag course of experimental groping in the dark."[26] Dealing with periods that preceded the existence of actual television services, this scope of this section is decidedly international. As it demonstrates, both the technological ideas about devices for seeing by electricity and the utopian and dystopian cultural attitudes toward these prospects freely floated across national, discursive, and disciplinary boundaries.

Chapter 1 locates the initial conceptions of moving image transmission within the intermedial context of the late nineteenth-century electrical telecommunication systems. Drawing on technical discourses as well as on utopian and science fiction literature of the era, it argues that the concurrent emergence of cinema and moving image transmission media is best seen as two distinct but interrelated (or even dialectical) manners of mediating modernity's oft-theorized transformations in sensory perception and the configuration of time and space. Chapter 2 maps the technological history of early schemes for moving image transmission devices onto the history of the changing notions of vision in the nineteenth century. The chapter demonstrates how the first designs for electrical visual media were modeled after the manner in which modern physiologists depicted the structure and function of the human eye. This consideration of image transmission technology as essentially imitating the human sensory apparatus offers an understanding of television as a prosthetic medium that extends the powers of human vision and therefore intersects with histories of other modern media and with various modernist conceptions of a new, technologically enhanced human. In chapter 3 I turn to the period of early cinema and hypothesize that just as cinema played a role in the formation of early concepts of moving image transmission, so too did moving image transmission media influence the cultural context of the initial reception of cinema. This intermedial exploration brings to light the fact that during the early history of moving image media, the distinctions between recording and transmission were not mutually exclusive but rather contingent, continuous, and destined to converge.

Part II, "Debating the Specificity of Television, On- and Off-Screen," considers television's experimental era, starting with the realization of mechanical television apparatus by pioneers such as Charles Francis Jenkins and John Logie Baird and ending with the launching of regular public television services in the mid-1930s, shortly before the project of television largely halted for the duration of World War II. The experimental era saw not only technological development in moving image transmission devices and infrastructure, but also intensive economic, cultural, and regulatory processes that would lead to the eventual formation of the autonomous mass media institutions of television. As the chapters in this section illustrate, the medium-specific properties of television did not come into being alongside the arrival of the technological apparatus; rather, they were established by way of ongoing cultural practices and debates that attempted to distinguish the new medium from the old dominant medium of cinema. The experimental era also marks the period during which the project of television became bound to national settings and specific political and economic conditions. Therefore, my consideration of the formation of television's media identity in this period focuses on different national settings—the United States, the Soviet Union, and Germany (and partly Italy). These distinct cases demonstrate how, as Lisa Gitelman has argued, the identity of media forms is never neutral and fixed but is always defined in historically and culturally specific terms.[27]

Chapter 4 concerns how the American film and radio industries responded to advances in moving image transmission technologies and how the broadcasting model came to shape the future of television in the late 1920s and early 1930s. During that period, television was considered cinema's rival, as well as its "stepbrother" or "cousin"; as an inevitable future formation of cinema; or simply as a technology for the wireless distribution of motion picture films.[28] The chapter delineates how ideas of televisual medium specificity came into being as part of the industrial debates about the control and use of the medium, namely, as part of Hollywood's pragmatic defenses of its industrial interest and the radio networks' efforts to expand into visual broadcasting. To complement the discussion of how television came to be understood as ontologically distinct from cinema, the chapter also discusses two early instances of intermedial overlaps: the notion of "films on television" is explored in a study of the first experimental broadcasts of motion pictures on television, and the notion of "television in films" is demonstrated by early cinematic depictions of televisual devices. The final two chapters change the setting to different national and cultural contexts as they examine the impact of television on the cinematic avant-garde and early film theory. In these chapters, my focus is on two of the figures most identified with the concern for film's aesthetic and ontological specificity. The topic of chapter 5 is the reception of the idea of television in the Soviet Union. It revisits filmmaker and theorist Dziga Vertov's early writings on television in order to consider the early history of radical avant-garde deployments of the medium. As this chapter shows, despite his perceived affinity with high-modernist cinematic aesthetics, Vertov was quick to regard television as a superior media form that was destined not only to replace film but also to fulfill the revolutionary objectives of Soviet cinema. The formation of medium-specific notions of television is taken up again in chapter 6, which turns to the national settings of interwar Germany and Italy and concerns the work of film critic and perceptual psychologist Rudolf Arnheim. This chapter shows how the efforts to come to terms with nonfilmic moving image media necessitated classical film theory to engage with questions of intermediality and media change that decades later became central in media theory. In closing, the book's conclusion offers observations about how the history of the emergence of television may inform further considerations of the present mediascape in film and television studies.

PART I

Archaeologies
of Moving
Image Transmission

1   Ancient Affiliates

The Nineteenth-Century Origins of Cinema
and Television

The study of the early history of television necessitates us to forsake assumptions about linear historical developments, pursuits of a singular original idea that would mark the medium's historical stating point, and considerations of the nature of the medium as seen retrospectively through the lens of its present dominant configuration. Instead, the history of television, as with all other media, has multiple starting points and is deeply embedded in a complex of cultural and media practices of the time.

Writings about moving image transmission technologies started appearing in numerous fictional scenarios, technical proposals, cartoons, news reports, and hoaxes that were published in different countries in the late 1870s. These accounts used different names for the technological devices, attributed them to different inventors, and proposed different ways in which they could be put to practical use. Uniformly, however, they all described variants of electric apparatus that allowed seeing on an optical instrument the instantaneous reproductions of images captured at the same time by a remote corresponding instrument. As a New York paper put it in 1877, with such an apparatus, "objects or persons standing or moving in any part of the world may be instantaneously seen anywhere and by anybody."[1] Reports of this sort about the introduction of various moving image transmission technologies continued to appear in the press through the turn of the twentieth century.

As with early cinema, the initial writings about moving image transmission repeatedly evoke intermedial references in descriptions of its novelty and discussions of its origins and possible uses. As François Albera has noted, early commentators on cinema did not think the new medium had appeared from nowhere. Rather, they "constantly attempted to establish its *connections* with the moving images, reproductive and projection devices, toys and apparatuses that existed before it."[2] In such historical intermedial reference, I would argue, lies the chief distinction between the histories of the emergence of the two media, for in contrast to the discourses on the beginning of cinema, the early commentators on inventions of moving image transmission technology repeatedly pointed toward its connections with the telephone. A pioneering article titled "Telephony, Telegraphy and Telescopy," published in 1878 by Portuguese physicist Adriano De Paiva, argued that the technology for the transmission of moving images is "a very natural consequence of the discovery of the electric telephone."[3] In a rather technologically deterministic manner, De Paiva contends that ever since the introduction of the telephone, "we could not help thinking that soon another scientific invention would appear; the application of electricity to telescopy, or the creation of electrical telescopy."[4] A hoax published in the American press in 1880 by a writer who claimed to have invented an image transmission device dubbed "the diaphote" similarly claimed that the idea first came to the inventor when reading of Bell's early telephone experiments.[5] Early encounters with the telephone also inspired several individuals around the turn of the twentieth century to write to Thomas Edison with suggestions to invent "telephones that could display pictures of the person speaking at the other end of the line."[6]

The popular imagination associated the idea of future visual transmission technologies with real figures in the field of electric communication. In 1878 *Punch* magazine published a famous cartoon, featuring an "electric camera obscura," supposedly invented by Thomas Edison, which in combination with the telephone "transmits light as well as sound"; another humoristic magazine published an illustrated column on a similar invention, attributing it to a "Professor Goaheadison" (figure 1.1); in 1880, rumors claimed that Bell had invented an electric distance seeing machine, and by the end of the nineteenth century, newspapers reported that Nicola Tesla was working on developing one.[7] Even the names given to the variety of moving image transmission devices in nineteenth-century writings—a

PROFESSOR GOAHEADISON'S LATEST.

A. I am much distressed in my mind. I am told that I cannot be

cured unless I consult Sir Settemup Pilliboy, the eminent physician, and it's such a tremendous journey to London from here——

B. L o n d o n ? What the deuce do you want to go to L o n d o n for? Haven't you heard of Professor Goaheadison's F a r-Sight Machine? Bless my soul—you *are* behind the times! Oh dear, yes. Wonderful man is Goaheadison! Just invented a machine by means of which a person in Nyork can actually see another person in Shicago, or Borston, or even 'Frisco. You just stand at a street corner in Nyork, and drop a dollar in the slot, and pull out a drawer, and there you see the party you want to have a look at, with a white choker on, and his hair all beautifully curled and oiled. If you keep on dropping dollars in the slot, bless your soul! you can keep your eye on him all day long—follow him in and out of all the saloons, and everything. Look here, these machines are not exactly laid on as yet in England, but that Goaheadison is such a smart chap that there's no doubt if you just drop a twenty-pound note in the slot—any slot —and pull out a drawer—any drawer—you'll find one of the machines in it.

A. Dear me! Well, this beats all! Here is the machine as you predicted! Lorks! Now, do I just lay it on to Doctor Pilliboy in Harley Street? Like so? * * * By Jingo! there he is, standing in his consulting room and smiling at me. He's motioning me to do something—but I can't quite grasp—what a pity I can't hear what—

B. My dear boy, simplest thing in the world—just drop a jubilee four-shilling piece (be careful that it *is* a four-shilling piece, as Mr. Boehm's coinage is carefully kept free from any means of identifying its value; that's its chief artistic merit—its problematical value. If you want to find out the value of a British coin you take it to a chemist to weigh, and then you go home and carefully work out how much such a weight of silver is worth)—just drop in a jubilee problem, and pull out a drawer, and you have a telephone laid on. There, now!—you can consult your London physician perfectly. * * Can he see your tongue?

A. Oh, yes, beautifully; but there's a difficulty about s o u n d i n g my chest.

B. Difficulty? Pooh! Just lay on a microphone, and connect it with the telephone, a n d there you are.

A. Well, I *am* glad you turned up just in time to tell me about Goaheadison's inventions! I do feel so much better already! What a wonderful man Fullspeedaheadison must be!

B. Rather! and I see in the papers that it's all owing

to his method of keeping up the nervous tension while at work. He does all his thinking seated on a powerful dynamo from which wires are

1.1. "Professor Goaheadison's Latest."
Illustration by James Sullivan.
Fun magazine, July 3, 1889.

variety of neologisms such as "telephote," "telephane," "télé-chromo-photo-phono-tétro-scope," and "telectroscope"—suggest that the emergent technology was considered to be affiliated with the telephone.

However, if we are to consider that, as William Uricchio has noted, "the televisual, as a technological construction, was born with the invention of the telephone in 1876," it is crucial to consider a longer trajectory that this intermedial influence took part in.[8] While it was telephony that "sparked an anticipatory interest" in the possible future development of visual transmission media, the invention of the telephone itself also derived from another media technology—the telegraph. The original telephone patent that was issued to Alexander Graham Bell was titled "improvements in telegraphy" and concerned a method for sending multiple telegraphic messages simultaneously. The ability to transmit sound was a by-product of this development. Bell's telephone operated on the same principle as the telegraph: it permitted long-distance communication by means of electrical transmission of signals, but it allowed transmission of voices, whereas the telegraph sent only textual signs. The initial newspaper reports about the telephone referred to it as "a revolution in telegraphy," or "a speaking telegraph."[9] Being the "last word" in telegraphy, a dramatic development that extended the capacity of the electric medium, the invention of the telephone opened up possibilities for further speculation about potential progress in telegraphic communication. It made possible a series of ideas and fantasies that revolved around an imaginary trajectory of technological configurations, where the invention of each new medium signified the coming of another. This trajectory starts with the telegraph (the initial electric medium for the transmission of textual messages), continues with the telephone (a telegraph that sends speech by electricity) and moving image transmission media (which allows "seeing by electricity"), and finally culminates in a technological compound that would allow long-distance audiovisual communication.

A commentator in a British technical journal writing as early as 1877 about the introduction of the phonograph and the telephone remarked on "the wonders yet to be accomplished" in the field, specifying "the reproduction of written characters, and, indeed, of any possible motion at any distance—say, across the Atlantic, and of light at a distance."[10] Similarly, in the view of an American journalist writing on the laying of the transatlantic telegraph cable, it appeared plausible that within a few years one would also be able to conduct long-distance telephone conversations, and soon after, with the aid of a telectroscope, "we shall also be enabled to see from here what is going on at the moment in China or Japan."[11] Much in the spirit of modern faith in technological progress, newspaper reports were quick to announce that the emergent technology for moving image transmission would also be superior to the existing electric media forms, describing it as "an invention that beats the telephone," that would "supersede in a very short time the ordinary methods of telegraphic and telephonic communication" and make them obsolete just like communication via smoke signals.[12] French author Albert Robida best expressed these sentiments when he delineated, in his 1882 science fiction novel *The Twentieth Century*, a genealogy of electric media from an imaginary retrospective position:

The old electric telegraph—that primitive application of electricity—was replaced by the telephone, and later, the telephone was suppressed by its supreme culmination, the telephonoscope. The old telegraph enabled someone to communicate with a distant correspondent or an interlocutor. The telephone allowed one to hear them. The telephonoscope tops it all by making it possible to see them as well. What more could they want?[13]

Outside of the firm belief in progress, the conception of an inevitable progressive trajectory that would lead from the telegraph to sound and image transmission technologies also emerged in association with contemporary scientific and philosophical developments. Many early texts on moving image transmission refer implicitly or explicitly to theories of waves and vibrations, which attempted to provide evidence of common principles that govern disparate phenomena in nature. Key figures in all branches of science argued during the nineteenth century that light, sound, electricity, other forms of energy, and even matter itself were all manifestations of different frequencies of vibrations in the ether-filled world and as such were essentially interchangeable.[14] In the same way as the telephone transformed sound waves to electric signals, it appeared realistic that light, too, could be similarly transformed to signals. The analogy to the operation of the telephone proved foundational for early discourses on moving image transmission technologies, especially since it was understood that light and electricity are essentially manifestations of the same thing.[15] Alexander Graham Bell himself was quoted in the American press as saying, "There is no theoretical reason why the well-known principles of light should not be applied in the same way the principles of sound have been applied in the telephone," although he admitted that "it will be very much more difficult to construct such an apparatus, owing to the immensely greater rapidity with which the vibrations of light take place when compared with the vibrations of sound."[16]

Even if wave theory never provided a readily applicable solution to the problem of transmitting moving images (since, as Bell indicated, no vibrating membrane that effectively responded to light waves was to be found), it did suggest that the realization of such technology was feasible. Indeed, starting in 1879, several scientists and technicians attempted to fabricate devices for the transmission of still and moving images. Some of them claimed to have experimented with the construction of transmission apparatus, while many others published theoretical proposals and some patented their methods.[17] By the beginning of the twentieth century, over twenty different technological schemes for such devices were published in scientific journals in North America, Europe, and Britain. The discursive inventions and media fantasies became a practical scientific project.

The scientists and technicians who were engaged in the development of the earliest schemes for image transmission apparatus in the nineteenth century came from varied backgrounds. Among them were electricians, physicists, telegraph technicians, and engineers. Significantly, they worked in almost complete isolation from the lanternists, photographers, opticians, mechanics, chemists, and showmen who were to become the pioneers of cinema.[18] Although the development of image transmission technologies started in more or less the same years that saw major achievements in the field of animated pictures, the science and engineering journals that published ideas on the many concurrent international pursuits of transmission devices constituted a largely separate professional discourse.

The separation between the two professional circles is most explicitly evident in the exceptional case of Charles Francis Jenkins, a prolific American inventor and perhaps the only individual to make significant contributions to the early development of both film and television. In July 1894, Jenkins published in an electrical engineering periodical a scheme for "transmitting pictures by electricity."[19] Jenkins did not construct such an apparatus until the 1920s, and did not pursue experimentation in this area until several decades later, but by the end of 1894 he had also applied for patents on an improved version of Edison's kinetoscope viewer and on a movie camera–projector compound. Nonetheless, the detailed history of moving image devices from the phenakistoscope to the cinema that Jenkins included in his 1898 book *Animated Pictures* completely excludes any mention of his or others' ideas of image transmission devices. For Jenkins—or, perhaps one should say, *even* for Jenkins—they did not belong in the lineage of cinema.[20]

At the same time, references to optical devices that are usually associated with the origins of film appear very infrequently in the early technical writings on moving image transmission. To be sure, the very idea of the moving image drew on the contemporary notion of the persistence of vision, which, in turn, was indebted to the philosophical toys of the early nineteenth century. Yet only a couple of technicians explicitly mention optical devices such as magic lanterns or Japanese mirrors in their proposals for technological schemes for moving image transmission.[21] Much more consistently, the early scientific publications on image transmission devices use analogies to other electric communication media, describing their object as "apparatus intended to reproduce telegraphically at a distance the image obtained in the camera obscura," or as apparatus for "seeing by telegraphy" and "visual telegraphy."[22]

More than mere rhetorical devices, these intermedial associations indicated the technical principles that guided the project of constructing a practical image transmission apparatus, which aimed at emulating the telegraphic and telephonic methods of conveying text and sound by electricity signals. The technicians envisioned an electric apparatus consisting of two instruments, a sender and a receiver, connected by wire. The sending instrument in these schemes consisted of a camera obscura that captures images and, with the aid of a light-sensitive component, converts them to electric signals that could be transmitted over the wire. The receiving instrument, attached to the other end of the wire, then converts the electric signals back to a visible form, displaying them virtually simultaneously as the images are transmitted. This technological scheme introduced three main (but by no means exclusive) challenges. First the pioneering technicians had to find a light-sensitive material suitable to function as an optical pickup device in the sending instrument, a visual variant of the microphone that could dissect the images to discrete components and convert them to electric signals. Then they had to construct quick-enough means for displaying the images via the receiving instrument so that an impression of movement could be achieved. Finally, they needed a method to keep the sending and receiving instruments synchronized. These challenges were not satisfactorily met until the 1920s. During the decades of experimenting with different technical solutions, a number of scientific discoveries and inventions altered the ways moving image transmission technologies were envisioned. Those included, most notably, wireless transmission and the cathode ray tube. But even these landmark technological developments came into being initially as improvements on the existing fundamental scheme of moving image transmission apparatus that was formulated by the late nineteenth-century technicians and remained unchanged until the realization of working television prototypes.

Although the technological schemes for moving image transmission technologies were not yet close to being practical, many of the early publications on the subject suggested ways in which the proposed devices may be put to practical use. Most commonly, the late nineteenth-century commentators regarded moving image transmission devices as complements to the telephone, which in combination with the sound medium would allow one to see and hear a distant interlocutor. But as ubiquitous as this conception became, it was by no means the only proposed application. The early discourses about the transmission of moving images evoked a wide and diverse range of possible applications. Already in 1877, an American newspaper report noted that apart from allowing people to see their relatives and loved ones from afar, the novel technology could also allow merchants to exhibit their goods to customers worldwide, police authorities to identify fugitive criminals in any part of the world, painters to exhibit their works in multiple galleries simultaneously while still in the studio, scholars to consult manuscripts from any museum, and operas and plays to be reproduced in any given theater.[23] Another newspaper article suggested that when the technology would be realized, military officers could use it to send images from the battlefield to the generals in the headquarters and reporters could send pictures of distant scenes to be reproduced in newspapers.[24] According to another report, the emerging technology could be of use for train dispatchers in overseeing railway traffic and avoiding collisions, by jailors for observing prison cells, and by doctors for examining patients from their home. "The scope of its usefulness," it noted, "will be almost unlimited."[25]

Strikingly, all of these many proposed uses for image transmission devices are rather different from the practice that in the mid-twentieth century became the dominant use of television. At the same time, it is also notable that while the apparatus for seeing by electricity was celebrated as a fascinating novelty, none of its proposed uses was actually new. To borrow the term used in André Gaudreault's study of the coming of cinema, it could be argued that the moving image transmission media emerged in the late nineteenth century as a product of "intermedial meshing." Gaudreault (following Eric de Kuyper) refers to intermedial meshing as the complex of existing techniques, cultural practices, and representational codes that new media forms characteristically emulate, "in a rather servile manner," from other media before developing their own medium-specific distinctive institutions and traits.[26] Indeed, since the mid-nineteenth century, long before it was proposed as an application for image transmission media, railway companies had been using the telegraph to administer train departure. As telegraphic communication allowed the sending of messages faster than any train, police officers similarly used the telegraph to distribute information about fugitive criminals. Starting very early on in the medium's history, the telegraph served the printed press in gathering news reports from around the world and businessmen in carrying out international trade deals by wire. By the mid-nineteenth century, telegraphy was also employed in the battlefield, when officers telegraphed information back to the generals in the headquarters.[27] Likewise, when the telephone was introduced, point-to-point conversation was only one of several practices it was deployed for. In the 1880s, the European Théâtrophone services allowed customers to listen in on opera and theatrical performances. The telephone's possibilities for detection, monitoring, and surveillance attracted a great deal of attention in the vibrant discourses that surrounded the introduction of the new medium; while it is unlikely to have been a common practice, the idea of doctors efficiently diagnosing patience from afar was entertained by several commentators shortly after the introduction of the telephone.[28]

In sum, the concept of seeing by electricity was initially conceived in the late nineteenth century as an *extension* of other media.[29] In terms of its discursive formation, devices for the transmission of moving images existed in the nineteenth-century imagination as the next inevitable step in the lineage of telecommunication technologies that started with the telegraph; in terms of material construction, technicians and scientists considered the realization of visual transmission devices as further development, or even perfection, of the mechanisms of telegraphic and telephonic signal communication; and finally the media practices designated for the emergent technology of moving image transmission were variants of practices already carried out by the telegraph and the telephone, with an added visual dimension. In this respect, once more, the distinction between the initial ideas about moving image transmission media and the cinema is striking. Whereas the earliest discourses on devices for the transmission of moving images considered them as extensions of the nonvisual media of telegraphy and telephony, early cinema exhibition practices (and the content of many of the early films themselves) borrowed from existing practices of lantern projections, magic shows, the vaudeville stage, and scientific imaging techniques. This divergence demonstrates how the two forms of moving image media emerged concurrently but out of two different media environments, and initially developed in two parallel trajectories while incorporated into the established media habits, institutions, and practices of their respective intermedial contexts. It suggests, in other words, that the distinction between television and the cinema goes beyond their ontological differences and material capacities and exists on a more fundamental level, in the very conditions that enabled their conception and shaped their emergence.

Identifying television's origins in the intermedial context of the electric tele-communications media of the nineteenth century holds historiographical significance beyond revealing the conditions for its initial conceptions; it also provides us with an opportunity to trace the early cultural attitudes toward the emergent medium. As a great proportion of the late nineteenth-century writings on seeing by electricity indicates, the telegraph and the telephone not only provided the context for the multiple inventions of moving image transmission media but also associated them with a web of var-ied cultural sentiments, habits, and beliefs that typified the technological-utopian discourses on novelties of electric technology.

Read in this light, the speculative early writings on moving image trans-mission media appear not as mere abstract dreams on inexistent machines but, rather, as an inherent part of a cultural-technological discourse that was very much grounded in its time. The period of the late 1870s and the early 1880s, when the first publications about the prospects of moving image transmission came out, also marked the beginning of large-scale application of electricity in industry, transportation, leisure activities, and ultimately in the domestic sphere. These years saw, for instance, the introduction of the electric light bulb and the opening of the first commercial power plant in the United States. Around the turn of the twentieth century, electricity was considered "the wonder of the age, the hallmark of progress."[30] Beyond be-ing a technical phenomenon, electricity also meant, on a metaphorical level, "novelty, excitement, modernity, and heightened awareness."[31] Such views become common throughout cultural expressions of the period. As Kristen Whissel puts it, "The hallmarks of modernity . . . are unthinkable without electricity."[32] James Carey and John Quirk identified a "rhetoric of the elec-trical sublime" in American literature of the late nineteenth century, which "has invested electricity with the aura of divine force and utopian gift and characterized it as the progenitor of a new era in social life, which somehow reverses the laws and lessons of past history."[33] At the same time, according to Carolyn Marvin, the popular magazines "were filled with accounts of one electrical invention after another, and with bright dreams of affluence and fantasies about the routines of work and play in a world where electricity has transformed the lives of ordinary people."[34]

It was such enthusiastic (and at times also puzzled and overwhelmed) at-titude toward electric technology that informed the formation of the tech-nological imaginary of moving image transmission media. This way, long before the visual medium became practically feasible, a collective vision about its identity and anticipated capacities was in place, serving as a frame of reference not only for literary and journalistic speculations but also for the ongoing technical efforts to construct visual transmission devices.[35] Such historical feedback loops of influences between imaginary ideas and technological design existed by the 1880s and 1890s, when some technicians working on schemes for image transmission devices openly admitted to have been influenced by fictional depictions of such technologies, and when characters based on real-life scientists appeared in science fiction literature.[36]

Since the cultural context of the initial encounters with electric technologies was a crucial factor in the construction of the technological imaginary of moving image transmission media, it is important to recall that the cinematic apparatus that emerged in the same period was considered largely to belong to a different category. Film technology, principally, is not (or rather not necessarily) electrical. While in several models of cinematic devices electric power has been applied to run the film camera's motor or provide the illumination in the projection apparatus, these functions could be carried out manually and by using gaslight. The Lumière cinematograph, for example, was not an electric instrument in any respect. Admittedly, some of the rhetoric about early cinema adopted vocabulary from electric technology (particularly in referring to early movie houses as "electric theaters"), and scholars such as Kristen Whissel, Carolyn Marvin, and Tom Gunning have pointed to important cultural and historical affinities between early cinema and the concurrent growth in electrification.[37] Nonetheless, even in the views of some film pioneers, cinematic technology occupied for the most part a different cultural space than that of the many electrical instruments of the late nineteenth century. In the opening of their 1895 monograph on the invention of the kinetoscope, W. K. L. Dickson and Antonia Dickson explicitly distinguish the cinema from the electrical world, writing that Edison went on to pursue the fabrication of the kinetoscope only once "the great issues of electricity were satisfactorily under way. The incandescent light had received its finishing touches; telephonic and telegraphic devices were substantially interwoven with the fabric of international life; [and] the phonograph was established on what seemed to be a solid financial and social basis." At that point, the Dicksons indicate, Edison finally "felt at liberty to indulge in a few secondary flights of fancy" and dedicate himself to developing the motion pictures.[38]

My interest here, however, is not to try to prove that electric transmission media was more important to the nineteenth century and that the cinema was of secondary significance. My aim is, rather, to distinguish the specific cultural traits of the discourses that informed the expectations, development, and reception of moving image transmission technologies in order to elucidate their particular correspondence to the culture of nineteenth-century modernity. Clearly, the very association of moving image transmission media with electric technologies such as the telegraph and telephone related it to the technological utopian (and at time dystopian) notions of novelty, energy, acceleration, efficiency, and influx—all of which were fundamental in the cultural discourse on modernization. Following this notion, I will focus here on two aspects that played a central role in the anticipatory discourse on moving image transmission media, both of which derived from existing notions about the telegraph and the telephone: the concept of the annihilation of space and time, and the configurations of networks.

In the simplest sense, the feted modern trope of the "annihilation of time and space" expresses a fascination with (and sometimes anxiety about) technology's conquests over natural conditions.[39] Frequently used in early discourses of the telephone and the telegraph, the origins of the trope in fact predated electric telecommunications. It was evoked before the emergence of the electric telegraph with respect to the unprecedented speed of railway travel, and even prior to that it was attributed to divine powers, on the one hand, and to the postal service, on the other.[40] Karl Marx ascribed a similar agency to capital, writing that "while capital must on one side strive to tear down every spatial barrier to intercourse . . . it strives on the other side to annihilate this space with time, i.e. to reduce to a minimum the time spent in motion from one place to another."[41] But it was the introduction of telegraphy's (and later telephony's) ability to convey information to great distances virtually instantaneously that seemed to truly fulfill the modern cultural aspiration to achieve total speed and triumph over physical distances and temporal gaps.

To be sure, the concept of "annihilation of time and space" must not be taken literally. According to Wolfgang Schivelbusch, it is more accurate to speak of "the alteration of spatial relations," as exemplified in the railroad's expansion of transport space and diminishing of transport time, two factors that radically changed the traditional experience of the time-space continuum.[42] Yet the many nineteenth-century commentators who evoked this trope should not be regarded as plainly naive. Just as no one believed that a train ride takes no time at all, telegraphic communication could not actually give a sense of elimination of duration—it took time for the clerks to transcribe telegrams to Morse code and tap them on the telegraph key and for the messages to be relayed between terminal offices on different branches of the telegraph system, and to be retranscribed at their destination and delivered to their addressees. Even the duration of the transmission of electric signals through copper wires was subject to measurements, as the early electricians knew that electric relay was not instantaneous. For example, in Charles Wheatstone's experiments in the 1830s, the speed of electric transmission was measured as 280,000 miles per second.[43] Nonetheless, as James Carey famously put it, the electric signals running through the telegraph wires allowed for the first time the dissociation of communication from transportation, making it possible to convey messages at speeds no messenger or vehicle could achieve. Distances thus started to matter less, and as a consequence, what was happening in distant places started to matter more. A London newspaper aptly declared that with the new technology, "time itself is telegraphed out of existence."[44]

Ironically, however, telegraphy's immediate influence on time was not to erase but rather to reinforce and standardize it. Answering the railroad's needs of coordinating train departure and arrival times in order to keep to their schedule and avoid collisions, the telegraph became instrumental in creating standard national time zones and ultimately the world standard time. The electric medium's ability to distribute seemingly instantaneous time signals made possible for the first time the synchronization of timekeeping in different distant places. As Lynne Kirby comments, "One's own time was now to be thought of in relation to the concurrent time in faraway places."[45] The standardization of timekeeping, in turn, brought about broad social and cultural changes in the consciousness of time. It found expression in modernist artistic styles and narrative forms that strived to convey a sense of simultaneity.[46] The late nineteenth and early twentieth centuries saw the rise of large-scale economic, military, bureaucratic, and political procedures that corresponded to the concurrent (and at times dependent) accelerating pace of modern capitalism and industrialization and required new systems of communication and management to control and coordinate these activities.

The novel possibilities of the so-called instantaneous communication media quickly gave rise to utopian ideas about an approaching new era in which electric technologies would change the relations among different cultures and nations and bring universal peace and harmony. Anticipating Marshall McLuhan's idea of "the global village" by almost a century, several mid-nineteenth-century commentators argued that the fast and almost effortless telegraphic communication would eliminate not only distances but also prejudices, hostilities, and cultural differences.[47] The telegraph quickly became seen as analogous to the nervous system: numerous commentators posited that the technological communication system had the power to unify, indeed make into one cohesive organism, entire nations and even the entire world.[48] An 1852 book titled *The Future Effects of Steam and Electricity upon the Condition of Mankind* went so far as to state that the telegraph is "destined to become the link of minds, the channel of intelligence and thought between all habitable parts of the globe," and that together with modern means of transportation, telegraphy will "draw all nations into more intimate connexion, and to convert the whole human race into one society."[49]

It was within such discursive contexts that the initial ideas about moving image transmission technologies emerged. An American newspaper suggested in 1913 that the telegraph and the telephone "are only the beginnings of what electricity will do for us in annihilating distance" when image transmission technologies arrive.[50] Early reports on the prospects of seeing by electricity stressed the emergent medium's capacity for simultaneity, attempting at times not only to describe "real-time" reproduction of images but also to visualize it in innovative ways. The aforementioned *Punch* cartoon of the telephonoscope exemplifies well how the imagined technology's capacity to annihilate time and space was conceived from its very beginning in light of contemporary ideologies of Western dominance and bourgeois values. In the cartoon, an elderly couple in a room in London is communicating with their daughter, who is in the Crown colony of Ceylon, using an electric transmission device that consists of a large screen and attached telephonic handsets (figure 1.2). On the large telephonoscope screen the couple can see an image of their daughter standing next to a badminton court surrounded by other colonialists and a native woman. The cartoon's caption reveals the content of the telephonoscopic conversation: the father asks the daughter to come closer because he wants to whisper, as he inquiring about "a charming young lady" he spots on the screen.[51]

At first glance, it is easy to see that the cartoon's depiction of the imaginary communication device expresses a colonial worldview typical of its era. The telephonoscope conversation between London and the Crown colony exemplifies a fantasy of advanced means for conveying the influence of the European hegemony on a global scale and keeping the imperial center connected to the settlements in the periphery. In addition, the situation depicted in the cartoon resembles not only an ordinary phone conversation

EDISON'S TELEPHONOSCOPE (TRANSMITS LIGHT AS WELL AS SOUND).

(*Every evening, before going to bed, Pater- and Materfamilias set up an electric camera-obscura over their bedroom mantel-piece, and gladden their eyes with the sight of their Children at the Antipodes, and converse gaily with them through the wire.*)

Paterfamilias (in Wilton Place). "BEATRICE, COME CLOSER, I WANT TO WHISPER." *Beatrice (from Ceylon).* "YES, PAPA DEAR."
Paterfamilias. "WHO IS THAT CHARMING YOUNG LADY PLAYING ON CHARLIE'S SIDE?"
Beatrice. "SHE'S JUST COME OVER FROM ENGLAND, PAPA. I'LL INTRODUCE YOU TO HER AS SOON AS THE GAME'S OVER!"

1.2. "Edison's Telephonoscope." Illustrations by George du Maurier,
Punch Almanac for 1879.

but also the conditions of surveillance. The telephonoscope enables two-way sound communication between the center and the periphery, yet the mediated exchange is in fact not quite symmetrical: while the parents can see the daughter on the screen, it does not seem that the parents are made visible in the apparatus in Ceylon. The daughter can only hear them via the "old" technology of the telephone, but not see them—vision is a privilege reserved to those in the Empire.

But beyond the expression of the imperialist fantasy of instantaneous global communication, the cartoon also offers a fascinating reflection on the new relations of space, time, and communication that new technologies constitute. It is significant (although rarely discussed, despite the cartoon's frequent reprinting) that the content of the telephonoscope conversation in the cartoon explicitly revolves around dichotomies of mediation and immediacy, distance and closeness, and the ability to be heard at a distance without being heard in the same room. When the father in London asks the daughter in Ceylon to "come closer," he speaks of diminishing her distance not from the British Isles, but rather from the telephonoscope device. The daughter's closeness to the telephonoscope allows him to whisper into the apparatus, which is so sensitive that the distant daughter can hear him while his wife—sitting right next to him—cannot.[52] In this scenario, the long-distance transmission apparatus alters the basic correspondence between proximity and the ability to communicate in a contradictory manner. On the one hand, it functions as a means for holding on to the traditional values at times when modernity (and in particular the colonial project) necessitated a greater degree of mobility across the globe, as it is used to maintain family unity despite geographical distance. On the other, it also poses a threat to ideals of domestic conduct, as it opens previously unavailable opportunities for the father to promiscuously peek at strange women while still in the domestic space. Technological mediation annihilates space, but it also makes distance apparent and troubling in new ways.

This brings us to the notion of networking. As powerful as the trope of the annihilation of space and time might be, the focus on the seemingly instantaneous temporality of electric media must not obstruct the fact that the extraordinary capacity of telegraphy and telephony derives from their configurations as *networks* of communication. If the telegraph and the telephone permitted swift long-distance point-to-point communication that came to signify the imminent unification of the world, it is precisely because they were structured in the form of a complex systematized apparatus. Correspondingly, in the nineteenth-century technological imaginary, moving image transmission media were conceived as taking the form of a networked apparatus, similar to that of telegraphy and telephony systems.

I evoke the term "apparatus" not just as a synonym to technical equipment but in order to point at something similar to the 1970s theorization of the cinematic apparatus, where (psychoanalytic vocabulary asides) the object of theory was taken to be not only the cinematic audiovisual text but also the particular arrangement of the screen, projector, camera, film frames, and lenses; the darkened theater; and the position of the spectator within it. In similar fashion, engagement with the telegraph and the telephone must concern not only the signals that are transmitted along the line but also the interconnected system of wires, relay stations, operators, switchboards, transmitters, and receivers.

It is important to note in this context that by conceiving of moving image transmission technology as an extension of the telephone and the telegraph, the nineteenth-century imagination associated it with a very different kind of network than we are accustomed to speak of today when referring to "television networks." The present notion of television networks relates to the mode of operation of chain broadcasting, that is, to the linking of a single source to several wireless transmission stations so that they broadcast the same signals simultaneously to a great (and, indeed, potentially infinite) number of scattered individual receivers. The form of telegraphic and telephonic networks, conversely, is very different from the centralized model of broadcasting networks. Resembling more the structure of the railroad system, the networks of telegraph and telephone are structured rather as a decentralized system, where transmission lines connect numerous points in the system to one another and thus allow two-way point-to-point communication between any two points in the network. Both Morse and Bell created their electric telecommunication inventions with the aim that they would take the form of vast networks. Already in 1838, before the commercialization of the telegraph, Morse envisioned that "the whole surface of this country would be channeled for those nerves which are to diffuse with the speed of thought, a knowledge of all that is occurring throughout the land."[53] Forty years later, Bell anticipated that just like networks of gas and water pipes, a network of telephone lines would connect private homes and businesses to regional central offices so "a man in one part of the country may communicate by word of mouth with another in a different place."[54]

Networked systems are not a product of the modern era, but the importance of communication and transportation networks in shaping the modern world cannot be overstated. Such decentralized network formations, in their ability to integrate dispersed entities into organized, controllable systems, corresponded to the new demands posed by the modern economy of the nineteenth century. Sociologist Manuel Castells described the extraordinary advantage of networks as organizing tools "because of their inherent flexibility and adaptability, critical features in order to survive and prosper in a fast-changing environment."[55] Networks thus permitted to extend the range of the effects of modernization, as they allowed not only urban centers but also peripheral rural areas to participate "in the topography of modernity."[56] Given their ability to expand outward, to new territories, as well as inward, multiplying the connection possibilities within themselves, the modern railway and telecommunication networks proved indispensable in organizing and facilitating flows of populations, information, capital, products, and materials. By doing so, they played a central role in enabling the growth of imperialism and industrialization, the strengthening of bureaucratic mechanisms, and the acceleration of territorial expansion. The American telegraph network, for example, grew 600-fold between 1846 and 1852, not only serving the railroad but also utilized by businesses, the stock market, the press, and private customers.[57]

Robida's *The Twentieth Century* offers an illustrative example of the conception of moving image transmission technology as taking the form of a decentralized network. In an early chapter in the novel, one of the protagonists, Mr. Ponto, is stretched out in his armchair after dinner in front of his telephonoscope device, discussing with his daughters what to watch that evening. They debate the choice between a tragedy and an opera, check what show starts at a convenient time, decide on a new operatic production of *Faust*, and dim the living room lights to watch the show. So far, the scene's setting of the middle-class home, where the family gathers for some evening entertainment, seems to predict quite accurately the typical experience of domestic broadcast television; indeed, Robida is often credited as a media visionary who foresaw the coming of television.

However, what is at play here is not a prediction of future television network but, rather, an adaptation of existing nineteenth-century media practices to an audiovisual media system. Ponto's house, we learn, is connected to the network service of the Universal Theatrical Telephonoscope media conglomerate (dubbed so thirty years before Carl Laemmle founded his film studio), which serves 600,000 paying subscribers and distributes a periodical program guide of all theatrical performances in the world, from which the viewers may choose any play they wish to see (minding the time difference, in case they wish to connect to theaters abroad). Hence, once the decision to watch *Faust* is made and Ponto switches on the telephonoscope, he picks up the telephone's handset and asks the switchboard operator, "Connection to the Opéra de Paris, please." Then, after the operator connects the family telephonoscope to the desired destination, the opera stage is revealed on the screen and the performance begins. Later in the evening, after a particularly impressive aria, Ponto establishes a line of communication from the living room to the stage so that the family members can join the opera house audience's applause to convey their appreciation. Elsewhere in the novel, Robida describes large-screen crystal telephonoscopes that are installed in public spaces and display commercials, telephonoscope offices that allow travelers to contact their homes while away, and portable pocket telephonoscopes with which news reporters around the world can transmit images from events as they happen. In short, the telectroscope in *The Twentieth Century* is a truly ubiquitous medium in more than one sense. It is a global networked medium that permits its users not only to see instantaneously what happens in distant locations but also to be connected to a system that can establish audiovisual connection with any given point: to see and to be seen, as it were, anywhere.

In another pioneering text on moving image transmission technology, Adriano De Paiva puts forth an even more compelling, and far more hyperbolic, conception of the medium's network configuration. De Paiva's treatise on the prospects of "electric telescopy" discusses a vast network of wires that carry images and sounds through all parts of the world. In a utopian manner that supersedes the optimism of Morse's and Bell's predictions, De Paiva extends the nervous system metaphor to its extreme, bringing an explicitly Darwinian perspective to the discourse of media change. The advent of electric communication technologies, De Paiva writes, will eventually produce a more advanced life-form:

> Conducting wires charged with all important missions will cross and re-cross at the surface of the earth; they will be the mysterious duets which will bring to the observer the impressions received by artificial organs, which human genius has made to compass any distance. And, just as the complexity of nervous filaments can give an idea of the superior perfection of an animal, those metallic filaments, nerves of another order, will testify to the high degree of civilization of the monster organism—humanity.[58]

Utopias and Dystopias of Seeing: Televisual Media Fantasies

The anticipation of moving image transmission technology provided the most useful material for the flourish of utopian and science fiction literary works that enjoyed widespread popularity in the last decades of the nineteenth century.[59] Having witnessed the introduction of new media technologies, particularly the way in which novel applications of the new and still-mysterious powers of electricity had radically transformed everyday life, utopian and science fiction novelists of the fin de siècle depicted future worlds dominated by advanced media. Many writers in these genres depicted different devices of seeing by electricity in fictional works that dealt with the near future or with a distant future still dozens of centuries away. If Louis Lumière predicted at the end of the century that film was an invention without a future, it is tempting to say that after 1880 it was hard to imagine a future *not* saturated with new electric transmission media.

These utopian and science fiction depictions of future societies and future devices were not necessarily prophecies; much more so, they were commentaries on the writers' own times, engagements with possible consequences of current social and technical transformations, and often political statements in the form of parables on future or distant worlds. As such, they may be read as "media fantasies," to use a term Carolyn Marvin coined in her study of the hopes and fears about the possible social and cultural effects of new media. In Marvin's words, even imaginary depictions derive from perceived reality and thus "reflect conditions people know and live in, and real social stakes."[60] Media fantasies, therefore, make for valuable historiographical resources in the study of early television history. They not only consist of depictions of imaginary forms of technologies but also depict them as a full-blown media—that is, as technologies put to practical application and functioning within a given social context. Read this way, futuristic stories about seeing by electricity may reveal the ways in which the anticipation of moving image transmission corresponded to the culture of modernity, as their depiction of future media reflects attitudes toward technologization and, in doing so, toward modernization.[61] Like all other speculations regarding modernization, futuristic visions of image transmission technologies took different forms. I will not attempt to present here an exhaustive account of such literary depictions. Instead I look at a selection of examples illustrating the range of ideas about the emergent medium that nineteenth-century authors entertained, as well as some recurring themes among the varied depictions.

Some nineteenth-century writers shared Robida's view and regarded (either wishfully or mockingly) the coming of media like the telephonoscope networks as signifying a future bourgeois utopia that promised a comfortable life of luxury and consumption of high culture in the safety, isolation, and convenience of one's home. Directly inspired by Robida, the short story "In the Year 2889" by Jules Verne (although reportedly written by his son, Michel) tells the story of such a technology-saturated prosperous future.[62] The people of the twenty-ninth century, according to Verne, "live continually in fairyland" of technological novelties, so they become "indifferent to marvels." The future marvels mentioned in this story include air travel, climate control, and tubes that transport food directly to the home, as well as instantaneous long-distance visual communication and newspapers that are delivered to its subscribers audiovisually and in real time through "a system made possible by enormous development of telephony."[63] Another fin-de-siècle account, musing about the ten-thousandth century, similarly posited electric moving image media within a future of great technological development that releases mankind from the need to work and to obey laws. Presented as "an optimist's picture of the future," this account depicts the future world as governed by uniformity.[64] Its inhabitants live in identical houses built in identical cities made entirely of aluminum and glass. Through a centralized supply system, they are provided with the same attire and a universal diet. In this view of the future, moving image transmission media functions to reinforce uniformity and support centralized control: the Department of Public Supply deploys electroscopes to observe every detail in the factories and farms, an electric display system projects on the walls of each future city's central hall a never-ending moving panorama that tells the history of the universe, and a system of wires simultaneously transmits a reduced version of the panorama to every house.

Other utopian narratives rejected the view of the future as progressing toward the fulfillment of middle-class ideals and proto-Fordist utopias and instead described socially progressive possibilities for electric communication media. For example, in Edward Bellamy's *Equality*, the 1897 sequel to his celebrated *Looking Backward*, the protagonist is introduced to a futuristic invention—the electroscope, an audiovisual device that allows one to see any point on earth, as it is "connected with a great number of regular stations commanding all scenes of special interest."[65] He uses the electroscope not in order to consume highbrow entertainment but rather to connect to a distant classroom and view an examination on the topic "The Hopelessness of the Economic Outlook of the Race under Private Capitalism."[66] More interested in the portrayal of a future socialist order than in the description of imagined media, Bellamy discusses new technologies in order to characterize the culture of the futuristic utopia. Thus, even when his protagonists are viewing a theatrical performance on the electroscope later in the novel, Bellamy departs from Robida's and Verne's celebration of new technologies that provide high-class domestic entertainment to middle-class urban dwellers; rather, he emphasizes how the medium contributes to the democratization of culture by making it accessible to all as part of an overall socialist move toward the sharing of resources and equalization of conditions of living. By that, his account diametrically opposes twentieth-century leftist critiques of mass media as the rise of the "culture industry," as for him the electroscope network is instrumental in elevating the general artistic level of cultural production. "This ability of one troupe to play or sing to the whole earth at once," Bellamy writes, "has operated to take away the occupation of mediocre artists, seeing that everybody, being able to see and hear the best, will hear them and see them only."[67]

Against both kinds of bourgeois and leftist utopias, late nineteenth-century dystopian novels associated electric transmission media with tyranny and oppression. Image transmission media appeared to be particularly apt surveillance systems in the hands of totalitarian leaders. Instead of facilitating two-way communication, the surveillance media allow one to see everyone without being seen. A device of this sort is featured in W. N. Harben's *The Land of the Changing Sun* from 1894, an antisocialist novel set not in the future but in a distant country built in suboceanic caves and lit by an artificial electric sun.[68] Harben describes an electric optical surveillance system that allows the local police to observe the entire population and to identify politically rebellious individuals. The surveillance system—a "telescopic invention" made possible with the application of electricity and the ever-clear atmosphere of the suboceanic land—comprises an expansive system of observatories spread throughout the land. Each observatory reflects images of its surroundings to the central underground auditorium, where police officers or the king can observe the entire kingdom, as in a panorama.

Outside Harben's evocation of the moving panorama analogy, his description of the futuristic surveillance system also brings to mind Michel Foucault's discussion of the Bentham panopticon, a similar perfected disciplinary mechanism. It is worth noting, however, the distinctions between the transmission system in *Land of the Changing Sun* and Bentham's model: The panopticon is a fixed mechanism, a central tower that oversees the space arranged around it. The dystopian novel, however, models the surveillance instrument after the telegraph. It depicts a network of interconnected observation towers, each located in different parts of the controlled territory and partaking in the overall creation of social control. This latter model in fact more closely resembles what Foucault describes as Bentham's farther-reaching dream, when he "set out to show how one may 'unlock' the disciplines and get them to function in a diffused, multiple, polyvalent way throughout the whole social body" by transforming them into "a network of mechanisms that would be everywhere and always alert, running through society without interruption in space or in time."[69]

Surprisingly, an example of an electric image transmission device within a prison setting can be found in another futuristic text from the same era, although in an opposite scenario from that of panopticon practice. In Mark Twain's science fiction short story "From the London Times of 1904," a networked visual transmission apparatus dubbed "telelectroscope" is used to send pictures of the outside world into a prison cell as a means of transcending physical confinement. The story's protagonist, Lieutenant Clayton, is imprisoned, awaiting his execution for the murder of his former associate, the telelectroscope inventor (whom Twain modeled after the real inventor

Jan Szczepanik). In an attempt to divert his mind, Clayton uses a telelectro-scope instrument that is set in his quarters to virtually wander around the world, look at strange sights, and talk to people from distant countries, all of which allows him to feel "almost as free as the birds of the air, although a prisoner under lock and bars."[70] The night before his execution, Clayton wishes to see the sun one last time. He connects the telelectroscope to Pe-king, where it is midafternoon. Then, just as he is being taken away, the face of Szczepanik—who is not dead but has escaped to China—appears on the screen, proving Clayton's innocence.

In short, whereas fin-de-siècle media fantasies presented varied depic-tions of moving image transmission media and their possible applications, a consistent characteristic can be identified across all of them. Whether they evoked the moving image transmission medium in order to signify a uto-pian or dystopian future, and whether they located it in a bourgeois liv-ing room or in a prison cell, all these scenarios fantasize a medium that functions as a universal optical network and provides visual mastery by allowing its users to see *everything, everywhere, at all times.* By doing so, they relate the conception of the medium to a principal modern cultural obsession with obtaining visual mastery. The nineteenth century saw the emergence of numerous visual technologies and cultural practices that in-troduced novel modes of seeing, including the gigantic 360-degree hyper-realistic images of the panorama, the flâneur's impassioned mobile urban viewing practices, the unobstructed points of view from the hot air balloon, the look outside the train car window that "transformed the world of lands and seas into a panorama that could be experienced," and, of course, the cinema and other screen practices and photographic media from the magic lantern travel lecture to the stereopticon.[71] All of these nineteenth-century phenomena, among many others, played part in the modern "fantasy of om-niscience," which according to historian Chris Otter links total knowledge to total visibility.[72] In this context, the early imaginations of image trans-mission media must be seen as responding to the desire to bind together the promise (and threat) of electric technology and the modern dream of an all-powerful, all-knowing gaze.

However, the media fantasy that expresses the most extreme vision about the possible future effect of electric transmission media describes a seeing-by-electricity apparatus that does not (or does not only) transmit actual images or deliver information. This scenario is presented briefly but evoc-atively in the little-known 1884 American science fiction novel *The Disk: A Tale of Two Passions.* The novel tells the typical story of a lone inventor who constructs a "photo-electrophone," a large round illuminating disc that can be used "for the transmission of almost anything to any distance."[73] The photo-electrophone, as in many other fictional accounts, is put to a range of uses, from point-to-point communication to the transmission of stage shows. But alongside these applications the novel also indicates that the ambition of the photo-electrophone's operators is far greater. As the novel's protagonist claims, the new capacity of the invention to transmit images suggests that it also opens "the possibilities of all future lighting. By it, light may be conveyed over a wire from place to place, however remote." The photo-electrophone company thus goes on to construct a network of interconnected transmission stations all over the world, so that each station can capture sunlight during the day and relay it by wires to parts of the world where it is dark, ultimately creating a global "atmosphere of perpetual sunlight."[74] As the novel goes on to note, the global system of reciprocity is incomplete, and some areas remain dark for a few hours every day, since Asia "proved backward in adopting the invention" and no stations were constructed there. But outside this obstacle (which ultimately opens up new economic possibilities of growth for the company), the goal is achieved, and thanks to the photo-electrophone "Darkness Forever Rolled Away!"[75]

By exploring the possibilities of seeing-by-electricity technologies to perform something else besides transmitting images and instead provide artificial illumination, *The Disk* describes a scenario that comes very close to McLuhan's famous claim about electric light being "a medium without a message."[76] According to the intermedial schema McLuhan describes in *Understanding Media*, "the content of any medium is always another medium." Yet he considers electric light to have a distinct logic. "Without any content to restrict its transforming and informing power," he writes, the message of electric light is, "like the message of electric power in industry, totally radical, pervasive, and decentralized."[77]

While the effect of the electric network in *The Disk* is most certainly radical, pervasive, and decentralized, the novel's scenario is of interest not only for illustrating media theory concepts but also in its correspondence to specific historical conditions and cultural concerns. Read as an allegory, the story offers an indication of what was at stake with the growth of international networks of electric media in the nineteenth century. The photo-electrophone light transmission system does not facilitate fast communication or the diminishing of transportation time, but it represents the ultimate fantasy of the annihilation of space and time: it allows the disavowal of the very primal, natural marker of the passage of time and creates, instead, a manufactured ecology. *The Disk*, in this sense, describes a fantasy of a total annihilation of time by means of a decentralized networked system that quite literally connects the entire world together to a single time zone, a single interdependent reciprocal entity. In this perfectly rationalized and coordinated network, every sender is also a receiver, as the roles change repetitively in twenty-four-hour cycles while also annulling the very significance of the twenty-four-hour cycle in place, quite literally, since the beginning of time. To quote Marx's observations on capitalism once more: "In place of the old wants, satisfied by the production of the country, we find new wants, requiring for their satisfaction the products of distant lands and climes. In place of the old local and national seclusion and self-sufficiency, we have intercourse in every direction, universal inter-dependence of nations."[78] Similar to the other networks of communication and transportation that ushered in the modern era, the photo-electrophonic system is also a political-economic enterprise, operated by a global corporation in a manner that bears an obvious similarity to the aspiration of colonial projects. Following a distinctly imperialist logic, the network's goal is to establish flows of resources and capital over an expansive territory on which, as was once said about the British flag, the sun never sets.

Although the photo-electrophone network is in many ways a prototypical nineteenth-century technological-capitalist project, it is also strikingly compatible with key notions and metaphors from twenty-first-century media and social theories that set out to critique today's notions of the "network society" and of the postindustrial or information age. For example, the effect of the networked electric technology on markers of natural temporality in *The Disk* appears to be an *avant la lettre* illustration of Manuel Castells's conception of "timeless time." For Castells, this temporal category characterizes all dominant processes in contemporary society: work and social relationships are created across different time zones, scientific breakthroughs alter the temporality of life cycles, and new technologies accelerate and desequence labor trajectories.[79] In similar fashion, the temporality of the photo-electrophone could be understood in accordance with media theorist Wendy Chun's recent observation about new media networks as operating with a constant urgency and condensation of time that she describes as an ongoing endless state of "crisis, crisis, crisis."[80] More recently, Jonathan Crary wrote of a real-life Russian-European experiment in creating perpetual sunlight in his treatise about the relentless "24/7" logic of late capitalism, when "global infrastructure for continuous work and consumption" subjects humans to unnatural demands of continuous effective functioning under the guise of progress and development. As he notes, "No moment, place, or situation now exists in which one can not shop, consume, or exploit networked resources."[81] The ultimately failed project Crary discusses took place in the 1990s but bears almost uncanny resemblance to the storyline in *The Disk*. It intended to enable outdoor work around the clock by launching into orbit a chain of synchronized satellites equipped with a mirror that would reflect sunlight onto earth. Crary refers to this project to exemplify the 24/7 logic taken to its extreme.[82] "An illuminated 24/7 world without shadows," he writes, "is the final capitalist mirage of post-history."[83]

I do not cite these contemporary theoretical and critical notions in order to suggest that the scenario described in *The Disk* is significant for its prophetic qualities. Rather, I take the novel to exemplify a science fiction mode of writing that, as Steven Shaviro has argued, "addresses events in their potentiality" and thereby "conjures the invisible forces—technological, social, economic, affective, and political—that surround us."[84] What is important to note here, then, has to do with the novel's present, not its fictional future. It was, after all, the late nineteenth-century social-technical conditions that allowed the novel's authors to conceive of a scenario that foreshadows much later observations about the information society, new media, and late capitalism. Put differently, this media fantasy on seeing by electricity (alongside many other of its contemporaries) is quintessentially modern, not only in terms of the technologies and social situations it responded to, but also in its conceptualization of the furthest potential possibilities of electric networks and the endeavor to annihilate time and space, which touches on a core experience of the transformations brought about by modernization. The fantasy of the photo-electrophone takes the liberty to depart from speculations about communication media per se. Rather than narrating the possible consequences of the broadening and accelerating circulation of information, it instead engages with the concept of networking itself. Its depiction of a radically interconnected world, in turn, exemplifies a view on the potential of modern media. And just like the effect that McLuhan attributed to pure message-less electric light, the potential is, in two words, "total change."[85]

The Fleeting and the Permanent, the Discontinuous and the Interconnected

As I have attempted to demonstrate in this archaeology of television, the initial conceptions and early technological development of moving image transmission media were contemporaneous with key moments in the emergence of cinema, but they developed in a distinct parallel trajectory and in association with different traits than the ones that characterized early cinema. In this light, rather than regarding television as a postcinematic variant of moving image media, it would be more accurate to suggest that the very concept of moving image media came into being in the nineteenth century in two different forms, each corresponding to a different contemporary media environment. Photography, phonography, the magic lantern, and a range of other optical devices provided the intermedial context to the coming of film, whereas television appeared to be an extension of the technologies and practice associated with electric telecommunication media. The question that remains open, therefore, is how to interpret the emergence of the two distinct media against the same historical-cultural backdrop of the last decades of the nineteenth century. I will dedicate the remaining pages of this chapter to discussing two ways in which the emergent forms of cinematic animated pictures and of moving image transmission media relate to one another *dialectically*, as two alternative technological media forms that answered in different ways to the cultural needs, anxieties, and desires of their time.

First, I shall address the topic of temporality, perhaps the most obvious distinguishing feature between the two media: film is a medium of recording, which involves the production of (ideally) permanent pictorial inscriptions on a durable material basis; televisual transmission, conversely, is not durable but fleeting and thus allows for seemingly instantaneous reproduction of images at a distance. Nonetheless, while these traits are fundamentally distinct, in the context of the culture of modernity the temporalities of recording and transmission are historically and conceptually intertwined and in fact unthinkable without one another. As I showed in the discussion of the initial cultural responses to telegraphy and telephony, the instantaneous temporality of transmission media both shaped and was shaped by the emblematic nineteenth-century cultural desire to "annihilate time and space." The new technologies of transportation and communication refashioned the experience of time and space, gave a sense of a gradual "shrinking of the world," and were celebrated not only as scientific achievements but also as humankind's triumph over fundamental physical conditions of existence. The compression of space and time also had considerable social and cultural consequences as it brought, in turn, an expansion and acceleration in the mobility of commodities, population, and all material and spiritual products.[86] William Uricchio's important contributions to television historiography have demonstrated how this cultural fascination with instantaneity and speed fed into the fantasies of instantaneously seeing at a distance by means of image transmission technologies. The temporal nature of television, in this sense, is consistent with the cultural sentiments of the late nineteenth century and modernity's utopian notions of social and technological progress.

By letting this conception of simultaneity overdetermine our understanding of the origins of moving image media, however, we undermine the significance of technologies of inscription, recording, and preservation to the culture of the same period. Mary Ann Doane's study of the relation between cinema and modern notions of temporality has shown that "the nineteenth century witnessed an upsurge of interest in archival processes," which resulted in, among other things, the emergence of "new archival technologies" such as photography, phonography, and the cinema.[87] Discourses surrounding early cinema indicate that cinema, too, was considered a technology for the annihilation of time, although in a different sense. Numerous commentators on early film wrote about cinema as a medium for freezing and storing time and for representing the past, repeatedly referring to it as "a machine that conquers death," because of its ability to fix and represent duration and movement. "When these cameras are made available to the public," wrote a French journalist as early as December 1895, "death will have ceased to be absolute."[88] Along similar lines, Bolesław Matuszewski published three years later what appears to be the first call for a foundation of a film archive, noting that film's capacity to record and preserve images of actual events would make it an ideal "new source of history."[89]

We have, therefore, two different historiographic conceptions of moving image media and temporality in modernity: Uricchio deems the main interest of late nineteenth-century culture to be in simultaneity and thus gives precedence to the early ideas of instantaneous moving image transmission as representations of what was anticipated from modern moving image media. As he suggests, "It might be argued that *television rather than film* occupied the central place in the nineteenth-century horizon of expectations."[90] Doane, on the other hand, sees the archival drive as typifying the modern concern with time and thus regards cinematic storage and representation of time as emblematic of the era's conceptions of temporality. Consistent with her line of argument, works by media scholars such as Friedrich Kittler and Lisa Gitelman, for example, have emphasized the central role of inscription media in reshaping social, cultural, and epistemological notions in modernity.[91]

However, even if the cinema and seeing by electricity technologies may be seen as ontologically dissimilar in their temporal features, modernity's concerns with simultaneity, on the one hand, and with archiving and recording, on the other, are themselves not distinct, but dialectically related. By claiming this I do not attempt to find a happy middle ground between Uricchio's emphasis on modernity's interest in simultaneity and Doane's emphasis on the contemporaneous interest in storage and preservation. Rather, what I wish to show is that the cultural impulses they both discuss must be seen as inherently inseparable. This point is manifested in the way Doane's own argument suggests that it was modernity's "obsession with instantaneity and the instant, with the present," that led to "the *contradictory* desire of archiving presence."[92] As she shows, the same modern preoccupation with the fleeting and transient—as manifested in fashion, the cult of the new, and so on—brought about the cultural interest in technologies for the storage and preservation of time. These technologies were considered as a means to give material form to the instant so it could be studied, represented, and experienced.

In this light, the emergence of electric transmission media may be seen as consistent with modernity's concern with acceleration, speed, instantaneity, and the aspiration to annihilate time, while recording media are consistent with the contradictory, yet consequential, drive to store, archive, and make permanent inscriptions of the passing and temporary. The nineteenth-century conception of the moving image thus found manifestation in both ways: in anticipatory fantasies of television as a medium of transmission, and in cinema as a medium of recording. Both of these media forms were conceived in relation to modernity's dialectic temporal concerns, which, as I have shown, *no single medium could embody.*

Second, a similar argument can be made about the differences between the modes of representation in early cinema and in the nineteenth-century conception of moving image transmission media. Both early cinema practices from around the turn of the century and the early imagined forms of seeing by electricity share the fantasy of total visibility, in what may be understood as an attempt to cater to what Tom Gunning described as the modern culture's "lust of the eye" and the "unquenchable desire to consume the world through images."[93] Early films provided visual access to the modern world with all its multiplicity, complexity, sensations, and thrills. They epitomized—and, in turn, escalated—the unprecedented increase in visual intake of the fin-de-siècle generations. Elsewhere, Gunning noted that the film catalogues of early production companies "present a nearly encyclopedic survey of this new hyper-visible topology" of the modern world.[94] Film historian Ben Singer had argued that early cinema "seemed to show the entire world, show *everything*, the whole panoply of modern life, representing virtually the sum of all conceivable contemporary settings and states of affair."[95] In a similar fashion, as repeatedly demonstrated in the various utopian and dystopian fictional descriptions I have surveyed here, the still-imaginary media forms of moving image transmission were also associated with such ability to create visual links to everywhere in the world. From stage performances and news events of international interest to loved ones in distant countries and trains approaching from afar, media for seeing by electricity promised a view of the world in its entirely.

It is significant, therefore, that the two moving image media differed in the respective methods of displaying "the whole panoply of modern life." The dominant visual mode of early films has been commented on extensively by film historians during the past decades. Particularly influential among these studies are the writings of Gunning and Gaudreault, which analyze the "cinema of attractions" as the dominant mode of early filmmaking. In their account, the cinema of attractions is invested less in conveying a narrative and more in pure exhibitionist display that emphasizes movement, trickery, surprise, constant change, and assault on the senses. As Gunning puts it, early films borrowed from existing aesthetic strategies deployed in arcades, world fairs, billboards, and amusement parks, as they "categorized the visible world as a *series of discrete attractions*."[96] In light of these observations about early film aesthetics, scholars of early cinema and modern visual culture have investigated the correspondence between the early cinematic attractions and the processes of urban-industrial modernization, highlighting the fact that the style and visual address of the early films reflected the fragmentation, discontinuity, and constant shock and eruption that typified the experience of the ever-shifting spatiotemporal relations of modernity. To quote Gunning once again: "Attractions both mime and compete with the succession of shocks and distractions of modernity through an equally aggressive purchase on the spectator. . . . [They] trace out the visual topology of modernity: a visual environment which is fragmented and atomized."[97]

Yet the experience of modernization did not exclusively mean the sensation of shock, assault, discontinuity, and fragmentation that the early cinematic representations reflect. Modernization was a fundamentally ambivalent phenomenon. It also involved what Gunning refers to as the "dialectical flipside" of its explosive and disorienting dimensions—namely, the centrality of the systematic processes, scientific planning, control, bureaucratization, rationalization, and standardization, as emphasized by theorists such as Zygmunt Bauman and James Beniger.[98] The historical significance of networked systems of transportation and communication, which established themselves as the quintessential systematic organizational structures in urban-industrial modernity, exemplifies how such qualities of coordination and rationalization played a central role in shaping modern societies.

Thus, while the cinema of attraction presented moving images in a manner that drew on aesthetic forms that mimicked the shock experience of modernity, the imagined media for seeing by electricity may be understood as drawing rather on the rationalized and systematic aspects of modern life. Admittedly, it would be impossible to speak of "televisual aesthetics" in the context of the late nineteenth century, given that no images were actually transmitted or viewed during that period. But the considerable body of speculative, scientific, and fictional writings on the prospects of the emergent medium gives us a very good sense of the various ways in which the nineteenth-century imagination envisioned the uses of media for seeing by electricity. In these imaginary depictions, the future visual media share some of the qualities of the railway and the telegraph networks, which offered reliable, fast, coordinated means of transportation and communication. The media fantasies of a visual technological network similarly emphasized their ability to efficiently facilitate the visual access to any person, object, or event by linking their users to any of the other devices that are interconnected to the network. In the various early media fantasies, image transmission networks offer a way to "consume the world through images" in an easy, efficient, and speedy manner from the comfort and safety of any location where a televisual device is available. It is not surprising, in this light, that a number of the initial uses proposed for the emergent medium considered it suitable to be deployed in prisons, clinics, train dispatch stations, and police headquarters—all hallmarks of modern administration, discipline, and control.

As in the case of the dissimilar temporal registers of cinema and image transmission media, I emphasize this distinction between the modes of vision associated with the two emergent media not in order to determine which mode is a more authentic expression of modern culture. Rather, I wish to stress that they offered *alternative* means of mediating the visual experience of modernization: one based on discontinuities and shocks, the other on mastery and rationalization. In the case of cinema, the visual experience of the discrete attractions of early films produced a particular type of gaze, one that "seems to be pushed and pulled in conflicting orientations, hurried and intensified, and therefore less coherent or anchored."[99] By producing this gaze, early films not only demonstrated the medium's capacity to reflect the experience of modernity and provided a particular kind of pleasure. They also offered a means to adapt oneself to the rapid transformations of perception and experience brought about by the conditions of modern life. In her study of Walter Benjamin's writings on cinema and modernity, Miriam Hansen observed that the experience of filmic sensual thrills offered a kind of training for the senses, producing a stimulus shield from the overwhelming assaults of modern environment.[100] Drawing on this concept, Gunning's analysis of the cinema of attraction ties the particular early film aesthetics to a certain timely response to the experience of modernization.

The mode of vision associated with technologies for seeing by electricity produces a very different gaze, although I argue that it was also conceived as responding to the very same conditions of sensory disorientation of urban industrial modernity. Simply put, the imaginations of media for seeing by electricity present a radically dissimilar conception of the task of visual mediation. Instead of fragmentation, they offered coherence; instead of reflecting the visual shocks and discontinuities in order to adapt the viewing subject to the modern environment, they held the promise of an omnipotent combination of the eye and the networked transmission system. With moving image transmission media, one could survey the visual world thoroughly and systematically from a position of mastery and control. While this visual experience could not be more dissimilar from that of the cinema of attraction, its goal, ultimately, is identical: to mediate the troubling experience of the shifting modernizing world. As one commentator articulated very potently in the very end of the nineteenth century,

> If the new telectroscope can be practically applied at low cost . . . distance will, indeed, be vanquished. Friends may talk with each other face to face in spite of intervening mountains and seas. Niagara may be seen and its thunder heard without leaving our homes. *The world will be at our feet.*[101]

By the early 1900s, many believed that television was finally becoming a reality. "The only question about distance moving pictures is not 'can it be done soon?' but 'how soon will it be done?,'" remarked an American newspaper in 1913.[102] But soon afterward, the outbreak of World War I brought the technical efforts to realize moving image transmission media to a halt. When the work on developing television renewed in the early 1920s, the mediascape was once again fundamentally altered, and both cinema and transmission came to have different cultural, technical, and social meanings than they had at the turn of the century. I discuss these periods in more detail in chapters 3 and 4. First, however, I turn to a discussion of the development of television technologies, shifting from questions about *what* kind of ideas of image transmission existed in the late nineteenth and early twentieth century to questions about *how* they were materialized.

2   Severed Eyeballs and Prolonged Optic Nerves

Television as Modern Prosthetic Vision

In February 1928, a few days after John Logie Baird demonstrated for the first time transatlantic transmission of moving images, the *New York Times* published an article that contained some detail on the process that led to this remarkable achievement. The article, titled "Eye Taken from Boy Aided Television," quotes at length Baird's description of how he attempted to resolve the problem of the insufficient light sensitivity of the television camera, which he considered a major obstacle to realizing long-distance televisual communication. One of these attempts, reportedly, involved the fabrication of an experimental camera that contained visual purple, a pigment that was understood to be the light-sensitive substance in the human retina. According to Baird's account,

> I had persuaded a surgeon to give me a human eye which he had just removed, in order that I might try by artifice to rival nature. . . . As soon as I was given the eye I hurried in a taxicab to the laboratory. Within a few minutes I had the eye in the machine. Then I turned on the current and the waves carrying television were broadcast from my aerial. The essential image for television passed through the eye within half an hour of the operation. On the following day the sensitiveness of its visual nerve was gone. The eye was dead, but

it had enabled me to prove an important theory on which I had been working at the time. . . . It was essential to get some of this visual purple in the natural setting of the human eyeball in order to use it as a standard of perfection in completing the visual parts of my apparatus.[1]

Whether such a grotesque experiment actually took place or, as television historian Albert Abramson suggests, the whole claim is simply "nonsense," is unclear.[2] This scenario, however, has been quoted by several authors, and Baird himself retold it many years later in his autobiography *Television and Me*, where he provides a similar account of the experiment but concludes with different results. In that version, after tricking an ophthalmic surgeon into thinking he was a doctor, Baird received a freshly dismembered eye wrapped in cotton wool, but failed to extract from it the substance he needed for his camera. "I made a crude effort to dissect this with razors," writes Baird, "but gave it up and threw the whole mess into the canal."[3]

Read today, these descriptions of slicing open a boy's severed eye in order to install it inside a machine appear to fit better alongside two other iconic dissected and abused eyeballs of 1928, namely those featured in Georges Bataille's *Story of the Eye* and in Luis Buñuel's *Un chien andalou*, than in the technological history of television. But Baird's account, clearly, was not an avant-garde fable. It was a part of an ongoing popular-scientific discourse that served to familiarize the public with the novelty of television. What the story of the dissected eye and the experimental apparatus does, in fact, is take to its limits (if not slightly beyond) the logic behind one of the frequently recurring tropes in the early discourses about moving image transmission: the metaphor of the television apparatus as an eye that "sees" by electricity.

As several media historians have noted, early writings about the functioning of television constantly evoked the human eye metaphor as a way to anthropomorphize the new technological medium and thereby to counter the "human fear of an incomprehensible technology" as well as "anxieties fostered by the uncanniness of seeing at a distance."[4] Consistent with such writings, the reports about Baird's experimentation with visual purple essentially convey that human vision and the so-called machine vision rely on the exact same properties (and thereby describe a unique medium that is not strictly "an extension of man," as Marshall McLuhan famously put it, but rather one in which a human body part extends the technology's capacities). Admittedly, while Baird's Frankensteinian combination of an electric apparatus armed with a boy's retina does little by way of soothing the anxiety regarding new technologies, it quite literally functions as an embodiment of the ubiquitous television-eye metaphor.

In the late nineteenth century, however, such conceptions regarding the similarities between the televisual apparatus and the eye did not only serve a rhetorical function in descriptions of the technological novelty to the unacquainted public. On a much more fundamental level, contemporaneous scientific studies of the human faculty of vision also informed the manner in which the earliest moving image transmission devices were conceptualized, designed, and constructed. In the following pages, I offer an alternative archaeology of television, one that maps the origins of moving image transmission technologies onto the history of modern scientific conceptions of vision in the nineteenth century. I shall demonstrate how both the earliest technological schemes for image transmission devices and popular imaginary discourses that surrounded them were continuously intertwined with aspirations (as well as several actual attempts) to complement or even substitute for human perception with prosthetic vision devices.

The goal of this inquiry into the historical relationship between the eye and the emergence of television is to claim the place of the medium's early history within studies of nineteenth-century visual culture and modern conceptions of vision. I am referring here mainly to art historian Jonathan Crary's prominent book *Techniques of the Observer*, which situates the nineteenth-century appearance of photography, cinema, and a range of earlier optical devices against the backdrop of the rise of modern understandings of vision.[5] As Crary has shown, nineteenth-century philosophy and physiology gave rise to conceptions of vision as an embodied, subjective, and contingent phenomenon. These conceptions, in turn, became constitutive of the rich and vibrant visual culture of modernity, as physiological studies of the limitations and manipulability of the eye informed the construction of many of the optical devices of the nineteenth century, such as the stereoscope, the phenakistoscope, and ultimately the cinema. As the present chapter demonstrates, the history of moving image transmission media, too, corresponds to the emergence of modern physiological conceptions of vision—but in a markedly different fashion. Central to the historical lineage I trace here is the fact that modern physiological studies of embodied sensation, particularly of the function of the optic nerve and the transmission of nerve impulses to the brain, came to serve as something of an *ur*-medium of image transmission, which the televisual apparatus was initially modeled after. I begin this chapter, therefore, with an account of earlier discourses about the affinity between electrical technology and human vision.

Long before the technologies for "seeing by electricity" were first debated in the late 1870s and the early 1880s, it has been widely accepted that in fact, as one journal later put it, "all seeing is seeing by electricity."[6] In particular, two distinct influential scientific discourses of the time linked electricity to vision. The first, of course, originated from James Clerk Maxwell's theory of electromagnetism. Effectively blurring the line between optics and the electrical sciences, Maxwell suggested that visible light is a specific form of electromagnetic radiation that differs from other forms of electromagnetic disturbances in the ether only in its particular wavelength. This ground-breaking theory led some scientists to make new inferences with regard to vision: if the human eye is sensitive to light and if light is an electromagnetic phenomenon, then the eye may be understood to be an electric instrument susceptible to certain electromagnetic radiation.

The first scientists to conduct experiments in electromagnetism focused not on the prospects of wireless communication but, rather, on the investigation of a series of analogies between optical principles and electromagnetic waves.[7] One of the key developments in this area of research resulted from Oliver Lodge's experiments with the reflection, refraction, and polarization of Hertzian waves in the early 1890s. For his experiments, Lodge had fabricated a system consisting of an oscillator and corresponding receivers, with which he generated and detected electromagnetic radiation.[8] Today Lodge's electromagnetic system is best known as a pioneering radio apparatus that allowed wireless signals to be sent and received at a short distance. But at the time, Lodge was interested not in communication but in the connections between light and electromagnetism. He thus considered his system an *electric eye*—"a sort of artificial sense organ," and "an electric arrangement which can virtually see intermediate rates of vibration."[9] Following Maxwell's theory, Lodge stressed that both the detectors in his system and the human eye are essentially receiving instruments; just as his detectors were capable of receiving a definitive range of electromagnetic frequencies, so is the eye sensitive to different colors within the range of visible light. Further, Lodge drew on these analogies when he proposed "an electrical theory of vision," which also set out to explain the physiological phenomenon of the persistence of vision.[10]

Lodge's theory may be seen today as rather unconvincing (and indeed it did not prove very influential), but it does offer a striking example of how, as Iwan Morus has argued, during the nineteenth century "the human body was becoming technologized in that it was becoming interchangeable with items of machine culture and could be approached with the same practices and assumptions."[11] Indeed, versions of the hypothesis that the eye functions like an electric instrument had also been entertained outside the scientific milieu in the popular culture of the period. H. G. Wells draws on such a notion in his 1895 science fiction short story "The Story of Davidson's Eyes," which tells the story of a scientist named Davidson who survives a lightning strike while working with an electromagnet in his laboratory. As Wells explains, due to "some extraordinary twist given to his retinal elements through the sudden change in the field of force," the accident temporarily alters Davidson's sense of vision.[12] Davidson gains access to a fourth dimension, where the normal measures of distance do not apply. He can no longer see his immediate surroundings; instead, he sees what occurs at the same time eight thousand miles away, in the South Pacific. Even though the story does not depict any imagined technologies, Wells does suggest in the story's preface that the invention of new systems of artificial vision might be possible, as he notes that Davidson's experience "sets one dreaming of the oddest possibilities of inter-communication in the future, of spending an intercalary five minutes on the other side of the world, or being watched in our most secret operations by unsuspected eyes."[13]

Nineteenth-century studies of the physiology of the senses shared the belief that knowledge about electrical technology is applicable to the understanding of the human body, and vice versa. This notion is best demonstrated in the ubiquitous nineteenth-century metaphor of the nervous system as a kind of electric telegraph network. In this case, too, the claim for similarities between the organic and the technological systems was not merely a figure of speech. According to Laura Otis, it was not only that "the telegraph and the nervous system appeared to be doing the same things and for the same reasons" but also that the groundbreaking experiments of electric engineers and physiologists "stimulated one another in a complex 'feedback loop,'" as their objects of studies came to be understood in terms of one another.[14] Both the telegraph and the nervous system were conceived as types of apparatuses that facilitate virtually instantaneous transmission of signals that carry information through a network of interconnected communication lines; they were both seen as serving the purpose of maintaining control and organization of disparate entities and were both considered to consist of a central organ (the brain, or the central post office) that governs all transmissions and interprets the meaning of the conveyed information.

Thus, while the electric telegraph was often described as "the nervous system of society" (or, in other accounts, the nation, or even the whole world), it also provided scientists with a key to understanding how the real nervous system actually works. Prominent physiologist Hermann von Helmholtz considered the electric telegraph method of conveying information by signals a model for how sensations and perceptions are transmitted in the form of nerve pulses through the neural pathways of the body, and he utilized devices adapted from the telegraph industry in his measurements of nerve transmission speed.[15] In the mid-nineteenth century, the specific material properties of the nervous system were still unknown, and some physiologists maintained that the nerves actually conducted electric current to and from the brain. For example, Otis cites Emil Du Bois-Reymond's assertion that muscles and nerves "are endowed during life with an electromotive power"—a concept that, despite being refuted by other physiologists, had resonated in the popular imagination for several decades.[16]

Following renowned physiologist Johannes Müller's theory of specific nerve energies, the transmission of sensations in the nervous system became a chief topic of inquiry in nineteenth-century studies of the senses. Müller discovered that each specific nerve type in the body could determine only one kind of distinct sensation. From this discovery followed the crucial notion that sensations are not dependent on the sense organs themselves; rather, they are effects of the nervous system.[17] Thus, in Müller's view, visual perception was not necessarily related to the impression of light in the eye, given that multiple other causes—including the application of electric current—may stimulate the optic nerve and produce an identical sensation. As contemporaneous physiological studies of the eye had shown, the conversion of light to transmittable nerve pulses is performed by specialized light-sensitive elements in the retina. These light-sensitive elements—eventually dubbed the rods and cones—function as transducers that modify light excitations in the eye and transform them to signals that are transmitted along the fibers of the optic nerve. In short, modern physiology of the senses regarded the eye, the optic nerve, and the visual centers in the brain as forming an electric signal communications system. Timothy Lenoir has summarized this scheme, noting that via the telegraphic model of sensation suggested by Helmholtz (himself a student of Müller), it becomes possible to understand vision as a process during which the image created on the retina "dissolved into a set of electrical impulses, data to be represented by symbols as an 'image' in the brain through a perceptual analogue of Morse code."[18]

Jonathan Sterne has proposed in his history of sound reproduction the modern physiological conception of each sense as a "functionally distinct system . . . [that] could be mapped, described, and subsequently modeled," which allowed for the abstraction and imitation of sense organs in the form of artificial mechanisms.[19] This is very much true in the case of vision as well. In the late nineteenth century, the alleged similarities between human vision and electrical technologies inspired new, ambitious plans to fabricate artificial eyes. Particularly instrumental in opening up a possibility to model an electrical device that could imitate the eye was the discovery of the photoconductive properties of selenium. In 1873 British engineer Willoughby Smith observed that selenium plates alter their electric conductivity proportionally to the amount of light shone on them. Further experiments by German engineer Carl Wilhelm Siemens highlighted how this property of selenium could be seen as analogous to the function of the human eye. In an 1876 demonstration before the Royal Institution of Great Britain, Siemens presented some ramifications of the novel discovery of selenium's property, using an instrument he had dubbed "an artificial eye."[20] This instrument (figure 2.1) consisted of a selenium cell—an electric circuit connected to a plate of selenium—that Siemens mounted inside a hollow ball, opposite a circular opening covered by a glass lens. The similarities between the structure of the device and the eye were self-evident: the ball represented a human eyeball, the selenium substituted for the retina, and the opening opposite the selenium plate functioned as the pupil. In addition, Siemens furnished this artificial eye with artificial eyelids in the form of two sliding screens that were placed on the top and on the bottom of the lens.

Siemens placed an illuminated screen in front of the artificial eye's lens. The light was then focused on the selenium plate, thereby causing its resistance to decrease and change the amount of electric current in the circuit. As Siemens demonstrated, changing the color of the illumination caused the selenium to conduct varying amounts of electricity. Furthermore, Siemens suggested the possibility of attaching an electromagnet to the sliding eyelids and connect it to the selenium cell's electric circuit. This way, when strong light fell on the selenium, enough current would be supplied that the artificial eyelids could close themselves and block the light—just as if they were protecting the eye from overstimulation and allowing it to restore the selenium's original resistance.

Artificial eyes of various sorts existed, of course, long before Siemens

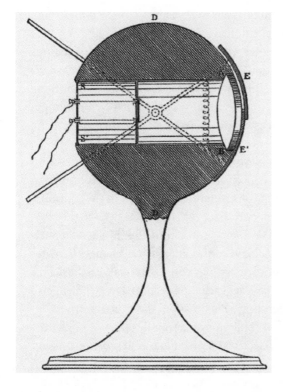

2.1. A sketch of Siemens's Selenium Eye. *Scientific American*, December 9, 1876.

invented the selenium eye. Wooden or brass artificial eyes in the form of small hollow spheres with attached lenses existed as early as the seventeenth century.[21] Used as scientific instruments for demonstrations of optical principles, those artificial eyes were based on early conceptions of the eye as the organic equivalent of the camera obscura. Photography pioneers also drew parallels between their inventions and the eye: Nicéphore Niépce described an early model of the camera he attempted to fabricate in the mid-1810s as "a kind of artificial eye," and Louis Daguerre's photographic camera was similarly dubbed an "artificial retina."[22] But Siemens's instrument was radically different from the artificial eyes that preceded it. While the camera obscura instruments and the photographic cameras resembled the eye in their shape and optical methods of imaging, it is hard to call the selenium eye an optical device, since it *did not involve the creation of images* at all. Rather than being modeled after the geometrical and optical principles of its human counterpart, Siemens's artificial eye exemplified what John Durham Peters has described as nineteenth-century technologies of "neurophysiological mimicry," fabricated to serve as "artificial portals to the human (or sometimes animal) nervous system."[23] According to Siemens's own explanation, the selenium eye was an artificial organ "sensitive to light and to differences in color, which gives signs of fatigue when it is submitted to the prolonged action of light, [and] which regains its strength after resting with closed lids."[24] He went on to suggest that, given these similarities to the characteristics of human vision, his experiment might be "suggestive to physiologists as regards the natural conjoint action of the retina and the brain."[25]

The operation of the selenium eye was indeed remarkably consistent with the way modern physiologists conceived of visual perception as occurring not in the formation of an image on the retina but, rather, in the transmission of excitations in the optic nerves. To quote Helmholtz (who in the 1850s worked closely with Siemens's brother Werner in the Berlin Physical Society), "The first concern of physiology is only with material changes in material organs, and that of the special physiology of the senses is with the nerves and their sensations, so far as these are excitations of the nerves."[26] Siemens's artificial eye demonstrates precisely this function: the light-sensitive selenium reacted to the "excitation" of light by altering the amount of current that ran through the circuit of electrical wires, much as in the transmission of excitations in the nerves.

Unlike many other inventors, whose media technologies aimed at supplementing or perfecting the human sensorium, Siemens opted, rather, to mimic the human eye complete with its deficiencies, time lags, and imperfections—all of which were issues of great concern in nineteenth-century physiological examinations and measurements of the senses. In particular, Siemens paid attention to the eye's susceptibility to overstimulation and fatigue. His statements thus emphasized not only the similarities between his instruments and the human eye, but also the fact that the selenium in the artificial eye was subject to fatigue: after being affected by bright light for a long duration, it needed to reestablish its vigor behind closed artificial eyelids.

The study of strategies for preventing or minimizing fatigue became a key concern in the nineteenth century, a time when emerging forms of industrial capitalism demanded an increase in productivity and efficiency.[27] As Mary Ann Doane argues, fatigue functions in modernity as a mark of "the body's finitude, the limits of its endurance and its capability of storage/retention and is a recurrent theme in much nineteenth century thinking."[28] Considered within this cultural context, the artificial eye not only demonstrated the properties of selenium and the similarities between electrical technologies and the nervous system but also offered new means to study the causes and possible treatments of eye fatigue. Siemens's device, therefore, encapsulates an intersection of two dominant discourses of modern culture. It participated in the period's scientific, economic, and philosophical obsession with notions of fatigue—and it did so by means of a technological mimicry of the human body.

The Origins of the Human Television System

Historians of early television have long agreed that the discovery of selenium's photoconductivity properties played a crucial role in the realization of image transmission technology.[29] As a 1950 volume of a history of television stressed, "The conception of transmitting pictures over distance . . . goes back a surprisingly long period, to the time of the discovery of the light-sensitive properties of selenium."[30] Yet the scientific discovery of the properties of selenium could not in and of itself spontaneously give birth to the idea of image transmission. More accurately, it offered a potential solution to one of the fundamental problems in realizing a technology for image transmission. As I discussed in the previous chapter, the initial ideas of moving image transmission technology emerged in the late 1870s in response to the invention of telephony and largely independently of practical considerations of their scientific plausibility. The first technicians who proposed schemes for image transmission apparatuses aspired to send images at a distance in much the same way that the telephone transmits sounds—by converting them to electric impulses that may be relayed at a distance and reconstituted in perceivable form by a receiver. What was still missing, then, were suitable pickup and display devices, visual equivalents of the telephone's mouthpiece and earpiece.

Following Siemens's demonstration of the artificial eye, it appeared that the selenium cell could offer an apt solution to the challenge of constructing visual transmitting devices. Portuguese physicist Adriano De Paiva's pioneering essay "Telephony, Telegraphy and Telescopy" from 1878 explicitly points out that it was Siemens's "curious instrument" of the artificial eye that provided an answer to his search for a feasible method of transforming the energy absorbed by a plate inside a camera obscura into electric current that may be transmitted at a distance. Following the published accounts of Siemens's experiments, De Paiva recognized that selenium could help in realizing such an apparatus, which—again like Siemens—he referred to as an "artificial organ."[31] Years later, one very enthusiastic newspaper article

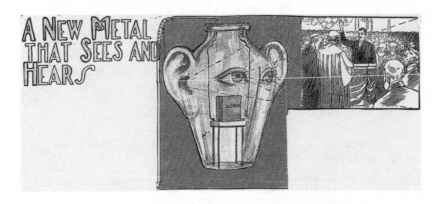

2.2. Illustration for a story about the wonders of selenium. *St. Louis Post-Dispatch*, November 7, 1909. Image produced by ProQuest LLC as part of ProQuest ® Historical Newspapers, www.proquest.com, and published with permission of ProQuest LLC. Further duplication is prohibited without permission.

about the prospects of seeing by electricity included an illustration of a slab of selenium inside a test tube equipped with human eyes and ears. As the article put it, selenium was "a metal [*sic*] that sees and hears" and could make possible "'electric telephotography,' or sending light waves by wire in pictures" (figure 2.2).[32]

Selenium cells offered a means to convert, so to speak, light to electric current, but given that every image is composed of numerous elements illuminated in varied intensities, a single selenium cell was not sufficient for the transmission of an entire image. Starting in the late 1870s, the most common method for resolving this challenge involved an even greater approximation of the human eye, down to the microscopic level of the composition of the retina. Generally speaking, systems designed according to this method consisted of two devices: a transmitter device in the form of a camera, within which a mosaic of numerous small selenium cells was placed opposite the lens, and a receiver device similarly designed as a mosaic of small light-emitting units.[33] A bundle of electrical wires then connected the two devices so that each single wire connected a cell in the transmitter to a corresponding unit in the receiver. As the transmitter's camera formed an image on the mosaic, each individual selenium cell would conduct electric current to the receiver apparatus in proportion to the degree of light falling on it. This way, each unit in the receiver apparatus would light up and effectively become, in the complete reproduced image, what we now call a pixel (figure 2.3).

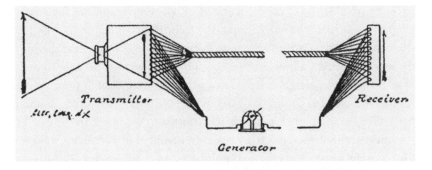

2.3. A diagram of Charles Francis Jenkins's initial scheme for image transmission. *Electrical Engineer*, July 25, 1894.

As was made explicit in the writings of several technicians who proposed such devices, the design of the mosaic of selenium cells took its inspiration from the arrangements of the photoreceptors in the eye. For example, in a letter published in an 1879 volume of *English Mechanic and World of Science*, Irish inventor Denis Redmond reported, "By using a number of circuits, each containing selenium and plutonium arranged at each end, just as the rods and the cones in the retina, I have succeeded in transmitting built-up images of very simple luminous objects."[34] The following year, in a paper read before the Cambridge Philosophical Society, Henry Middleton proposed a facsimile model for reproduction of pictures at a distance (using not selenium but a "mosaic of thermocouple elements"). Middleton emphasized "a striking analogy between the camera of the instrument and that of the human eye," noting the similarities between "the thermoelectric elements of the instrument and the rods and cones of the eye," and between "the conducting system of insulated wires emanating from the plate of the instrument and the optic nerve."[35] More decisively, an 1890 column in *The Electrician* argued that moving image transmission devices "must resemble the retina of the eye in being differentiated into a vast group of minute independent structures, sensitive electrically to light," so that they could emulate the function of the retinal photoreceptors and simultaneously feel all the detail of the image falling on them.[36]

Years later, John Logie Baird referred to these early schemes for image transmitters as "the human television system," for it was designed "in imitation of the human optical system."[37] Indeed, the similarity between the mosaic transmission devices and the principal structure and function of the human eye is striking. Correspondences between the two exist both in the physical shape of the devices and in how they reproduce the physiological mechanism of vision. First, the technological device and the eye share the same structure of a camera obscura that can capture images from the external world and focus them on an internal surface. Second, in both cases the focusing of light inside the camera obscura triggers a process that results in the transmission of pulses of energy (in the case of the human body, these would be nerve signals transmitted to the brain; in the case of the image technologies, electric current transmitted to a receiving device). Consider the similarity between the above schemes for image transmission technologies and the following passages from Helmholtz's *Popular Lectures on Scientific Subjects*, written in 1868, which discusses the structure of the retinal photoreceptors and the transmission of the excitation to the brain as follows:

> [The rods and cones] are ranged perpendicular to the surface of the retina, closely packed together, so as to form a regular mosaic layer behind it. Each rod is connected with one of the minutest nerve fibers, each cone with one somewhat thicker. This layer . . . has been proved by direct experiments to be the really sensitive layer of the retina, the structure in which alone the action of light is capable of producing a nervous excitation. . . .
>
> If an accurate image is thrown upon the retina, each of its cones will be reached by exactly so much light as proceeds from the corresponding point in the field of vision; and also the nerve fibre which arises from each cone will be excited only by the light proceeding from the corresponding point in the field, while other nerve fibres will be excited by the light proceeding from other points of the field. . . .
>
> We may assume that a single nervous fibril runs from each of these cones through the trunk of the optic nerve to the brain . . . and there produces its special impression, so that the excitation of each individual cone will produce a distinct and separate effect upon the sense.[38]

Given the multiple correspondences between the discourses in the physiology of the senses and in electrical engineering, it is clear that the conception of the image transmission technologies of the late 1870s and 1880s depended not only on recent inventions and the discoveries of affiliated technologies such as the telephone and the selenium cell but also, at least in part, on contemporary research on the human body and perception.

It is worth noting that the composition and location of the light-sensitive elements in the retina were not known until the early nineteenth century. They remained subjects of ongoing debate among scientists until the publication of German naturalist Gottfried Reinhold Treviranus's microscopic examinations of the eye in the mid-1830s.[39] According to Treviranus's observations, the optic nerve terminated in numerous fibers that spread through the retina and ended in swellings that he presumed were the first elements that light hits on entering the eye. Although Treviranus mistook the location of those elements for the front of the retina (instead of the back) and considered them to consist of one type of cells (instead of two), his discovery played an important role in modern physiological studies of the eye throughout the rest of the century. Over the following decade, further examinations distinguished between two kinds of light-sensitive retinal cells closely packed together in the aforementioned mosaic structure, which were dubbed rods and cones according to their distinct shapes (with the so-called visual purple being a component of the rods), though it remained unclear which retinal cells functioned as the light-sensitive elements. Eventually, anatomist Heinrich Müller established in the mid-1850s that the rods and cones are in fact the ones responsible for the phototransduction of light to nerve signals.

The impact that other physiological discoveries from the 1820s and the 1830s had on the creation of moving and stereoscopic optical devices is well documented in media historiography. Namely, Joseph Plateau's 1829 experiments and measurements of retinal afterimage and Charles Wheatstone's 1838 discoveries about binocular disparity and depth perception have become important landmarks in the making of modern visual media. Television, though it of course also involves the creation of an impression of movement, is rarely considered part of the visual culture that formed in light of nineteenth-century modernity. Yet given how Treviranus's discovery had informed the earliest schemes for electric image transmission technologies, it is possible to claim in much the same way that the history of television was also influenced by studies of the eye that date back to the same impactful decade of the 1830s.

Crary's account of modern conceptions of vision and the history of optical media makes the assertion that the nineteenth century saw a "modulation in the relation between eye and optical apparatus."[40] In post-Enlightenment thought, when vision was primarily theorized according to the model of the camera obscura, the relationship between the eye and the camera obscura was "essentially *metaphoric*" (or more accurately analogic), as the two "were allied by a conceptual similarity." Conversely, modern optical novelties such as the stereoscope and the zoetrope were not regarded as similar to the eye. Rather, with the reconfiguration of vision in the early nineteenth century, "the relation between eye and optical apparatus becomes one of *metonymy*," since "both were now contiguous instruments on the same plane of operation, with varying capabilities and features. The limits and deficiencies of one will be complemented by the capacities of the other and vice versa."[41] The design of the early moving image transmission devices subverts such a dichotomy between metaphor and metonymy. On the one hand, by virtue of displaying moving images, the electrical devices were designed to work on the eye by manipulating the retina's susceptibility to afterimages. But on the other hand, the devices also imitated the human eye and optic nerve. The transmission devices thus shared many of the characteristic of other nineteenth-century visual media, but at the same time they also introduced an entirely new kind of optical apparatus that imitated the human faculty of vision as it was radically reconfigured in light of modern sciences and concepts of subjectivity.

Electrical engineers and technicians did not take long to realize that in order to reproduce a complete and clear image, the transmission apparatus consisting of a mosaic of multiple selenium cells had to employ an enormous number of cells and wires connecting them to an equally enormous number of light-emitting units in a receiving device. The impracticality of constructing such an apparatus led even proponents of the method to agree that there is "more hope of seeing through the proverbial brick wall than of seeing through a copper wire."[42] Paul Nipkow's 1884 invention of the scanning disc allowed the dissection of the image to individual lines that could be scanned serially, and thereby opened up the possibility of constructing an image transmission apparatus by employing a single selenium cell (figure 2.4).

Most technological schemes that were proposed after Nipkow, including the first working prototypes of television in the mid-1920s, employed such means of mechanical scanning instead of the multicell method.[43] In fact, some mechanical television systems lost any resemblance to the eye by doing away not only with the retina-like mosaic of photocells, but with the camera altogether. Early television studios were often equipped with a pickup device dubbed the "flying spot scanner." In these systems, a Nipkow disc was used not to scan a captured image but in conjunction with the light source, so that it illuminated the scene itself with a rapidly moving, intensely bright ray of light. Instead of a camera, the light reflected from the "prescanned" scene was picked up by a battery of light-sensitive cells that

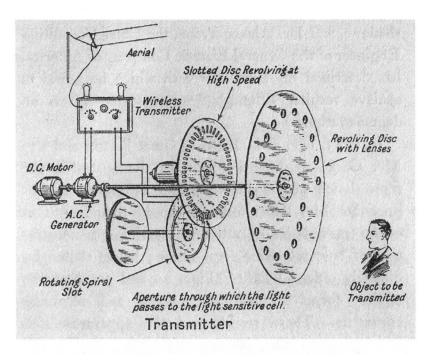

Labels within figure:

Aerial

Slotted Disc Revolving at High Speed

Wireless Transmitter

Revolving Disc with Lenses

D.C. Motor

A.C. Generator

Rotating Spiral Slot

Aperture through which the light passes to the light sensitive cell.

Object to be Transmitted

Transmitter

2.4. The Nipkow disc. Illustration from Edgar Larner, *Practical Television*, 1928.

converted it into a corresponding electric signal (figure 2.5). In a sense, television transmission using the flying spot process functions less like the eye, and more like a camera obscura turned inside out.

In the 1930s, the first working electronic television apparatus replaced the mechanical scanners with vacuum tubes and electronic image scanning and reproduction, and this remained the dominant television technique well into the broadcast era. The method of employing a mosaic of selenium cells thus became obsolete before being successfully put to use. But even if it ultimately led to a technological dead end (unless we see charge-coupled-device sensors in digital cameras as later variants of such designs), the short history of this early technological scheme remains significant for the understanding of the origins of television. As the first plausible blueprints for image transmission devices, they launched the ongoing technical project that fifty years later culminated in the realization of practical television and also set in motion an anticipatory popular discourse about the prospects of the future media form. And as numerous arguments and predictions exemplify, the conceptual similarity between image transmission devices and the eye

2.5. Photocells in a flying spot system. Illustration from
The Technocrats' Magazine, 1933.

remained a fundamental notion in the anticipatory discourse well beyond the turn of the century and into the age of electronic television. Russian physicist Boris Rosing, who designed a pioneering model of a cathode ray tube receiver, evoked the old trope of the "electric eye" in his prophecy that with television, "we shall see what no human being has seen":

> The "electric eye" fitted with a powerful lamp and submerged in the depths of the sea, will permit us to read the secrets of the submarine domain. . . . The electric eye will be man's friend, his watchful companion, which will suffer from neither heat nor cold . . . and facilitate communication between all members of human society.[44]

When Rosing's protégé Vladimir Zworykin presented his electronic television, *Popular Science* magazine referred to it as a "mechanical eye" and a "robot eye," claiming that Zworykin had achieved "man's nearest mechanical approach to the human eye."[45] The analogy has become so pervasive that a 1928 Bell Laboratories booklet about television devoted a number of pages to explaining that practical television "*cannot* be patterned on the eye"—although ironically the booklet itself bore the evocative title *Through Electrical Eyes.*[46]

Modern Media Prostheses

The proclaimed similarity between television technology and the human eye, therefore, found its fullest expression in the recurring trope that described image transmission devices as prosthetic eyes. This claim might come across as yet another variant of a common theme in media theories. The genealogy of the concept of technological media as sensory prostheses may be traced back to the popular discourses that surrounded the coming of virtually every new technological medium. Correspondingly, various key theorists, writing in different contexts and traditions, have evoked similar metaphors that relate technological media to prostheses. Freud writes of modern technologies as auxiliary organs that have turned the human into "a kind of prosthetic God," although they "still give him much trouble at times"; McLuhan's theory is founded on the notion that all media are extensions of human limbs and senses; and while Friedrich Kittler had reservations with regard to McLuhan's methodology, he also made the sweeping assertion that media "begin with a physiological deficiency" that needs to be overcome.[47] More recently (and in a more historical and material-specific consideration of the concept), James Lastra has demonstrated that the consideration of media as prosthetic sensory apparatuses was, alongside metaphors of writing and inscription, one of the two "master tropes through which the nineteenth century sought to come to grip with the newness of technologically mediated sensory experience, and together they set the boundaries for describing, understanding, and deploying new representational technologies."[48] Nevertheless, I argue that the late nineteenth-century conception of electrical image transmission media as sensory prosthesis constitutes a unique discourse that must be understood in its own specific terms.

Most "media as prosthetics" arguments in historical discourses and theoretical writings are made metaphorically.[49] Media technologies are understood as prosthetic sense organs because they simulate human sense faculties, not because they function as prostheses. For example, the ubiquitous idea of the movie camera as prosthetic eye is based on several principal characteristics the camera and the eye share: both are hollow opaque objects equipped with a lens that focuses an image on a surface made of light-sensitive particles.[50] Yet the camera cannot serve as a prosthetic substitution for a missing or deficient eye. In the late nineteenth century, however, electrical moving image transmission devices were indeed thought of as prosthetic artifacts in the most literal sense of artificial substitutes for the human eye. Proponents of this idea based their arguments on Müller's notion that external stimuli of the optic nerve may cause a sensation of light regardless of the existence of any impressions on the eye, claiming that it is also possible to externally stimulate the impression of complete images. For example, Alexander Graham Bell—who was inspired by Helmholtz's physiology of the senses and engaged in research on the treatment of deafness—proposed in an 1893 interview that direct electrical stimulation of the brain may allow blind people to see.[51] In 1899 an American newspaper reported that a Russian physician named Peter Stiens had invented an apparatus with which "the blind may be made to see, even when their eyes are hopelessly destroyed."[52] Like many other inventors of the time, Stiens described his invention as a visual telephone. But rather than reproducing the image on a remote screen, the new apparatus was meant to send electric signals to a device that conducts pulses to its user's head. One journalist claimed to have subjected himself to an experimentation with the new invention. According to his account, Stiens blindfolded him and connected his head to the apparatus until he "began to see a dim light," and later on (as the suggestive illustration that accompanied the report shows) could also see the physician's fingers stretched before his covered eyes (figure 2.6).

In several publications from the early 1900s, the technical discourse on visual technologies converges with the utopian discourses on visual prosthesis, indicating that for a time it was possible to envision moving image transmission devices not as screen media but as artificial eyes that connect directly to the human nervous system. As one American inventor suggested in a letter to the *New York Times*, "The solution of the problem for seeing by electricity would ultimately be found in electrically exciting the retina or nerves of the eye, independently of the external or light process."[53] In 1906, reports on an invention of a new instrument for the electrical transmission of images provoked another inventor to speculate about using it as a prosthetic device, asking, "Why should it not be possible that when these 'televue' instruments . . . are perfected, by the means of two wires from the instrument, one to each optic nerve, [they can] produce sight to the blind?"[54]

Alongside such utopian ideas about the power of moving image trans-

2.6. Illustration from a news report on Peter Stiens's artificial seeing apparatus. *Cincinnati Enquirer*, September 30, 1899. Image produced by ProQuest LLC as part of ProQuest ® Historical Newspapers, www.proquest.com, and published with permission of ProQuest LLC. Further duplication is prohibited without permission.

mission technologies to fix or complement the human senses, other contemporary accounts expressed more ambivalent sentiments. Anticipating what more recent theorists have described with regard to the double logic of the prosthesis, these ambivalent accounts recognized the promise of electrical visual technologies to extend the human senses but also considered them a potentially disturbing factor for human embodied experience.[55] For example, a 1889 Belgian journalistic report about the invention of a moving image transmission apparatus dubbed "telephote" described it as a device for "transporting sight to the distance." According to the report, once telephote connection will be established between Marseilles and Paris, "one could, so to speak, transport his eyes to the Cannebière and follow without effort everything passing at the point." The report goes on to comment not only about the viewer's eye but about the entire body, noting, "One believes he dreams when he thinks that one day the eyes will plant there the human body and will go travelling incognito in different places they are ordered to explore."[56]

To the late 1880s reader, the trope of the eye leaving its place in the body and going to explore distant visual representation would be familiar from previous discussions of visual media. A memorable commentary on the ste-reoscope, for example, argued in 1861 that its three-dimensional impres-sions produce "a dream-like exaltation in which we seem to leave the body behind us and sail away into one strange scene after another, like disem-bodied spirits."[57] But unlike such descriptions, the commentary on the tele-phote imagined the device not in terms of disembodied vision but in terms of technology that alters the visual experience deeply rooted in the body. In doing so, this short figurative allusion points at the inherent complexity of the human relationship to its technological perceptual prosthesis. It de-scribes the telephote as enhancing the perceptual capacities of the eye and therefore—much as though we were to take Marshall McLuhan's famous dictum very literally—as an extension of the limited and finite human body. At the same time, this description also implies that while the mobile and far-reaching prosthetic vision machine is subordinated to the orders of the viewer, it also renders the viewer's body fixed, immobile, "planted."

It is thus not only the conflation of the transmission device with the eye but also the fascination with the instantaneous temporality of televisual transmission that led to such speculative comments about technology's ef-fect on the body. Since with the telephote one could be in a certain place while seeing what was taking place in a distant location *as it was happen-ing*, the medium was imagined as capable of separating perception from presence—or, more precisely, *sensation* from *perception*. Put this way, the body and the eyes could still be imagined as linked together, but with the mediation of the transmission apparatus. Most aptly in this respect, the nar-rator of Edward Bellamy's 1897 novel *Equality* describes the distant vision technology (here dubbed "electroscope") as a mechanical apparatus that "serve[s] the purpose of a prolonged optic nerve."[58]

In the previous chapter, I described how Bellamy's writing expresses the utopian fascination with the electroscope. It is important, nonetheless, to note how he describes a rather disturbing aspect of the same technology. Several instances in Bellamy's novel about a nineteenth-century man who wakes up one day in the twentieth century express the confusing and troublesome effect of one's first encounters with a technology for seeing at a distance. The first time the narrator uses the electroscope, he watches from his friend's home a lecture that is given in a distant school. Perplexed, he asks his friend, a native of the twentieth century who acts as his Virgil, "Are we here or there?" His friend answers, "We are here certainly . . . but our eyes and ears are there."[59] In this scene, the protagonist does not confuse the transmitted image with reality (as common myths about early interactions with film often suggest), nor does he comment on the ghostly nature of the images. The disturbing impact is not in the reception of the televised images, but in the fictional spectator's body. The novel's protagonist feels as if his eyes are in the distant school while his body is with the receiver. Once again, the notion of a transmitted image is conveyed as so radical that the nineteenth-century man is more likely to believe his eyes are the ones that are being transported. Later on the novel's protagonist uses the electroscope to explore what has changed in the world while he was asleep. "Without leaving my chair, I made the tour of the earth. . . . I had but to name a great city or a famous locality in any country to be at once present there so far as sight and hearing were concerned."[60] He describes at length his fascination with looking at metropolitans and natural wonders from around the world, but within one hour the fantastic experience becomes too unsettling: "With all my conceptions of time and space reduced to chaos, and well-nigh drunk with wonder, I exclaimed at last: I can stand no more of this just now! I am beginning to doubt seriously whether I am in or out of the body."[61]

This moment stands out in Bellamy's novel, where imagined advanced technologies are otherwise celebrated with utopian optimism. What is at play here is the flip side of the empowering effect of the prosthetic extension of the senses, a troubled adaptation to new media, which demonstrates the intuitive manner in which the nineteenth-century notion of technologically mediated vision was linked to notions of alteration of the embodied experience of time and space. The exclamation of Bellamy's character exemplifies the sense that, decades later, McLuhan theorized as the troubling effect of the adaptation to auxiliary organs. For McLuhan, the conventional response to new media technologies tends to be "the numb stance of the technological idiot," precisely because humans feel alienated from technologies that so forcefully and intimately modify their existence.[62] In such cases of inappropriate engagement with technology (what McLuhan would call the misunderstanding of media), the effect is not of extension of a particular organ or sense but, rather, of amputation. When new technological extensions introduce unfamiliar heightened physical sensation, the body's self-preservation mechanism responses by numbing or severing the sensation. "In the physical stress of superstimulation of various kinds," McLuhan writes, "the central nervous system acts to protect itself by a strategy of amputation or isolation of the offending organ, sense, or function."[63]

Bellamy imagines the interaction with the electroscope along strikingly similar lines. By conceiving of the electroscope as an extended optic nerve, he anticipates McLuhan's consideration of electric technologies not as mechanical extensions of the limbs but as extensions of the nervous system itself. In the world of *Equality*, the electroscope might not be a new technology, but it offers an audiovisual experience that is radically new to the narrator and results in the sensation of being separated from his own eyes—that is, isolated from his extended organ, which he mistakes for his eyes. In the end of the scene, the narrator's twentieth-century friend—who is more fully adapted to technology—advises him to go for a brisk walk, as some physical exercise and unmediated engagement with the outside world appear to be the appropriate remedy for the troubling experience of using the electroscope.

Overall, this scene in Bellamy's novel is significant not for how it predicts the coming of television but for how it depicts technological modernity's impact on the senses. The image transmission device is a synecdoche or a placeholder for the anticipated shocks introduced by the modern technologically altered experience of time and space. Not surprisingly, the twentieth-century man in the novel does not find the experience of the electroscope so unsettling—he is already properly "trained" to interact with the world through the mediation of modern technology. As F. T. Marinetti famously put it in 1910, "The nonhuman, mechanical species" of the future "will be endowed with unexpected organs adapted to the exigencies of continuous shocks."[64]

By the time of the introduction of television broadcasts and the commercial institutionalization of the new medium, the prevalent metaphors of television as a visual prosthesis and a means of seeing by electricity gave way to new tropes. One of the most dominant new tropes was the description of television as "a window on the world," which appeared prominently in publicity texts and popular discourses on the new mass medium.[65] Whereas the conception of televisual transmission as analogous to vision was inherently linked to late nineteenth-century scientific and philosophical notions of subjectivity, temporality, and manipulability, the "window on the world" metaphor presented an entirely different visual mode that instead repressed the modern acknowledgments of the subjective and imperfect nature of vision. The window metaphor suggests that television spectatorship, just as in the case of looking out a window, allows a direct and unproblematized (though admittedly a limited and predetermined) means of visual access from an enclosed interiority to a separated outside world, through a framed opening and a transparent pane. Structurally, this trope may be seen as an updated variation of the seventeenth and eighteenth centuries' understanding of vision, which relied on the metaphor of the camera obscura in its articulation of the spectator's position in relation to the world. If in the camera obscura model the observer was considered fixed within a dark interior space, separated from the outside world while given an ideal view of it, the postwar trope of window on the world retained the notion of separation and updated it to fit the contemporary ideals of domestic space and conduct. Instead of the observer's mind, it was the living room that was the (relatively) dark chamber, which with the aid of television—now conceived as a domestic medium—became a space for a safe, stable, carefully coordinated, and autonomous view on the world.

This resemblance to classical notions of vision demonstrates that the mid-twentieth-century "window on the world" trope came into being as a product of the pervasive ideological discourse reformation that obliterated the modern terms in which television had previously been understood. Yet the earlier modernist "prosthetic" tropes played a central role in the history of television, since it was through constant references to human vision that television technology was conceived, designed, experimented with in laboratories, and imagined in popular fiction during the first decades of its long emergence. At the same time, the concept of television as a seeing-machine, an imitation of the embodied human visual apparatus, took many different forms. As I have shown, the ideas of television as an electric eye continuously shifted throughout the speculative stages of television history; in several instances the technological medium appeared to be identical to or interchangeable with the eye, while in other instances it appeared to be a complementary extension of the body, or even a superior substitute to the eye that makes the human organ of vision unnecessary. In this sense, the range of ideas about television is emblematic of the ongoing modern debate about the consequences of rapid technologization, which oscillated between utopian regard for omnipotent technologized bodies and anxious reliance on technology to make the body better suited for the demands of the modern era.

3 Happy Combinations of Electricity and Photography

Moving Image Transmission in the Early Cinema Era

In chapter 1, I located the origins of cinema and television in two distinct formations of moving image media that were conceived simultaneously in the late nineteenth century: one based on animated photographs, the other on electrical transmission. This chapter continues the historical inquiry into the relationship between the two forms of moving image media by turning to the period of early cinema, which spans roughly two decades between the invention of the kinetoscope up to the beginning of World War I. As standard media histories have it, during these years the trajectories of cinema and television unfolded independently of one another, with the development of moving image transmission technology lagging decades behind the realization of cinema. Motion picture film was first demonstrated in the 1890s and quickly became the dominant visual medium of the period, while moving image transmission media remained in the realms of speculation and technological experiments and only effectively interacted with the cinema following the formal launch of television broadcasts.[1] The following pages seek to offer a different account of this history of the intermedial dynamics by taking on a media-archaeological approach. Particularly attuned to imaginary media formulations, failed experiments, unrealized ideas, and details that remained on the margins of official histories, media archaeology makes manifest that the histories of the different moving image media are inseparable from one another. In this respect, my argument in the present chapter is fairly simple: I wish to contend that just as cinema played a role in the formation of early concepts of moving image transmission, so too did moving image transmission play a part in the history of cinema. While the coming of animated photographs fundamentally changed the mediascape within which the slow emergence of moving image transmission took place, the early anticipatory discourses about moving image transmission also played a role in the formation of the cultural context of the initial reception of cinema.

In fact, the most important lesson from the archaeology of turn-of-the-twentieth-century media is that photographic and electric moving image media were not necessarily understood as separate, mutually exclusive entities at the time. Here the argument of this chapter becomes more complex. The historical discourses about the moving image were not oblivious to the difference between filmed and transmitted images, but they also often confused the two categories, merged them together, or presented them as parts of a continuous linear trajectory of media development. Some early commentators on film saw it as a step toward the realization of electric transmission technology, while others regarded electric transmission as an imperfect recording medium or, quite frequently, as a component of a future combined media system for both transmission and recording. For example, a 1910 French chromolithograph illustration, originally a part of a cigarette card series about life in the year 2000, depicted a "cinematic-phonographic-telegraphic" visual communication medium consisting of a phonograph horn, a film projector, a large screen, a telephone handset, and a complex set of wires—complete with a telegraph operator who administers the transmission (figure 3.1). Such imaginative speculations about future compound media effectively sketch new genealogies of media: they suggest a cumulative trajectory of development that culminates in audiovisual transmission and thus renders cinema a mere component in the prehistory of seeing by electricity.

As this chapter shall demonstrate, long before theorists of cinema and media attended to the issue of the ontology and temporality of visual media of storage and simultaneity, debates about the distinctions between different moving image media came into being in the late nineteenth century. Then, the early arguments about the specificity of cinematic and transmitted moving images were made against the backdrop of existing discourses in which the two appeared to be conflated or continuous.[2] By emphasizing the histo-

3.1. An imaginary cinematic-phonographic-telegraphic device, illustration by Villemard for a 1910 French postcard.

ricity and discursive formation of these medium-specific distinctions, I do not claim that they are false—they certainly are not, in terms of the media ontologies. To be sure, a telegraph wire does not create a permanent record of the electric signal running through it, and a celluloid sheet cannot relay images at a distance. But if we were not just to consider the technological properties of cinematic and televisual apparatus but also to relate to the overall medium as a set of materials and cultural practices, which more often than not function within an amalgamation of machines and procedures, many instances of hybridization and overlap come to light, proving the notion of the recording/transmission dichotomy somehow inadequate. In addition, as the historiography of early cinema demonstrates, the temporality of a medium is not exclusively a matter of its material properties. While film is a recording and playback medium, filmic representation took on various different temporal registers. During the first two decades of cinema history, films transitioned from being chiefly understood as documentation of reality (that is, preserving and displaying the temporality of the visible world) to being predominantly providers of narrative (with autonomous constructed and manipulated temporality). In this light, the attempt to compare the temporality of image transmission media to the temporality of cinema already deals with a moving target. The following account, therefore, traces the initial ideas about the relationship between the new media and the formation of notions of medium specificity between the 1890s and the 1910s, through the examination of several real and imagined technological inventions and of early films that reflected on the status of cinema vis-à-vis the emergent technology for image transmission. But first I shall start—how else?—with Thomas Edison.

The Promise of a Perfect Medium

Although none of the inventions of moving image transmission technologies of the late 1870s and 1880s led to actual concrete results, in the years around the turn of the twentieth century the vibrant popular and scientific discourses on the emergent media technology sustained a great deal of attention. One technical journal commented in 1898 that "in the sensational literature of the day, 'seeing by electricity' is becoming a periodic headline."[3] Thomas Edison, who famously had a flair for public relations, was quick to exploit the anticipation of this technology already in the very initial stages of developing his motion picture apparatus. As early as September 1889, just a few months after the initial work on the kinetoscope had started in the Edison laboratory, he claimed in an interview to the press: "I am at work on an invention which will enable a man at Wall street not only to telephone to a friend near the Central Park but to actually see that friend while chatting telephonically with him," and even argued further, "I have already obtained satisfactory results in reproducing images at that distance, which is only about 1,000 ft."[4]

Promoting the exhibition of the kinetoscope he intended to hold at the Chicago World's Fair two years later, Edison again promised to display a novelty of visual transmission technology, "a happy combination of photography and electricity," though he no longer envisioned it as an optical auxiliary of the telephone.[5] Instead, he was now speaking of a machine that would provide screen entertainment. "I hope to be able by the invention to throw upon a canvas a perfect picture of anybody, and reproduce his words," he announced.

> I have already perfected the invention so far as to be able to picture a prize fight—the two men, the ring, the intensely interested faces of those surrounding it—and you can hear the sound of the blows, the cheers of encouragement and the yells of disappointment. And when this inven-

tion shall have been perfected . . . a man will be able to sit in his library at home, and, having electrical connection with the theatre, see reproduced on his wall or a piece of canvas the actors, and hear anything they say.[6]

This description grossly misrepresents Edison's invention. While the kinetoscope was eventually used for the display of boxing matches and theatrical performances (first through a peep-show viewer and shortly later projected on a screen) and at times was paired with a phonograph that reproduced sound accompaniment, Edison here contradicts his own earlier statement about the kinetoscope doing for the eye what the phonograph does for the ear. Unlike the instantaneous transmission device Edison initially described, the kinetoscope was a device for reproduction of inscribed records—or, in Edison's words, "a way to write history."[7] With no records supporting the claim that Edison was actually developing an image transmission apparatus, historians have concluded that he chose to represent the kinetoscope this way because he believed that a true description of cinema would not make the same impression on the public. In his study of Edison's work, Gordon Hendricks deems these statements "a mass of exaggerated publicity." According to Hendricks, Edison prioritized other business ventures at the time and thus, "forced to scrape the bottom of the barrel to satisfy a public that was accustomed to getting new sensations from him," he exploited the established fascination with image transmission media.[8] More recently, Paul Spehr has confirmed that Edison never seriously experimented with such moving image transmission technology, suggesting that "perhaps the far-sight story kept moving images in the public mind while diverting attention away from what was really going on."[9]

Without refuting Hendricks's and Spehr's conclusions (especially given that Edison himself reportedly laughed at a journalist who inquired about his promises a few months after they were made), a different reading of these statements might prove plausible, if we are willing to assume that Edison distinguished between two stages in the creation of the kinetoscope.[10] Edison's use of the word "perfected" in the above quote is particularly indicative in this case. At the time of declaring that he had "already *perfected* the invention *so far as* to be able to picture a prize fight," Edison also announced a further intention. "When this invention shall have been *perfected*," he said, the projection apparatus would have an electrical connection with the theater. As he specified in another interview, "Arrangements can be made" so that the kinetoscope may be connected to a telegraphic device "a la stock and race ticker."[11] Could it be, therefore, that for Edison the project of the kinetoscope was not necessarily meant to be "perfected" by the 1893 World Fair and that what he intended to exhibit was an intermediate version? Is it possible, in other words, that Edison regarded the kinetoscope, as we have come to know it, as part of a longer trajectory of technological developments that, on perfection, would bring about the convergence of his various inventions in the fields of motion pictures, sound recording, telegraphy, and telephony?

Several inventions and statements from earlier stages in Edison's career suggest that, in his view, recording and transmission were never completely distinct properties. One of Edison's early successful inventions, the telegraph repeater, embodies the intermingled nature of recording and transmission media in an evocative manner. The repeater intended to solve the problem of electric telegraph signals growing weaker when sent at a great distance. Initially, telegraph companies employed human operators for the task of resending signals that had deteriorated along the way or had to be routed through different spokes in the network. Eliminating this need, Edison's telegraph repeater automated the process of receiving and resending messages. It created *inscriptions* of telegraph signals in the form of indentations on a sheet of paper, so that they could later be traced by a mechanism that *relayed* identical telegraphic signals farther down the wire.[12] Simply put, the repeater defies the commonly accepted dichotomy, being at once both a recording and a transmission device.

The particular logic of the telegraph repeater's mediation also came to play a central role in Edison's invention of the phonograph—a medium that does for the ear what the repeater does for Morse code. In 1888, Edison claimed that the initial idea of phonography came to him "almost accidentally" while working on a repeater. "In manipulating this machine, I found that when the cylinder carrying the indented paper was turned with great swiftness, it gave off a humming noise from the indentations."[13] The noise Edison accidentally produced inspired him to fabricate a sound-recording apparatus that worked in a similar fashion by inscribing sound on solid material. As John Durham Peters had commented, "A phonograph is a telegraph inside out, a sender that keeps on sending, an infinite repeater. Transmission implies recording. Similarly, a telegraph can be understood as a very fast phonograph whose playback occurs only once. Recording implies transmission."[14]

The phonograph, which came to be regarded as the *ur*-form of recording technology, not only was modeled after an auxiliary device for the telegraph, the *ur*-form of transmission technology, but also continued to be intertwined with transmission technologies in various different manners.[15] During the 1870s and 1880s, Edison envisioned several amalgamations of telephony and phonography where the sound-recording apparatus was implemented in a transmission system. Among those were a phonographic telephone-repeater, which allowed the relatively weak telephone signals to be relayed at long distances, and a method for creating permanent records of important telephone conversations. One of Edison's patent records notes that since the telephone and the phonograph work according to similar acoustic principles, a "very simple device may be made" that would enable the speaker "to simultaneously transmit and record his message."[16] He suggested attaching a phonograph player to the transmitting end of the telephone in order to enable newspaper correspondents to send spoken reports to the editorial office, and, conversely, attaching a phonograph recorder to the receiving end of the telephone, thus creating a preliminary variant of an answering machine.[17] In all of Edison's proposed intermedial combinations of sound inscription and transmission devices, each technology highlights the other's limitations while also rendering the other indispensable. "The phonograph will *perfect* the telephone," Edison declared.[18] For him, the combination of recording and transmission yields perfection. By this logic (and given that the kinetoscope was conceived of as an extension of the phonograph) it is possible that Edison may have indeed considered from the start that the "perfected" kinetoscope would consist of a moving image transmission device.

A Permanent Record for the Telectroscope

Irrespective of Edison's actual motivation, his declarations about inventing a moving image transmission apparatus ultimately backfired, at least on some occasions, when he presented the kinetoscope to the public.[19] While the new invention proved attractive and successful, several commentators pointed out that the novelty did not deliver all that Edison had promised. Responding to Edison's description of the new invention, a columnist in the British journal *Leisure Hour* noted that outside of some mechanical improvements and greater sensitivity to light, the novelty "adds nothing to our knowledge of the production of moving pictures on the system familiarized to us by Muybridge." "What is chiefly lacking in [Edison's] own report of the apparatus," the columnist concluded, "is an account of the transmission of his pictures by electricity, and the nature of his photo-electro motive cell. This is the most critical part of the kinetograph, upon which its claims will stand or fall."[20] Along similar lines, the *London Standard* contended that the kinetograph "is simply a combination of the phonograph and the camera." Calling attention to the discrepancy from Edison's earlier descriptions, the paper asserted that the kinetograph is "in no sense of the phrase a means of 'seeing by electricity' any more than looking at a photograph in London which has been taken in New York is entitled to that description.... It enables us to see not one foot further than we could before. It is thus not so quite striking an advance as the telephone."[21] Even commentators who found the novelty of motion picture film remarkable in its own right immediately offered speculations about the even more exciting future prospects of visual media. A British amateur photography journal stated confidently that "pseudo-life like representations of moving or animated objects and scenes cannot fail to prove attractive," though at the same time it also proposed combining the kinetoscope with a system of photo-telegraphy so that viewers could "contemplate a scene or incident . . . while it is actually taking place!"[22]

Responses of this sort, which considered the kinetoscope to be merely a development of photography and pointed out how it falls short of delivering the promise of electric image transmission, confirm claims made by several film and media historians about early cinema's relation to the unique temporality of transmission media. William Uricchio has compellingly argued that since modern culture has been fascinated with the notion of simultaneity ever since the invention of the telephone, cinema was initially received as a compromise, a partial success, or a "detour" on the way to the eventual realization of television.[23] Uricchio relates film's failure to live up to the temporal expectations of "liveness" to the predominance of actualities (nonfiction films documenting current events) in the era of early cinema. As he suggests, early filmic actualities—particularly of the popular variant of uninterrupted "timeless" natural scenes—attempted to simulate a sense of simultaneity by evoking in their viewers a sense of witnessing something as it was happening.[24] Along similar lines, though in different contexts, film historians Paul Young and Jonathan Auerbach have described early nonfiction filmmaking and exhibition practices that aimed at creating an association between telegraphy and cinema, an association that endowed the film-viewing experience with the "entertaining if not indispensable" effect of simultaneity.[25] In the words of one exhibitor writing in 1899, "The secret of moving pictures consists in the timeliness."[26]

Nevertheless, alongside expressions of dissatisfaction with the kinetoscope's inept temporal nature, the ambivalent and mutable mediascape of the late nineteenth century allowed also for opposite responses that privileged the power of recording media over transmission. What is striking, however, is that commentators from either perspective speculated time and again that photographic media and electric media would eventually intertwine, envisioning an intermedial trajectory that would lead to combinations of recording and transmission capabilities. For example, a Kansas newspaper reporter who confused the kinetoscope for a transmission device (perhaps due to Edison's initial claims) noted in 1893 that "the kinetograph is to the eye what the telephone is to the ear. Things occurring at remotely distant points are mirrored to the observer, who posts himself at the kinetograph, and by electric connection peers into quarters a hundred miles away." More than anything, the reporter found this technological advance alarming: "Let the reader suppose, that every act of which he has been guilty, good or bad, could have been reproduced in the houses of his neighbors ten squares away!" To this bleak prediction, the report adds an even more daunting one, suggesting that the combination with a recording device would make the new technology all the more troubling: "A little further along we may expect that a way will be found of *photographing the images* thus produced by the kinetograph and thus perpetuating them."[27]

A little-known and ultimately unrealized invention by an electrician identified only as E. August provides a particularly telling illustration of the early conception of recording and transmission media. August described his invention in an 1891 letter written to the journal *English Mechanic and World of Science* in response to previous publications about the kinetoscope and the telectroscope (one of many proposed devices for seeing by electricity from the period).[28] August's device, according to his description, combines properties of the zoetrope, the magic lantern, and the phonograph. It consists of a sensitized glass cylinder with microscopic photographs arranged on it in a spiral and a light source fixed in its interior. Thus, when the cylinder is cranked like a phonograph, the photographic images are projected outward in succession, creating an impression of movement. According to August, a cylinder "of certainly a manageable size could be made to last one minute—long enough to observe many interesting motions."

It is unclear if August was aware of Edison's previous work, but his motion picture apparatus bears striking resemblance to an early experimental model of a cylinder-shaped kinetoscope Edison designed a few years earlier.[29] Nevertheless, August's intention in devising this apparatus was markedly different from Edison's. While Edison conceived his kinetoscope as a visual counterpart to the phonograph, August conceived of his invention as a storage and replaying auxiliary device to a yet-inexistent image transmission technology. As he put it, he wanted the device in order to make "a *permanent record for the telectroscope.*"

No documents that I am aware of indicate that August ever constructed this apparatus (though, regardless, the task of recording moving images that are transmitted from afar would only become relevant several decades later). But even if August's invention remains an obscure and anomalous "imaginary medium," I find it invaluable in shedding light on the nineteenth-century mediascape: it demonstrates that just as we today think of television as a postcinematic technology, an opposite view was possible in the early days of cinema. Yet there is more to take from this invention than simply a reversal of linear history. Following Siegfried Zielinski, the August apparatus allows us to identify both "the old in the new" and "the new in the old."[30] On the one hand, it is possible to think of August's apparatus for the storage and retrieval of electrically transmitted images as a precursor to later inventions such as the videotape or today's TiVo and other digital recorders. On the other, it is also possible to see in the invention the very same logic that half a century earlier informed Morse's telegraph: the distinguishing trait that made Morse's telegraph system preferable to other models was that it consisted of an *inscription* mechanism fabricated in its receiving apparatus, which left permanent marks of dots and dashes on a strip of paper. Often called the "recording telegraph" or "marking telegraph," the Morse system thus eliminated the need of constantly attentive operators transcribing messages as they arrived by enabling the storage and retrieval of messages at any time.[31] Viewed this way, August seems to have followed Morse's example and conceived of an apparatus for recording and retrieval that could similarly complement the telectroscope.

While neither Edison nor August realized their ideas of hybrid transmitting and recording visual media systems, several later inventors presented models of media technologies that integrated photographic and telegraphic devices during the early twentieth century. As early as 1914, shortly after a system for telegraphing photographs became feasible, scientists reportedly attempted to employ this technique for the scanning and transmission of motion picture films.[32] In 1934, Gaumont–British Pictures deployed a similar method of telegraphing frame-by-frame newsreel footage of an airplane race from Australia to England by wireless telegraphy. Relaying eight feet of film from a wireless station near Melbourne to a station in London took sixty-eight hours, only three hours less than the duration of the race itself.[33]

In 1926, television pioneer John Logie Baird invented the phonovisor, a recording mechanism that inscribes televisual signals on a gramophone disc, thereby creating a permanent storage to the fleeting transmitted signal. But as Baird himself wrote later in his autobiography, the device might have been worth developing only "if the cinema had never been invented."[34]

The most influential and practical technologies that combined recording and transmission of moving images were developed by the young television industry during the interwar period in order to improve the performance of broadcasting units. As media historian Anne-Katrin Weber has shown, several film and television hybrid devices were designed during the 1930s in attempt to compensate for the slow and insufficient light sensitivity of early television apparatuses. In such hybrid technologies, footage captured by a motion picture camera was immediately developed and projected on a telecine image scanner, which converted the images to electric signals that could be broadcasted to distant television receivers.[35] If, as Weber has concluded, the existence of such systems demonstrates the blurriness of the conceptual and technological boundaries between film and television, the proposed systems of Edison and August prove that the respective autonomy of recording and transmission media was thrown into question already at the very beginning of the history of motion pictures.

The Invention That "Will Out-Edison Edison"

The novelty period of motion pictures saw an upsurge in scientific attempts at realizing moving image transmission technologies. The rise in commercial applications of electrical technologies during the late 1890s and early 1900s and the enthusiastic reception of the cinema led to an increase in the resources available to scientists working on eclectic media and in the public interest in new media developments.[36] The inventions of Edison and the Lumières did not directly affect the technical project of seeing by electricity, where the main challenge had still remained the fabrication of a feasible means of dissecting images and converting them to electric signals in rapid succession. But the coming of cinema introduced changes to the technical and popular discourses that surrounded the ongoing development of moving image transmission technologies. Alongside the intermedial allusions to telegraphy and telephony that had typified these discourses since the 1880s, turn-of-the-twentieth-century commentators started evoking frequent references to the motion pictures.

The work of Polish inventor Jan Szczepanik, who in 1897 patented his invention of a "Method and Apparatus for Reproducing Pictures and the Like at a Distance by Means of Electricity," known as the telectroscope (or, according to some sources, "telelectroscope"), sparked a particularly interesting discourse about the relationship between cinema and visual transmission media. In and of itself, Szczepanik's invention came to play only a modest role in the technological history of television. Most notably, he proposed a technique for image scanning that deployed oscillating mirrors, and, like others before him, conceived of a special prism system that would allow image transmission in natural colors.[37] But even though the Szczepanik telectroscope resembled the principal design of several existing technological schemes, it received a great deal of attention by virtue of being among the first advances in moving image transmission since the introduction of the cinematograph and the kinetoscope. Szczepanik and his associates, who were able to raise significant financial backing from investors, took advantage of the popular interest in visual media in the promotion of the technological novelty in the press. They not only attempted to create an association between the telectroscope and the kinetoscope but also fashioned the public persona of Szczepanik after the maverick self-made promising young inventor persona of Thomas Edison. On different occasions, journalists introduced Szczepanik as "The Edison of Europe," "Another Edison," "A Second Edison," "A Hungarian Edison," and "The Austrian Edison."[38] One commentator, stressing the enormous potential of the moving image transmission technology, also claimed, "He will out-Edison Edison."[39]

Just as Edison promised to display the kinetoscope in the Chicago World's Columbian Exposition in 1893, Szczepanik announced the plan to debut his moving image apparatus in the 1900 Paris World Fair. Rumors had it that the fair promised to pay the inventor a sum of 6 million francs for displaying the telectroscope and intended to designate for it a building capable of seating five thousand people.[40] According to one report, Szczepanik intended to establish a connection between Paris and Le Havre so that visitors to the fair could see a steamboat arriving from America and perhaps recognize friends among the debarking crowd—a plan that likely drew inspiration from contemporary nonfiction film exhibition practice that capitalized on the audience's potential familiarity with the filmed subjects and characters.[41] Ultimately, just as Edison failed to exhibit his invention in Chicago, the telectroscope remained absent from the Paris Fair and was never realized.

Many of the newspaper reports on the telectroscope's anticipated debut at the Paris fair included intermedial reference to cinematic devices in descriptions of the invention and its possible uses. For example, an 1898 newspaper article noted that the moving images projected by the telectroscope are "something like that exhibited by the kinetoscope."[42] Another article claimed that the kinematograph provided the inspiration for Szczepanik's invention and that the transmitted images not only resembled those of the kinematograph in appearance but also shared their imperfections and similarly appeared "shivering like these" when projected on the screen.[43] Other commentators made a case of a media-historical trajectory that begins with precinematic media and ends with the telectroscope. One report argued that the telectroscope is "as far ahead of the kinetoscope as the latter is ahead of the common photograph," and another maintained that while the cinematograph is nothing but a refined zoetrope that can project moving images, the telectroscope is nothing but a cinematograph that can transmit images at a distance and in natural color.[44] An illustrator for *San Francisco Call*, whose drawing accompanied a big article on Szczepanik, imagined the telectroscope as very similar to filmic apparatus, with a large-screen projection in a theatrical setting (figure 3.2). Yet the illustrator also emphasized the telectroscope's simultaneous reproduction of images by dividing the drawing in two: on the top of the page we see a group of operators setting an electric device across from the Eiffel Tower, and on the bottom of the page another device projects a large picture of the tower onto a screen in a theater in New York. These two frames, in turn, are linked by a drawing of a bundle of wires that run between the transmitter and the receiver devices, winding between the columns of the article as if representing the entire distance that the wires would need to cross between the continents, and reinforcing the fact that the two illustration should be regarded as concurrent, not successive. Such careful depiction of the entire stretch of the electrical wires that connect the receiver and transmitter apparatus became a recurring motif in several contemporaneous illustrations of the telectroscope (figure 3.3).

Szczepanik's own view of the telectroscope's relation to the cinema offers a more nuanced consideration of the properties of the moving image. At times, he too made references to motion pictures in order to describe his technological novelty in familiar terms. The patent record of the telectroscope notes that the transmitted images would be projected in succession that would create an impression of motion "exactly as in the case of the stroboscope, kinematograph, and the like," and in a later interview Szczepanik claimed that the device was already capable of projecting images "with all the clearness of the cinematograph."[45] In another interview from

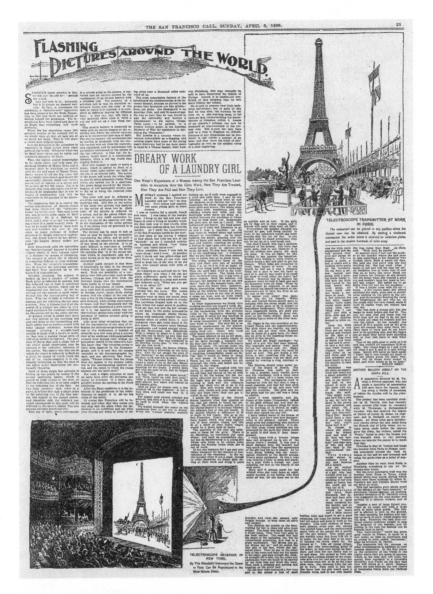

3.2. The telectroscope transmitting images from Paris onto a screen in New York. Illustration from *San Francisco Call*, April 3, 1898.

DISTANCE SEER TO BE A FEATURE OF PARIS FAIR

SZCZEPANIK'S METHOD OF TRANSMITTING TELE-PHOTOGRAPHY.

3.3. The telectroscope transmitting images from Cairo onto a screen in Paris. Illustration from *Chicago Daily Tribune*, December 3, 1899. Image produced by ProQuest LLC as part of ProQuest ® Historical Newspapers, www.proquest.com, and published with permission of ProQuest LLC. Further duplication is prohibited without permission.

1898, however, Szczepanik chose to evoke the cinema not in order to stress its affinity with the telectroscope but in order to distinguish between the two visual media. Providing a technical explanation of how the telectroscope may transmit both still and moving images, he argued that this is possible because in the case of the transmission apparatus, "it is the *actual picture* which is reproduced, and not a *mere record*, as in the case of the cinematograph."[46]

While this comment might strike us as dubious and theoretically unsound, it nonetheless merits particular critical attention, for it exemplifies a pioneering attempt to articulate medium-specific characteristics of the moving image. The argument itself concerns the particularities of the telectroscope's technical operation: Szczepanik simply notes that the electrical connection between the transmitting and the receiving components of his invention allows the reproduction of either static and moving images, for what is displayed on the telectroscope's screen corresponds to whatever is captured at any given moment by the camera apparatus in connection with it. In this sense, he indicates that the distinction between still photography and motion picture film technology is not applicable to the case of transmission media. What is noteworthy in this example, however, is Szczepanik's particular choice of terms, namely "actual" to describe the transmitted image and a "mere record" to describe the filmic image—both of which, crucially, relate his technical explanation to larger concerns of the possibilities of cinematic representation. Contrary to the contemporaneous discourses that considered moving image transmission media as belonging to the same historical-technical lineage as the cinema and being destined to intertwine with it, Szczepanik argues here for an ontological difference between recorded and transmitted images. In the context of the 1890s discourses on visual media, his insistence on the distinction between filmic "records" and the telectroscope's "actual" images boldly aims to beat cinema at its own game: the game of authenticity and affinity with the real. The earliest discussions about cinema dealt extensively with the medium's unique capacity to register, store, and represent imprints of the real visible world (which, in later periods, was theorized as the indexical nature of the film). To a great extent, as Mary Ann Doane has demonstrated, the cinematic image was considered a reliable record of what existed in front of the camera because of its privileged relation to time—if not in terms of simultaneity, in terms of storing and representing duration—which allowed the cinema to offer "new standards of accuracy, memory, [and] knowability."[47] In Szczepanik's logic, however, the very material properties of photochemical inscription reduce the status of the cinematic image to "a mere record," because it can only show reproduced images of prerecorded event. Contrasting this property of cinema to the alleged instantaneity of the telectroscope, a transmission medium that operates free of the archival procedures of inscription and retrieval, Szczepanik makes a case for his invention's superior ability to display "actual pictures" of events in real time.

The use of the word "actual" in this context (which was also evoked in a British newspaper report about the telectroscope's capacity to show "actual scenes" or "an actual battle") turns on its head the celebrated notion of filmic actualities.[48] In contrast to the contemporary discourses on cinema, Szczepanik based the argument for the alleged "actuality" of the telectroscope's transmitted image not in indexicality but in the temporal coinciding of the represented and its referent—something the film medium can never achieve. By this, he anticipated a conclusion Doane arrives at in her analysis of the temporality of actualities. "The aspiration to convey the 'real time' of the event," Doane writes, "is only ever that—an aspiration—despite its claim to be grounded in the technological specificity of the medium. . . . The actuality is destined to produce only the sign of time."[49]

In 1898, such arguments about the distinct ontologies of the moving image remained on the margins of the speculative discourses about the emerging media of moving image transmission. But in the discourses that surrounded the launch of broadcast television in the 1940s, a revised variant of this argument had come to govern the understanding of the difference between television and cinema. Although the critical discourse on broadcast television emerged within distinct economic, ideological, and intermedial conditions, it is striking that Szczepanik foreshadowed the manner in which early proponents of television broadcasting championed the new medium's capacity of "liveness" as its essential attribute in order to distinguish it from the cinema.[50] In 1952, for example, critic Gilbert Seldes argued that "the essence of television techniques is their contribution to the sense of *immediacy*." Much as in Szczepanik's argument about "actuality" from over half a century earlier, Seldes highlights the mediation involved in cinematic representation in order to deny the mediation of the "live" transmission and make a case for the alleged immediacy of television. As he argues, television viewers "feel that what they see and hear is happening in the present and therefore more real than anything taken and cut and dried which has the feel of the past."[51]

"Television Next?": Media Divergence in the Transitional Era

After the promises made by Szczepanik and several other individuals who claimed to have developed devices like the telectroscope proved unfounded, the next actual breakthrough in the field did not occur until 1907. That year, German scientist Arthur Korn and French engineer Edouard Belin, who had been conducting experiments separately for several years, demonstrated the long-distance telegraphic transmission of still photographs. The initial promise of phototelegraphy, as this process has been called, was in conjunction with print media, since it allowed a significant increase in the speed with which photographs of news events could be supplied to illustrated newspapers. But the publicity of the initial phototelegraphic experiments also quickly reawakened the interest in the prospects of realizing moving image transmission media. The *New York Times*, for example, described Korn's invention as "a discovery that makes one other great step on the road to 'seeing by wire.'"[52] Once the phototelegraphy devices demonstrated the ability to scan photographic images, transmit them at a distance, and reconstitute them in visual form, it appeared that the construction of moving image transmission devices depended only on the ability to speed up the process so that pictures could be relayed and displayed quickly enough to create an impression of movement. This was still a far-off ambition— in Korn's experiments the transmission of still photographs at a distance of several hundreds of miles took six to twenty-four minutes—but many considered the goal realistic. As the headline of a *New York Times* feature

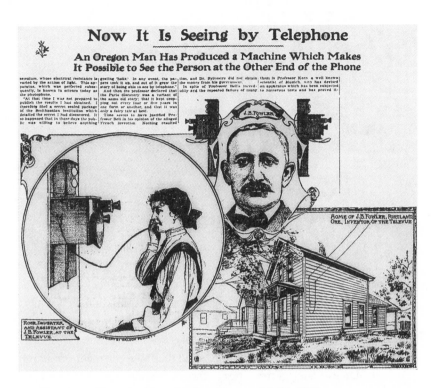

Now It Is Seeing by Telephone

An Oregon Man Has Produced a Machine Which Makes It Possible to See the Person at the Other End of the Phone

3.4. The televue, illustrations from *Southern Mercury*, July 26, 1906.

on telephotography questioned, employing a neologism coined a few years earlier, "Photographs by Telegraph: Television Next?"[53]

The enthusiastic responses to the first experiments in phototelegraphy gave rise to another wave of rumors and hoaxes about the invention of moving image transmission in the popular press. In particular, rumors about two different inventions of a "seeing telephone" apparatus named televue met a great deal of interest and enthusiasm. "Infinite are the possibilities of the 'televue' in practical service," proclaimed one American journalist, who noted that the new technology may be put to use in communication, commerce, medicine, the dissemination of news and sports events, control of railway traffic, and in services for the deaf and mute: "The multiplicity of its utilization in everyday life may never be definitely realized."[54] Reports and speculations about the televue appeared in major newspapers and magazines and in syndication in local newspapers, sometimes with entire pages dedicated to descriptions and illustrations of the novelty. One company in 1907 even offered televue stocks for purchase (figures 3.4–3.6).[55]

₢he Televue
[Seeing by Wire]

means another step in the MARCH OF PROGRESS, and it may mean much to you to investigate it NOW, while stock can be bought.

FULL PARTICULARS AT

215 Byrne Building

3.5. Advertisement for televue stocks, *Los Angeles Herald*, February 17, 1907.

By contrast to writings about previous real or imaginary technological breakthroughs in the field of moving image transmission technology, published commentaries about Belin's and Korn's inventions and about the televue rumors only very rarely include references to the cinema. The early twentieth-century writers rather emphasized the emerging media's relation to the telephone and telegraph. The absence of reference to cinema may appear puzzling: only one decade earlier most journalistic items about Szczepanik's telectroscope speculated on the novelty's relation to the cinematograph, and undeniably the visibility and cultural significance of cinema had dramatically increased by 1907. Yet this very omission may also prove instructive for our understanding of the period's mediascape if we consider it a case of what Thomas Elsaesser (following Arthur Conan Doyle) has called "the dog that did not bark" evidence: the type of evidence whose absence itself is significant.[56] Viewed this way, the absence of references to the cinema in the 1907 discourse on image transmission is indicative of the contemporary changes in the institutions of cinema and the consequential shifts in the mediascape of the early twentieth century.

André Gaudreault and Philippe Marion's schema of the double birth of media forms is effective for the explanation of these changes. In 1898, still during the period of cinema's "first birth" as a technological novelty, many commentators intuitively understood it to belong in the same milieu as the telectroscope, for they perceived both as types of apparatus for the reproduction and display of moving images not yet associated with distinctive media habits, institutions, or protocols of use. But a decade later, while the technology for moving image transmission had not yet been realized, cin-

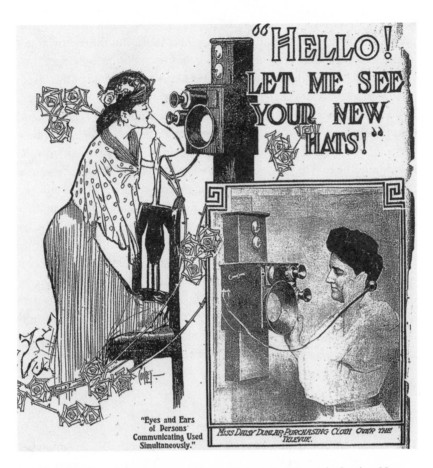

"HELLO! LET ME SEE YOUR NEW HATS!"

"Eyes and Ears of Persons' Communicating Used Simultaneously."

MISS DAISY DUNLAP PURCHASING CLOTH OVER THE TELEVUE.

3.6. Illustration for a feature about the televue. *St. Louis Post-Dispatch*, October 28, 1906. Image produced by ProQuest LLC as part of ProQuest ® Historical Newspapers, www.proquest.com, and published with permission of ProQuest LLC. Further duplication is prohibited without permission.

ema was approaching its "second birth," with the formation of a cinema-specific aesthetics, institutions, and protocols.[57] As cinema created for itself a distinct and coherent media identity, it charted new intermedial contexts and thereby distinguished itself from the sphere of transmission media.

The changes that the cinema had undergone in the first decade of the twentieth century were manifested in shifting conceptions and practices of cinematic temporality. Several film historians have pointed to the year 1907 as the end of the novelty period in cinema history and the beginning of a transitional era that saw the establishment of new production practices, the refashioning of spectatorship codes, and the emergence of dedicated spaces for movie screenings.[58] By 1907, as the popularity of actualities had declined, narrative films came to dominate film productions. Put differently, film's ability to record time became marginal, and its ability to construct time came to the fore. To quote Doane, "In the actuality, the time of the image is determined to a large extent externally," whereas "narrative constructed its own coherent and linear time, enhancing the autonomy of the film and the apparent self-sufficiency of the spectator."[59] The latter mode of filmic temporality departed markedly from the temporality associated with the imaginaries of moving image transmission media like the telectroscope. Decades later, designated broadcast studios equipped with electronic recording devices and multicamera systems allowed for more possibilities in televisual construction of time. But in the last years of the era of early cinema, the telectroscope was still understood in terms of the "real-time" transmission of the telephone and, to an extent, the telegraph. As such, it could be associated more readily with film actualities (which gave cinema the task of representing "a temporality outside itself") than with narrative films (which manipulated diegetic time).[60] The conception of the transmitted moving image, therefore, diverged from the dominant temporal register that typified the cinematic moving image and seemed once again to belong to a distinct milieu of media.

Projecting Television on the Early Cinema Screens

Thus far, my survey of the historical conceptions regarding the relation between cinematic and transmitted moving images has relied on writings of technicians and journalists who offered insights on the topic in various publications. Starting in the first decade of the twentieth century, however, the affinities between the different media forms were no longer exclusively the subject of debate in written form, but were also mused on in imaginative and playful ways in the motion pictures themselves. The earliest known films that depicted technologies for image transmission date back to 1908, in the midst of the period when interest in the emerging medium peaked due to Korn and Belin's demonstrations. That year, renowned French filmmaker Georges Méliès made *Photographie électrique à distance* (released in the United States as *Long Distance Wireless Photography* and in the United Kingdom as *Electrical Photographer*) and Lux released the now-lost *Le merveilleux telecinematoscope* (released in the United Kingdom as *The Marvellous Telecinematoscope*). In addition, an unidentified film known only by its Danish title *Dr. Ams Tram Grams Kikkert* (*Dr. Ams Tram Gram's Telescope*) also features a device for seeing by electricity and was presumably made in the same period.[61]

The depiction of moving image transmission devices in the two earliest surviving films, *Long Distance Wireless Photography* and *Dr. Ams Tram Gram's Telescope*, exemplifies unique cases of "remediation" as theorized by Jay David Bolter and Richard Grusin. Defining remediation as "the representation of one medium in another," Bolter and Grusin provided an influential analytical perspective on how new media forms make use of old media codes of representation.[62] What is at play in the early films is a reversal of the dynamic of remediation, as it is the "old" medium that represents the "new" inexistent medium and in fact gives the spectators first views of how the future medium might look and function. Similar to the situations described in contemporaneous newspaper reports about inventions of new image transmission media, both films depict inventors who demonstrate their new media technology to visitors in their laboratories. In *Dr. Ams Tram Gram* the invention is an electric telescope through which one can see every place in the world, whereas in Méliès's film the new machine instantaneously reproduces on a big screen both still pictures and living subjects (figures 3.7 and 3.8). In fact, the subject matter of Méliès's film is less imaginary or futuristic than it is often believed to be: the same year it was made, Danish inventor Hans Knudsen demonstrated an apparatus for wireless transmission of photographs, a development of Korn's invention that allegedly could "send pictures wherever Marconi can send messages."[63] Both *Long Distance Wireless Photography* and *Dr. Ams Tram Gram's Telescope* use the imaginary moving image transmission media as elements of attraction—the films depict them as spectacular machines and exploit them for visual jokes. For Méliès, the electrical photography machine offers opportunities to exhibit tricks of sudden transformation and of animating inanimate objects, as typical in his cinema. In *Dr. Ams Tram Gram's Telescope*, the transmission device allows a display of a series of documentary images in comical and swift motion. Most significantly, both films conclude with the destruction of the transmission devices and bursts of vulgar violence. In *Dr. Ams Tram Gram's Telescope*, the stereotypically depicted servant of the inventor tries to manipulate the electric telescope in order to observe images from India but accidentally breaks it; in *Long Distance Wireless Photography*, an elderly couple who visit the inventor's laboratory to act as living models in front of the technological novelty are offended by the grotesque appearance of their likenesses on the screen and cause havoc that leads to the device's destruction.

3.7. Screen reproduction of a photograph in *Long Distance Wireless* Photography, dir. Georges Méliès, 1908.

3.8. The televisual apparatus in *Dr. Ams Tram Grams Kikkert.*

3.9. Human subject televised in *Long Distance Wireless Photography,*
dir. Georges Méliès, 1908.

In both films, the new moving image transmission devices are "remediated" in manners borrowed from early cinema practices. When the close-up images of the elderly couple are reproduced on the screen of the electric device in Méliès's film, they appear frowning and making exaggerated expressions, and ultimately are even made to look like an ape (figure 3.9). The images in the screen-within-a-screen in these instances draw on the aesthetics of grimace films, a genre of film comedy that was popular at the turn of the twentieth century and consisted of close-ups of grotesquely distorted facial expressions. In *Dr. Ams Tram Gram's Telescope*, the transmitted images are not presented in a screen-within-a-screen but rather in a series of point-of-view shots with circular masking (by then a familiar convention for the depiction of a mediated view through a telescope). Standing out among the other shots of the otherwise narrative comedy film, these shots of the electric telescope's views consist of nonfiction film footage from different locations around the word that resemble (and were surely taken from) early film programs of actualities and travelogues (figure 3.19). In short, the early filmmakers represented the novelties of moving image transmission media as returning to modes of cinematic representation that by then could

3.10. A distant transmitted image in *Dr. Ams Tram Grams Kikkert.*

be considered "old"—and took delight in showing their malfunction and demolition.

The film *Amour et science* (*Love and Science*, 1912), a French production from the end of the era of early cinema, offers a particularly sophisticated filmic representation of moving image transmission technology, since it explicitly engages with themes of remediation and the relations between different moving image media. The romantic-comic plot of the film features both a film apparatus and a visual telephone device and plays them against one another in a way that delineates the potentials and limitations of each medium. In particular, the film gives a narrative and aesthetic form to the different conceptions of "live" and filmic temporalities; as such, it merits detailed consideration in the closing of this chapter.

The plot of *Love and Science* revolves around a motif that was well familiar to moviegoers by 1912. Like dozens of films, fictional stories, poems, stage plays, and cartoons from the early 1900s, it deals with an illicit love affair that is revealed when captured on camera. According to Stephen Bottomore, such narratives about the camera as witness that records evidence of infidelities or other indiscretions played a role in countering contemporary anxieties about the young medium, as they attributed a special moral quality to the cinema. In narratives of this sort—for example, *The Story the Biograph Told* (1904), *The Cameraman's Revenge* (Wladyslaw Starewicz, 1912), or *Erreur tragique* (Louis Feuillade, 1913)—the capacity of film to capture fleeting events in a credible manner turns the movie camera into an "all-seeing eye of God" under which no wrong deed goes without being observed and judged.[64] *Love and Science* presents an interesting modification of this trope: instead of an illicit act caught accidentally by a movie camera, an image transmission device captures evidence of an act of infidelity which is staged precisely in order to be seen.

The film begins with Max, a young inventor, working on the fabrication of a "seeing-at-a-distance" apparatus that could allow people to see one another while talking over the telephone. Unwilling to talk to anybody and never leaving his laboratory, he is obsessed with the invention to the extent that he contemplates suicide when his experiment fails. Frustrated about not getting to spend time with him, his fiancée, Daisy, decides to trick him into paying attention to her. After Max asks her one evening to test his invention, Daisy invites her friend Maud to come over and dresses her up as a man. When Max calls, he can see Daisy on the screen of the new apparatus. But at that moment, Daisy brings out her masqueraded friend from her hiding place and embraces her. The sight of his fiancée in the arms of (supposedly) another man shocks Max so profoundly that he takes out his gun and fires at the screen (once again, the cinema screen shows us the destruction of a televisual device).

The experience puts Max in severe emotional distress. Following his doctor's advice, Daisy hopes to bring her inconsolable fiancé out of his catatonic state by making him relive the traumatic moment. In order to do so, she visits a movie studio and asks a cameraman to film her talking on the phone in her room. She then places a film projector loaded with this footage behind the screen of the seeing-at-a-distance apparatus. In the film's final scene, Max is brought into his lab and calls Daisy, not knowing that what he is watching on the screen is in fact filmed footage of her (figure 3.11). The conversation goes on just like the previous fateful one, but this time when Daisy's friend comes into the frame to embrace her, she takes off her cos-

3.11. The ending scene of *Amour et science*, 1912. Eye Filmmuseum, Desmet Collection, the Netherlands.

tume and shows that she is actually a woman. Amused by the situation, Max is instantly cured. The film ends with Daisy and him kissing in front of the destroyed apparatus, behind which we can see the film projector.

Love and Science thus not only substitutes the movie camera with a visual telephone in the scene of witnessing the (apparent) infidelity, but also depicts its consequences in a markedly different fashion than the traditional renditions of the camera-as-witness trope. While in films like *The Story Biograph Told* and *The Cameraman's Revenge* it is filmic footage that provides the narrative conclusion by revealing the indiscretion, in *Love and Science* the mediated witnessing proves devastating, as Max's already-fragile psyche cannot stand the unexpected sight of the infidelity on the screen.[65] In this way, *Love and Science* anticipates arguments made by media theorists about the television's "liveness" and its affinity with catastrophe and interruption. Mary Ann Doane argues in her discussion of television temporality that, unlike film, television insists on the instantaneous and present-ness, and as such it "deals not with the weight of the dead past but with the potential trauma and explosiveness of the present."[66] When Max sees the images of his fiancée in the arms of a stranger on the transmission device's screen, it is precisely the explosiveness of the unpredictable present that traumatizes him.

In opposition to the shocking potential of the simultaneous transmission medium, the final scene of *Love and Science* presents cinema as capable of healing the traumatized inventor. The filmed footage that Daisy produces with the aid of the studio filmmaker enables Max to "work through" his trauma. According to film historian Anton Kaes, filmic metaphors were indeed deployed in the 1910s in discourses on the treatment of shell-shock victims. In that period, it was argued that hypnosis could allow the traumatized to recover forgotten or repressed troubling memories in a manner akin to a cinematic flashback.[67] The film-within-a-film in *Love and Science* functions as a simulation of such a flashback. It makes Max relive the startling experience, this time with a happy ending when the lover's true identity is disclosed.

This employment of the film camera for the creation of a staged, reenacted scene is indicative of how conceptions about the cinema had changed by 1912. In the earlier variants of the witnessing camera narratives, it was "real" illicit acts that were unintentionally captured on film. The movie camera in these narratives was nothing more than an instrument (often operated by non-professional filmmakers: detectives, amateurs, or children) that recorded an unplanned, contingent "temporality outside itself." In the 1912 film, cinema is created by professionals and the temporality of film is constructed, manipulated, and controlled. By contrast, it is now the visual telephony device that captures and reproduces images from the real world, in real time.

Love and Science, therefore, sets up a neat binary opposition between transmitted and filmed moving images. It aligns the visual telephone with the contingency of the real and susceptibility to shock, and the movie camera with constructed scenes and therapeutic possibilities. Yet the film introduces a further complexity, since the happy ending of the drama becomes possible not because of the difference between the two moving image media, but because of their similarity. It is only because the projected film and the transmitted moving images appear indistinguishable on the device's screen—even to the person who invented it—that Daisy's scheme works out. In this respect, *Love and Science* is ultimately a film about masquerading and passing, in more than one way. First, Daisy succeeds in getting her friend to masquerade as a man in a manner that fools Max. Then, the dramatic resolution occurs when she succeeds in having the film projector masquerade as the transmission device so that Max does not suspect that he actually is watching a film. Paradoxically, it is by depicting the capacity of the film projector to perfectly remediate instantaneous image transmission that *Love and Science* makes manifest the medium-specific property of the cinema. The scene of the reenactment of the telephone conversation, when Max is talking to the projected footage that he mistakes for an instantaneous transmission of Daisy talking back to him, highlights the radical temporal displacement of the filmic record. During these moments, in sharp contrast to the "real-time" operation of the visual telephone, the filmed footage belongs to a time that is at once before *and* after the time of the actual conversation: the preproduced footage was shot on an earlier day in order to be played back to Max at a specific time in the future, while at the same time it consists of a reenactment of the conversation that was already held in the past. Such complex temporal interplay, it transpires, is possible only in the cinema.

Love and Science concludes by establishing the volatile nature of the visual telephone and the creative possibilities of the filmic medium. But the intermedial melodrama in its ending offers a compelling variation of old tropes about the cinema and a playful self-referential commentary about the singular properties of recording media. Like many works that followed later in the twentieth century—both in film and in theoretical writing—it presents speculations about the merits and possibilities of cinema vis-à-vis encounters with a newly emerging visual medium that was about to alter the modern mediascape and cinema's privileged place within it. As such, it remains a valuable demonstration of how moving image media was understood in the early 1910s.

PART II

Debating the
Specificity of Television,
On- and Off-Screen

4 Cinema's Radio Double

Hollywood Comes to Terms with Television

In 1922, almost thirty years after his first engagement with the project of seeing by electricity, American inventor Charles Francis Jenkins filed a patent application for an apparatus for "transmitting pictures by wireless."[1] The centerpiece of the new transmission apparatus, which he developed as an offshoot of another invention in the field of motion picture projection technology, was a novel optical instrument dubbed the prismatic ring. Essentially a glass prism with variable angles between its faces, the prismatic ring could bend rays of light so that they would rapidly oscillate along an axis as the prism rotated. According to the initial intent, prismatic rings were to replace the shutter mechanism in film projectors and allow the use of continuously running film without intermittent motion. But Jenkins realized that in addition, a combination of several rotating rings could also allow for the rapid scanning of an entire picture in a visual transmission device. After successfully deploying the prismatic ring in the wireless transmission of still images, Jenkins turned to developing a moving image variant of the technology, and in late 1923 he held a private display of his new radio-vision apparatus. The crude early variant of the apparatus was capable of reproducing shadowy images, only a few inches wide, of objects held by the transmitter. Writer and inventor Hugo Gernsback, who witnessed the demonstration (and five years later started his own television station), reported that the apparatus was cumbersome, complicated, and "not as yet entirely perfected." Nevertheless, he also called it "the most marvelous invention of the age."[2] Jenkins followed up with another well-publicized demonstration that drew a great deal of public attention to his project. In 1928, after further improving the apparatus (and abandoning the prismatic rings in favor of scanning discs), he acquired a broadcasting license and started operating the first experimental television station to regularly broadcast in the United States.

Jenkins's achievements—alongside the pioneering works of inventors such as John Logie Baird in the United Kingdom, Dénes Mihály in Hungary, and Kenjiro Takayanagi in Japan—marked the conclusion of the decades-long speculative era in the history of moving image transmission and the beginning of what has become known as television's "experimental era." During that period, numerous inventors, independent enterprises, and major electronics and broadcasting corporations around the world engaged in concentrated efforts of research and development of television technology and launched transmission stations that begun experimental broadcasting on a small scale. By the second half of the 1930s, the initial technical standards for operating the new medium were established and the world's first regular television services had begun.

Even though the pioneering developments of moving image transmission technologies have been vital for setting in motion the process that led to the launch of television broadcasting, it would be wrong to claim that Jenkins (or any of his fellow inventors of the 1920s) invented television—at least not in the way that we have come to understand television. Jenkins invented a new technological apparatus, but not the cultural system of communication we call television, with its associated norms of representation, administration, and spectatorship. In fact, at this early stage Jenkins did not consider his invention a distinct medium in its own right; rather, he saw it as a modification of existing media technologies.

Consider, for example, how Jenkins first introduced two possible uses of the image transmission technology at the annual meeting of the Society of Motion Pictures Engineers in May 1922. First, he described the creation of "a service comparable to motion picture distribution," where motion pictures would be broadcasted from a single station to every theater in its area and thereby eliminate the costs and time loss of the operation of film exchanges.[3] Second, Jenkins drew inspiration from the success of Henry Ford's method of "selling standardized, quantity distribution article at a popular price," and suggested marketing small-screen receivers for individuals (thereby, remarkably, anticipating Max Horkheimer and Theodor Adorno's observations from decades later about mass media's subordination to rationalized industrial logic).[4] According to Jenkins, the screen could be attached to a home radio set instead of a loudspeaker and thus allow the reception of visual broadcasts. In both scenarios, then, the radio-vision apparatus becomes part of other media. In the first, the radio-vision technology is subsumed in the cinematic apparatus; the traditional means of recording motion pictures on film and projecting them in a theatrical setting are left intact and only the processes of duplicating and distributing film are replaced by the transmission device for the sake of greater efficacy. In the second, similarly, the visual element is merely an addition of one function to the existing system of radio broadcasting and its established uses in domestic entertainment.

In and of itself, the fact that the technological novelty of moving image transmission was not understood at first as a fully formed autonomous medium is not new. A number of media historians and theorists in recent years have argued that the emergence of new media forms must not be understood only according to the appearance of novel technical inventions but also in terms of establishing the cultural functions and social meanings that characterize these technologies. In his cultural history of sound media, Jonathan Sterne has demonstrated how early sound-reproduction technologies were not recognized to users as distinct media forms. Only when connected to distinct social practices and contexts did radio become identified specifically with broadcasting, the phonograph with archiving sound, and the telephone with point-to-point communication. Sterne describes the transition from technologies to media as a process of *articulation*, by which different phenomena are made into a recognizable social unity.[5] In a similar fashion, André Gaudreault and Philippe Marion describe the process by which cinema became an autonomous medium "worthy of its name" as the *institutionalization* of the medium—that is, the process of establishing industrial practices, cultural legitimacy, and representational norms that differentiated motion picture projection from other media forms it initially emulated.[6]

Television's experimental era encompassed precisely such processes of articulating and institutionalizing a defined set of media practices and characteristics. As Philip Sewell has put it, the period "marked the consolidation of a notion of what television should be, a *telos* in which television would reach its true purpose."[7] But as this present chapter argues, the process of developing television technology into a full-fledged mass medium was

unique in several respects. First, actual experiments with television apparatuses started some five decades after the initial conceptions of moving image
transmission appeared, and in the midst of a profoundly altered mediascape
dominated by new technologies and mass media practices. In this sense, the
formation of television's medial traits was in fact a radical re-formation of
the existing concepts in place since the 1870s. Second, whereas the historical formation of media such as the phonograph, radio, and cinema involved
an interplay between the trials and errors of producers, demands and adap-
tion of consumers, and exploration and tinkering of amateurs, the formation of television's characteristic traits occurred largely prior to its mass-
scale deployment and far from the public eye.[8] Due to the expansive and
complex infrastructure required for the wireless transmission of moving
images, only a few experimental television stations broadcasted programs
during the experimental era, and no more than a few thousand television
set owners, who had a limited impact on television's future, received these
programs.[9] Finally, unlike with other mass media, such as radio and cinema, television broadcasting was subjected to state regulation from its very
beginning, which diminished the scope of experimentation and bound the
new medium to a clearly defined matrix of political interests from day one.

The remaining chapters of this book will concern different aspects of the
relationship between moving image transmission and the cinema during
the periods that saw the institutionalization of broadcast television. In contrast to the transnational scope of the previous chapters, my focus in these
chapters is narrower. This shift in scope mirrors the change in the historical
development of moving image transmission in the late 1920s, when governmental legislators and telecommunication corporations became involved
in the development of the new medium, thereby associating it with specific
national enterprises rather than with the international imaginary that typified nineteenth-century concepts of seeing by electricity. As the following
chapters demonstrate, it is not only institutional, geographical, technical,
and regulatory differences between different nations that have shaped distinct television broadcast services, but also radically varied discourses that
surrounded the institutionalization of television in different political and
cultural contexts.

In the present chapter, I shall concentrate on the case of the emergence
of television network broadcasting in the United States, where the new medium emerged in proximity to two powerful and globally influential media institutions—the Hollywood film industry and the commercial radio
broadcasting networks. My focus here, therefore, will be on how television's

specificity and intermedial relations were negotiated vis-à-vis the economic interests and cultural function of other mass media institutions. In the two chapters that follow, I will examine early ideas about television in Europe, focusing on case studies in the contexts of the Soviet Union, Germany, and Italy.[10]

Triumph of the Broadcasting Model

It seems inevitable to begin any discussion of television's identity with the concept of network broadcasting, television's most prominent modus operandi. William Uricchio has noted that although television practices have taken many forms during the medium's long history, it is the particular configuration of network broadcast television that has "generated a referent for our notions of [televisual] medium specificity."[11] The association of television with network broadcasting—complete with the notions of its domestic setting, small- and low-resolution screen aesthetics, and the capacity for live transmissions—has remained so strong that even though we now have numerous alternative means by which to watch, download, stream, or record programs, we often regard those as "postnetwork" practices that deviate from the default mode of broadcasting.[12]

Network broadcasting was neither a natural nor an inevitable configuration for moving image transmission media when those first materialized in the mid-1920s. As the previous chapters detailed, early accounts on seeing by electricity from the late nineteenth and early twentieth century envisioned a wide range of deployments for the medium. Although some of these included wireless transmission or the transmission of visual entertainment to the home, they in no way foreshadowed broadcasting in the sense of one-way wireless communication from a single transmitter to numerous receivers. What the late nineteenth- and early twentieth-century authors envisioned, rather, were new configurations of the technical and communicative affordances of the telephone (as with, for example, Robida's novel *The Twentieth Century*, discussed in chapter 1, in which a switchboard operator facilitates individual transmissions from an expansive network of two-way communication lines). It is crucial to recall, therefore, that the history of moving image transmission and the history of broadcasting developed independently from one another and intersected only when radio networks and manufacturing companies observed the initial demonstrations of transmitted moving images and recognized the opportunity to incorporate television in their broadcasting operations.

During the first years of the experimental era, inventors had experimented with several different configurations of the moving image transmission. Most prominent among those, in terms of both technical capacity and draw of public awareness, had been the picture-telephone model that the American Telephone and Telegraph Company (AT&T) demonstrated in April 1927 alongside another large-screen model that intended to function as a "visual loudspeaker."[13] The picture-telephone model appeared not only as a realization of fantasies already in place since the 1870s, but also as a feasible extension of a communication system already in mass use. Indeed, as numerous magazine illustrations, motion pictures, and science fiction stories from the period testify, moving image transmission media was primarily understood in the popular imagination of the 1920s as a tool for two-way point-to-point communication (figures 4.1–4.3). In addition to the visual-telephone models, by 1930 several inventors experimented with systems for transmitting images onto large screens, hoping to deploy the new technology within the existing cultural and economic institutions of theatrical entertainment.[14] Others experimented with moving image transmission systems outside the realm of entertainment. For example, Jenkins developed the "aerial television eye," which intended to transmit airplane views to ground receiving stations, and Baird invented "noctovision," which allowed the reproduction of images of objects in the dark or through fog using infrared illumination.[15]

Unlike telephony and theatrical projection, broadcasting was still a novelty in the 1920s. The concept of commercial broadcasting came out of post–World War I radio culture, when American radio manufacturers conceived of using radio as a wireless variant of the music box or the domestic phonograph and started offering entertainment programs in order to stimulate sales of sets or to advertise their own organizations or commercial sponsors. During the same period, domestic media became a mass phenomenon: by 1920, 50 percent of American homes were equipped with phonographs and 37 percent with telephones.[16] Increasingly, electronics manufacturers targeted clientele beyond the technologically inclined hobbyists and began advertising prefabricated radio receiver sets for home use. The first nationwide broadcasting service was launched by RCA's National Broadcasting Company (NBC) just a few months after Jenkins and Baird first demonstrated their image transmission apparatus. A second network, operated by Columbia Broadcasting Services (CBS), launched two years later. With nationwide coverage (yet not without considerable gaps) radio became a uniquely powerful advertising tool as well as an instrument for the creation

4.1. Cover illustration of *Ralph 124C 41+* by Hugo Gernsback (1925 edition).

4.2. The telephot. Illustration from *Electrical Experimenter*, May 1918.

4.3. Visual telephony in *Metropolis*, dir. Fritz Lang, 1927.

of shared national culture—a notion that was of great concern during the time of the great waves of immigration to the United States in the 1920s. When the newly established Federal Radio Commission (FRC) took charge of regulating the use of the broadcasting spectrum in 1927, it preferred the commercial stations that allegedly operated in the "public interest" to those operated by amateurs or not-for-profit educational or political organization when it came to allocating higher power frequencies. Ultimately, these financial, regulatory, and technical advantages allowed the model of privately owned, commercially sponsored nationwide radio networks, now commonly dubbed "the American System of Broadcasting," to solidify its dominant role in American media culture by the time experimental work on television had started.[17]

American radio broadcasters and electronic manufacturers were quick to realize the potential of extending their operation to the visual realm and established themselves in the forefront of moving image transmission technologies research and development. Chief among them was RCA, which started an experimental television station in New York in April 1928. At that early stage, pursuing control of television did not simply involve seizing the best apparatus or business model; also at stake was conveying a compelling image of the future of television as a complete communication system of delivery and reception, cultural values, and aesthetic qualities. One important strategy of the broadcasting industry was to argue for its suitability to control the development and commercialization of television by way of making essentialist historical and ontological arguments regarding the affinity between radio and moving image transmission. Thus, the president of the Radio Manufacturers' Association stated in 1928, "Television is the next great step in the development of the radio art."[18] Later, NBC president Merlin Aylesworth similarly claimed, "We are not bringing to the public something totally new like radio; we are simply adding another dimension to radio."[19]

The most vocal and prolific advocate of commercial television broadcasting was David Sarnoff, who became president of RCA in 1930. In a number of essays in newspapers and popular magazines, Sarnoff stressed that the kinship between radio and television went beyond the technical capacity for wireless communication. According to Sarnoff, television not only marked "an entirely new era of radio communication" but also developed along a trajectory that ran parallel to radio's own course of development.[20] In a 1931 article for the *New York Times* he likened the current state of television to prebroadcasting amateur radio of the 1910s and predicted that television would be made available to the public when it was in a form comparable to the earphone stage of radio, from which it would develop further to match the "embryonic quality" of early crystal-set radio, and ultimately would reach the service quality of broadcast radio.[21] By drawing these historical parallels, Sarnoff intended to validate the claim that television was destined to take the form of a domestic broadcasting medium and adopt the commercial model of radio—a model which, as Sewell has convincingly shown, had by that period been associated with freedom from state control, as well as with the notion that it could offer unparalleled high-quality programming.[22]

According to Sarnoff's writings from the early 1930s, the new medium of television appeared in service of the old art forms of the theater, the opera, and the concert hall, which were "vying for the service of millions of homes."[23] Contra many contemporary critics of mass media, Sarnoff insisted that television had artistic merit and was going to uplift the nation's—if not the world's—cultural standards. Echoing notions that had been attributed to cinema in the 1910s, Sarnoff offered a utopian depiction of broadcasting as an agent of democratization and enlightenment, arguing that television's capacity to transmit images and sounds at a distance held the promise to take the fine arts out of their aristocratic isolation and bring them to the masses.[24] This popularization of the arts, Sarnoff posited, was not going to diminish their cultural significance; on the contrary, broadcasting was going to restore the original status of works such as classic dramas and Shakespearean plays, which as Sarnoff maintained, originated in what used to be considered the realm of popular entertainment. Further, Sarnoff declared that television was destined not only to provide cultural education but ultimately to sweep away the human physical limitations, extend the reach of the eye and the ear, and enable mankind to "encompass the whole world within the fraction of a second."[25] These strikingly proto-McLuhanesque assertions about the medium's relation to older cultural forms and its effect on human sense perception and embodiment come to a grand conclusion with Sarnoff's claim that television will bring "a new horizon, a new philosophy, a new sense of freedom, and greatest of all, perhaps, a finer and broader understanding between all the people of the world."[26]

While proponents of radio considered television a further evolutionary step in the history of sound broadcasting, other commentators thought television belonged within the historical trajectory of cinema. The almost-concurrent introduction of moving image transmission technologies and of sound film led many to speculate that television would be one of the future forms of cinema, alongside technological advances such as stereoscopic pictures, wide screens, and color film (all of which are typically associated today with Hollywood's later strategies of the competition with television but were already anticipated in the late 1920s). One studio executive argued in a film trade journal that television was an "inevitable development" of the motion pictures, and film trade journals listed items on television under the heading "applications for motion pictures."[27] Likewise, critic Paul Rotha wrote in the 1930 edition of his influential history of cinema, *The Film till Now*, that the American film industry "is thinking beyond the dialogue film, beyond even the color and stereoscopic film" and aiming at the development of television in order to achieve with its aid "complete control of the entertainment industry of the world."[28]

Other commentators drew parallels between various stages in the development of experimental television and key moments in the history of film, similar to how Sarnoff sketched the future of television parallel to the history of radio. Displaying an admirable familiarity with early film history, a newspaper report about AT&T's inaugural demonstration of television compared a vaudeville act that was transmitted as part of the event to Edison's 1894 kinetographic record of Fred Ott's sneeze.[29] In 1929, C. Francis Jenkins alluded to another early Edison film as he alleged that the pictures broadcasted from his experimental station were comparable to "a radio double of the old *Black Diamond Express* of sainted memory."[30] Nine years later, a *Variety* critic finally found a television play that came to stand as the new medium's equivalent of *The Great Train Robbery* (1903).[31] Television, in all these accounts, was moving ahead swiftly, but it still lagged over three decades behind the advance of cinema.

Like the radio broadcasters, Hollywood also expressed interest in the prospects of moving image transmission already in the 1920s. Film trade journals regularly reported on the progress of television starting with the first public demonstrations, and the president of the Motion Picture Producers and Distributors of America (MPPDA) requested to be kept updated on the status of the new medium as early as 1928.[32] When the Jenkins laboratories started marketing small television kits for radio amateurs, their customers also included Fox studios, the research laboratory of Eastman Kodak, and a number of movie theaters. This occasion, quite symbolically, became probably the first time that Hollywood lost money on account of television: according to the laboratory documentation, an engineer from Fox mailed Jenkins $2.50 for the kit, but did not receive one in return.[33] By the late 1920s and early 1930s, Hollywood's response to the new technology was a mix of futuristic enthusiasm and anxiety. The possibility of integrating image transmission technology into the cinema business appeared attractive and feasible to film executives. In 1928, for example, prominent exhibitor Samuel "Roxy" Rothafel stated, "We welcome the advent of television as an addition to progress. When the occasion arises we will harness it to our needs as we have radio. Speaking from the point of view of a motion picture producer, there is nothing to worry about."[34] A film trade journal reported the same year that Jenkins was about to collaborate with the Loew's theater chain on establishing such a "television movies" service, though clearly the state of the development of large-screen television made such a collaborative enterprise impossible.[35]

At the same time, the prospects of television also appeared to many to be a threat to the film business, primarily due to the competition already posed by the free domestic entertainment offered by radio. According to a *New York Times* report from June 1930, television became "a spectre-like problem" that haunted Hollywood, "creep[ing] into any serious discussion of the screen today."[36] One particularly alarmist column written by playwright Robert E. Sherwood for *Hollywood Spectator* warned in 1931 that "when Millions of television sets are in operation in homes throughout the land, the movie industry will undergo a reorganization as complete as Russia's" and will find itself reduced "to the humble estate of a subsidiary."[37] Sherwood emphasized in particular the threat television poses to theater owners, who in his view "are going to find themselves with tons of useless concrete, marble and red brocade on their hands."[38]

It would be wrong, however, to deduce that the film industry and the radio industry were two distinct rival parties that held opposite views about the prospects of television broadcasting. The reality of the 1920s and 1930s mediascape is considerably more complex. Whereas film theaters and radio services competed over the American consumers' attention and leisure time, there were no clean-cut distinctions between the cinema and the broadcasting businesses. The appearance of the first image transmission devices coincided with a peak of the film industry's involvement in radio.[39] By the time the first experimental television stations started operating, major electronics manufacturers played an important role in Hollywood's conversion to sound films and several studios and exhibitors operated radio stations. In addition, both radio networks NBC and CBS had affiliation with film studios: NBC's parent company, the Radio Corporation, established the RKO film studio in 1928 precisely in order "to protect itself when television becomes a fact."[40] CBS, in turn, partnered with Paramount, which had acquired a half-interest in the network in 1929. To quote Ross Melnick, by the end of the 1920s "there no longer was a walled-off 'film industry' but rather an 'entertainment industry' that produced motion pictures among a host of other products and media."[41]

Within this converged entertainment industry, the formulation of American television took place not only by way of competition between opposing broadcasting and cinema interests but also, in part, through business collaborations. By the end of the 1920s, several Hollywood studios acknowledged that their most critical disadvantage with respect to the development of television was a lack of necessary infrastructure and technological capacity. Consequently, they opted to pursue association with radio networks. Warner Brothers acquired substantial stock interest in an electronic company that held television technology patents, and Universal expressed interest in collaborating with a German company in developing television devices.[42] None of these efforts, however, amounted to actual achievements in launching television services. Even Paramount's partnership with CBS, which promised to give the film studio an effective new outlet and the radio network an access to experienced and esteemed producers of visual material, was ultimately short-lived. CBS executive William Paley viewed the collaboration with the film studio most enthusiastically, saying, "Just as the films have utilized the resources of radio science to give the screen a voice, radio broadcasting will eventually borrow eyes from the master minds of the motion-picture laboratory."[43] CBS started operating an experimental television station in the summer of 1931. However, according to Richard Koszarski, Paramount remained peculiarly indifferent to television efforts.[44] The main interest of the studio was to promote its stars and theatrical releases, and less than a year after the launch of the television station Paramount sold its part back to the network. Ultimately, due to the financial burden of the transition to sound and the effect of the Great Depression, which had a more severe impact on the film business than on radio, Hollywood proved incapable of playing a major role in the development of commercial television.

William Boddy has argued that with the exception of ongoing low-profile experiments with theater television, "alternative, nonbroadcast uses of television did not receive general public recognition or debate after the 1920s."[45] Several factors contributed to the quick and practically exclusive association of television with broadcasting. Among the various industries involved in what Joseph Udelson has termed the "great television race," broadcasting established itself as a highly profitable commercial model that could extend and absorb new technologies (though not without some considerable adaptations). Author and broadcasting consultant Edgar H. Felix observed so in a 1931 book:

Television will find a complete structure ready to commercialize it. Broadcasting stations have organized personnel and established contacts in the advertising field, the advertising agencies have specialists in handling radio problems for their clients, and the advertiser is already accustomed to radio as a medium of approach to the public. Consequently there will be no long period of adjustment and development. Advertising will be ready for the visual medium long before the medium is ready for advertising.[46]

Simultaneously, governmental regulation also favored the broadcasting model over other possible configurations of moving image transmission. The FRC, and later its successor, the Federal Communications Commission (FCC), played a crucial role in shaping the future of television, first and foremost by deciding to apply to it the same principles that guided the regulation of existing radio broadcasting—thereby implicitly framing television as a branch of radio from the get-go. The commission's responsibilities included issuing licenses for experimental transmission stations, allocating wavelengths for broadcasting in a manner that would prevent interruption of existing radio services, and eventually approving the commercialization of broadcasting. From the first years of its existence, the FRC's approach to television worked to the benefit of the radio companies. The commission required that applicants for experimental broadcasting licenses possess the necessary technical capacity and know-how as well as available capital for investment and operation of stations on a noncommercial basis. Licensing procedures also prioritized applicants engaged in technical improvement of television apparatus, particularly by offering higher picture quality while utilizing minimum radio frequency bandwidth. These requirements intended to discourage applicants merely interested in the commercial exploitation of the medium and instead encourage companies that would develop the state of the art, yet they were all but tailor-made for the experience and capacity of companies like RCA.[47] Thus, at a very early point in television's experimental stage, possibilities outside broadcasting were effectively blocked.

The state of the television race altered once again in the mid-1930s, when the introduction of Vladimir Zworykin and Philo Farnsworth's electronic television systems reawakened the interest of the public, which had become disappointed with the limited offering of mechanical television, since they allowed for dramatically improved image quality and screen size (at the time, electronic sets were capable of reproducing pictures of over three hundred lines of definition, compared with the average of forty-eight to sixty lines in mechanical sets). But new electronic apparatus was significantly more expensive to develop and operate. As a result, only a handful of large broadcasting and electronics corporations came to dominate the field, pushing out of the race many of the smaller and independent companies, including Jenkins's pioneering operation.

In light of this new situation, Hollywood's strategy with respect to television broadcasts during the second half of the 1930s involved attempts at both beating them *and* joining them. Some Hollywood studios entertained the possibility of pursuing alternatives to commercial broadcast television. For example, in 1938 Paramount Pictures acquired part ownership of the DuMont Laboratories television manufacturers principally in the interest of developing theatrical television.[48] But that second attempt of the studio to become involved with the television operations also remained in very low capacity. Another alternative involved offering pay-per-view services, a possibility that Samuel Goldwyn reportedly wished to pursue, though no actual progress on this front was seen until after World War II.[49] On at least one occasion, a society of independent exhibitors urged the FCC to dissociate television from the control of the radio industry by instituting public service broadcasting— that is, advertising-free television that would be funded by a service charge and regulated by a public body.[50]

At the same time, film studios continued seeking ways to associate themselves with broadcast television. A study of the status of television commissioned by the MPPDA in 1937 encouraged film studios to either purchase stations and form a new network or collectively purchase the control of one of the existing networks.[51] Such a step would have revolutionized the media industry, making television a subsidiary of the film business; obviously, however, the economic and regulatory condition rendered it implausible. A *Variety* reporter commented in an article succinctly titled "Pix Biz Chilly on Tele" that film companies opted instead to look after their interests in the business of motion pictures.[52] The studios prepared for the coming of television by adding new clauses to actors' contracts and to purchases of story rights, ensuring that they would also keep the rights to television appearances and adaptations in the hands of the studio, but by and large the film studios waited for further developments in television broadcasting under the control of the radio and electronics companies.

Outside of the activity of the radio networks and the Hollywood studios, the short history of the rise and fall of the picture-phone also offers an invaluable lesson with respect to the dynamics that allowed the broadcasting model to become the dominant formulation of television. As Luke Stadel has shown in his insightful history of television as a sound medium, shortly after AT&T's groundbreaking demonstration of the televisual apparatus in 1927, the company encountered a series of difficulties in matching the technical standards demonstrated by their competitors, establishing protocols for the two-way communication lines, and finding ways to commercialize their telephone-television model.[53] Consequently, work on the two-way model slowed down, and the development of the television apparatus was discontinued by the early 1940s. AT&T instead opted to solidify its role in developing infrastructure for television networks. By the mid-1930s, AT&T had developed coaxial cables that could sufficiently carry the wide range of frequencies required for high-definition visual transmission and thus connect local stations to central television studios—which effectively made the company into an important organ of the image-broadcasting industry.[54]

This shift from developing a medium for point-to-point communication to facilitating broadcasting networks is not only a matter of opting for different technological challenges or a business plan. It is also symptomatic of the changing role of technological media in the "emerging industrial-cultural order" of the interwar era, which saw an increasingly more controlled and centralized operation of mass media in concert with the new cultural and technical demands of vast and simultaneous connectivity.[55] Indeed, in Horkheimer and Adorno's *Dialectic of Enlightenment* the differences between the roles that the telephone and the radio prescribe for their respective users is specifically cited as an example of the subordination of modern media to the reign of the culture industry. For them, the telephone "liberally permitted the participant to play the role of subject," whereas radio "democratically makes everyone equally into listeners."[56] As Horkheimer and Adorno perceived, broadcasting came to embody a unique alignment of private economic and state ideological interests in the form of oligopoly capitalism.[57] With their unparalleled capacity for instantaneous and broad dissemination of information, broadcasting networks offered themselves as a strong apparatus for advertising as well as for the efforts of national unification and centralization of cultural power. Throughout the rest of the interwar period, this model proved more effective than any competing mass media configuration.

Television versus Film: Articulating Specificity

By the end of the 1920s, the association of moving image transmission with broadcasting appeared undisputed. In the United States, it was radio and electronics companies such as RCA, Westinghouse, and General Electric that spearheaded technical developments in the field. Many of the pioneering television engineers came from the radio industry and drew on transmission devices, electronic tubes, and even manufacturing facilities of radio, and published professional notes in broadcasting trade journals. This approach to television as essentially visual radio quickly came to dominate the popular discourse about the medium's future.

In the first years of the following decade, the performance of available television apparatus still left a lot to be desired, as the early mechanical models were capable only of reproducing low-resolution images of about sixty lines of definition on a screen no bigger than a few inches. Yet this period saw a boom in television activity and public interest in its prospects. By October 1931, Jenkins's pioneering enterprise was joined by no fewer than twenty-one other licensed experimental television stations in the United States, some of them operated by the NBC and CBS networks, some by local radio stations, and others by newspaper offices, educational institutions, and electrical manufacturers.[58]

Although experimental television operations had started in earnest and the coming of regular broadcasting services seemed "around the corner" (as the recurring trope of the period claimed), debates about the identity of television continued until the end of the decade, and questions about its aesthetic traits, the nature of its programming, and its relation to other media remained open. In particular, broadcasters as well as critics observing the emergence of the new medium made numerous assertions about what characteristics would distinguish television programs from motion pictures. For the proponents of broadcasting, it was crucial to present television as a new medium with its own unique expressive attributes and communication protocols rather than as a new subset of cinema. As long as cinema provided the sole technical and aesthetic standard for moving images, broadcasters could not offer television merely as a smaller, fuzzier version of the movies. The inevitable comparison to cinematic aesthetics was all the more pressing for broadcasters when it became part of the federal regulators' guidelines. The FRC acknowledged that the American public became accustomed to high-quality moving images in the cinema and determined that companies seeking television licenses must meet an unspecified degree of what they defined under the Marxist-sounding term "real entertainment value."[59]

Broadcasters, in short, needed to shape a discourse of television's media identity that would set it apart from cinema and allow for a consideration of its future possibilities in its own (still-nonexistent) terms. It was within this discourse that the notion of liveness—understood as the medium's unique capacity for virtually simultaneous transmission of events as they are captured on camera—became central. Remarkably, therefore, the discourses on television during the experimental era attributed to liveness a significance similar to what it would later get in television scholarship, where it prominently functions to define televisual medium specificity, ontological nature, underlying ideology, and claim for objectivity and truthfulness.[60] Television theorists usually trace the centrality of the idea of liveness back to discourses that surrounded network practices from television's golden age. Critical writings on live drama in the 1950s understood live transmission to be a manifestation of television's essence and championed the televisual "metaphysics of presence" as an aspect that strengthens programs' authenticity and intimacy. These critical responses simultaneously highlighted television's distinction from the affordances of cinema and attributed theatrical qualities to the new medium that was still striving for social recognition.[61] According to Robert Vianello's account of the politics of liveness in 1950s television, the broadcasting networks were also motivated to elevate liveness to the status of television's most fundamental trait, since the capacity for nationwide address allowed them to gain a more dominant position over their affiliated local stations.[62]

However, discourses that privileged television's instantaneous temporality may be traced back to a point long before television's golden era, before broadcasting services begun, and even before the term "live transmission" was coined in the mid-1930s. In the early years of the experimental era, claims about television's "spontaneity" or capacity for "direct pickup" were also instrumental in articulating the new medium's relationship to the cinema in terms of materiality, aesthetics, and social role. At times, the institutional discourse of the period strikingly resembles the arguments of modernist aesthetic criticism, as both seek to identify the unique material properties of a medium in order to deem them essential for its expressive possibilities. As early as 1928, an RCA engineer argued in a brief submitted to the FRC that simultaneity is an "absolutely essential" feature of the television, claiming that "a motion picture is a record of a moving scene, and a motion picture itself constitutes television, except that it lacks the essential element of simultaneity."[63]

Several technical and institutional factors distinguish the early discourse on television liveness from that of the 1950s. First and foremost, we must recall that live broadcasting as we now understand it was not possible in the early years of the experimental stage. Jenkins's pioneering work on television exemplifies well the historical-specific context of the liveness debates. Due to limitations of scanning speed, light sensitivity, and broadcasting frequencies, the first mechanical television apparatus operated by Jenkins's station was not capable of instantaneous wireless transmission of scenes caught on camera. Instead, in the very first experimental television broadcasts in the United States, Jenkins utilized filmed footage, which the crude television apparatus could more easily illuminate and scan. Correspondingly, Jenkins viewed live broadcasting as only a marginal part of what tele-

4.4. Charles Francis Jenkins and Florence Clark in the Silhouette Studio. Image from Jenkins, *The Boyhood of an Inventor*, 1931.

vision could achieve. Anticipating by several decades television theories that regard the coverage of unexpected disasters and catastrophes as the epitome of live television, Jenkins acknowledged that live transmission might fit "unusual news, like the tumbling down of the capitol building, the collapse of the Brooklyn bridge, or the dynamiting of Faneuil Hall," but considered it of little significance otherwise.[64]

In its early years, Jenkins's television station broadcasts consisted exclusively of filmed silhouettes, dubbed "pantomime pictures by radio." Jenkins first utilized animated films created especially for this service by the McCrory Animation Studios from New York. But in order to save the costs of production, a space at the Jenkins laboratory was converted into a makeshift film studio where new silhouettes pictures were filmed. Much as in Edison's Black Maria, the actors in the silhouette films were recruited from the laboratory staff, as was the director, Florence Clark—arguably America's first television director as well as last silent film director. The actors performed against an intensely illuminated white wall in front of a large mirror, while a motion picture camera captured the image reflected in the mirror so as to simulate a deeper focal length (figure 4.4).[65] Created under these particular conditions, the early television programs were made possible only through inherently intermedial combinations of transmission and film technologies.

In the early years of NBC's and CBS's experimental television operations, executives of both networks took a practical stance with regard to live programs and did not envision a service that would rely solely on live broadcasts. Even though the early experimental broadcasts of CBS consisted exclusively of live programming, Paley's initial assumption was that television subjects would consist of a mix of live studio transmissions and filmed performances.[66] Sarnoff, too, was of the opinion that live events were too unpredictable by nature and might not take place during hours when they could reach a sufficiently large audience. In his view, "television could be harnesses to the motion picture screen, so that a great event might be simultaneously recorded in a number of key cities throughout the nation and the talking motion picture film distributed again by television to millions of homes some hours after the actual occurrence."[67]

Nevertheless, during most of the 1930s, both networks became committed to a rhetoric that privileged live broadcasting as an essential quality of television and dissociated television from a dependence on filmed materials. This celebration of televisual liveness presented itself as a fairly smooth continuation of existing notions on sound broadcasting. Starting in the mid-1920s, NBC and CBS framed recorded programming as inferior and promoted a discourse that defined nationwide live transmission as the ideal form of radio services. Radio historian Alexander Russo has shown that this discourse intended to justify the economic interests of the two national broadcasting networks and preserve their oligopoly. In the view of the networks, the use of recorded material in radio threatened their hegemony, since it allowed for the decentralization of program production and the elimination of the need of network infrastructure for nationwide distribution. For the president of NBC, airing reordered programs meant taking away the supposed distinctive feature of radio broadcasting, which would eliminate the justification for the medium's very existence: "If radio is to become a self-winding phonograph it certainly is the end of network broadcasting, it would be better to disregard radio entirely and go back to phonographs and records."[68]

In practice, much as in the later case of filmed programming in early television, the networks' attitude was much more ambivalent. On the one hand, according to Russo, the major networks and other radio companies became involved in the business of developing sound on disc media in the 1930s, having identified it as a way to protect their interests. On the other, between 1927 and the mid-1930s NBC officially banned its affiliated stations from airing recorded music and lobbied for the FRC to restrict the use of recordings.[69] The commission shared the antirecordings sentiment, and in 1927 it ordered that stations broadcast announcements before and after each airing of recordings—thereby insisting on the need to single out nonlive material, while also acknowledging that the audience could not tell whether what they heard was live or prerecorded. The following year, the FRC's annual report stated that broadcasting frequencies should not be allocated to radio stations that mainly aired phonograph records because this kind of service "is not giving the public anything which it cannot readily have without such a station."[70] The commission's motivation, of course, had nothing to do with a commitment to medium-specific aesthetics but rather with the scarcity of available channels. Yet this policy essentially made an official ruling out of the notion that live broadcasting is a unique and essential trait of radio that other media cannot emulate.

The application of such notions of liveness to television services was also beneficial for the major networks. When experimental work on television began, the networks' experience in providing nationwide live programming was the most prominent advantage NBC and CBS had over their many competitors. Unlike the case of sound quality of electrical transcriptions, which were often degraded compared with the quality achieved in live studio performance, filmed materials allowed networks to air better-looking and more complex scenes. In addition to the other logistical challenges of producing live programs, television cameras of the 1930s still had limited light sensitivity and could capture in sharp focus only small areas. Nevertheless, in the eyes of the networks, live programming was still valued over the use of film. While the FRC did not rule against the use of filmed materials in television broadcasts (and nor did the FCC afterward), it is likely that the networks opted to conform to the existing regulations that privileged live transmission as long as they depended on the commission's approval to launch commercial service. Most importantly, according to Sewell, the discourse on liveness as essential for television remained central because the viability of televising filmed programs posed significant drawbacks to the network model: it made the need of a broadcast network superfluous and opened up a possibility for a competition with Hollywood film producers.[71]

Nevertheless, the networks' efforts to define liveness as the essential trait of television broadcasting ran ahead of the technical development of a nationwide infrastructure for the delivery of moving images. Television transmitters of the 1920s and 1930s were incapable of broadcasting signals to a radius bigger than fifty miles, and at the time no adequate technology existed for networking television stations by way of relaying signals of visual information. As an NBC technician described it in 1937, "Networking and field pick-ups by relay are a very essential part of a television system, because the life-blood of television is spontaneity."[72] Without such infrastructure, no single television transmission—live or not—could reach anywhere near "millions of homes" simultaneously. This was acknowledged as one of the pressing problems of television already at the very beginning of the experimental era, but discussions on the expensive and elaborate project of fabricating a coaxial cable network or a wireless relay system started in earnest only in the second half of the 1930s.[73]

Ironically, it was the discordance between the networks' valorization of nationwide service and the difficulties in actually fabricating a system for nationwide converge that opened a new opportunity for film companies to become involved in broadcasting. A survey on the state of television commissioned by the MPPDA and written by its former secretary Courtland Smith in March 1939 pointed out that, in lieu of a wired relay system, a simulated network could be established by distributing copies of filmed programs to individual transmission stations. Although Smith anticipated resistance from the side of the broadcasters to involve Hollywood in television operations, the current situation seemed to him to be working in Hollywood's favor. "For the time being television needs us, and very badly," explained Smith. "But most television people hope to relegate film to a minor position and bring the direct pick-up into all programs. In fact, if networks were now possible they might adopt the policy of excluding film as they excluded for years the transcribed radio programs. There being no networks, film will start unopposed and as an essential factor."[74] The idea of a simulated television network based on distribution of filmed programs remained one of the medium's many unrealized forgotten futures, but at that moment in 1939, on the eve of the launch of television services, it appeared to be in the film industry's best interest. For as Smith suggested, instead of keeping cinema distinguished from television, integrating film into the media system of broadcast television could disallow the new form of moving image technology to constitute its own separate rival media identity.

Smith's survey took a similar approach with respect to the competition that film exhibitors were facing from television broadcasts, and urged film companies to apply for broadcasting frequencies from the FCC in order to reserve them for the transmission of programs to theatrical venues once the appropriate apparatus became available. While such opportunity would allow the film companies to expand their business to a new area not threatened by competition with the broadcast networks, practical theatrical television was still years away even in the most optimistic views. Taking this into consideration, Smith argued that Hollywood must make sure the public remained open to future changes in the field of moving image entertainment. "We never should let the idea become generally accepted that television means pictures in the home instead of pictures in the theatre," his survey exclaimed. "It would seem to be wise to combat that idea at once."[75]

Smith's recommendations to the MPPDA bring to the fore an interesting parallel between the institutional rivalry over the control of television and the question of the definition of its media identity. Beyond identifying possible business strategies, Smith's survey urges Hollywood to intervene with the broadcasters' efforts to articulate an idea of television as an autonomous medium that is defined by its own specific properties. As I attempted to show in this section, the broadcasting industry promoted a particular formation of moving image transmission media that associated it with an ontology of liveness, in part as a means to distinguish it from cinema. Smith, who acknowledged the institutional strength of the broadcasting networks, suggested that Hollywood's response must be to contest the idea that television has a single and fixed meaning and instead to establish alternative visions of the medium, which do not segregate image transmission from film. Indeed, in both his suggestions—the creation of a system for distributing filmed programs to individual television stations and the broadcasting of programs in theatrical spaces—television is converged with cinema's tools and institutions. Ultimately, as the 1930s came to a close, the competition between Hollywood and the broadcasting companies was no longer about the control of television, but about the definition of its very identity and relation to other media.

Films on Television: The First Postfilmic Era

While the early debates about televisual medium-specific definitions took place, it also became evident that the introduction of moving image transmission technologies would bring about a significant change in the understanding of the nature of cinema. Now, not only was there a new and distinct moving image media form, but it also became possible to scan and transmit motion picture films that were initially created for the purpose of cinematic exhibition. Early experiments with the broadcasting of motion picture films had been undertaken by several television stations during the 1930s. Often held as part of technical tests or demonstrations of the capabilities of television transmission stations, televised motion picture films were not intended to meet wide viewership. Nevertheless, these experiments may be seen as marking a largely forgotten media-historical turning point, since they represent the first instances in which motion pictures were dissociated from film.[76]

On the one hand, the first experimental motion picture broadcasts exemplify a case of the remediation of cinema, to borrow a term from Jay David Bolter and Richard Grusin's famous discussion on how new media forms appropriate or refashion other media.[77] Indeed, television had borrowed fundamental representational practices from the cinema from the very beginning of the experimental stage. As early as 1930, the Jenkins laboratories manufactured television sets with screens in the aspect ratio of 4:3, in keeping with the standard dimensions of the frames in motion picture film (early sets manufactured by Baird, in contrast, were equipped with vertical rectangular screens).[78] In the decade that followed, even broadcasters who routinely emphasized television's need to develop its own specific tools acknowledged that it would first borrow techniques from the cinema.[79] But on the other hand, the broadcasting of motion picture films may be seen as constituting a distinct and more emphatic sense of intermedial relationship wherein television does not appropriate cinematic properties, but absorbs cinematic form altogether. Media theorist Alexander Galloway has commented in a different context that "television does not simply remediate film, it remediates film *itself.* The important issue is not that this or that film is scanned and broadcast as the 'content' of television . . . [but] that television incorporates film itself, that is, it incorporates the entire, essential cinematic condition."[80]

The first appearances of motion pictures on television gave rise to discussions that, when read today, seem to prefigure current scholarly debates about our alleged "postfilm" or "postcinema" era.[81] Much like film theorists of the late twentieth and early twenty-first centuries, who observe that the distinctions between media have become blurry and thus necessitate a reappraisal of the historically defined notions of cinematic specificity, commentators of the 1930s found themselves assessing what best defines cinema's distinctive quality in light of the newly emergent medium of television. Naturally, in the debates that surrounded the first broadcasts of motion pictures, the concern over the difference between televisual liveness and cinematic recording was pushed aside. Instead, the debates revolved around the consequences of what Francesco Casetti later termed the "relocation" of cinema—the process by which cinema separates from the medium of film, spreads to other media, and reestablishes itself in new contexts and environments.[82] As Casetti has shown, the process of relocation dissociates the object of film from the particular cinematic viewing experience in the context of theatrical projection. In so doing, the relocation of cinema emphasizes that the experience of the medium is defined not by its apparatus but by "a specific type of watching, listening, attention, and sensibility" as well as its surrounding environment.[83] While Casetti made his observations in the context of twenty-first-century digital media, already in the experimental era's discourses about the broadcasting of motion pictures we can find an engagement with a very similar set of concerns.

Even prior to any practical attempts to broadcast motion pictures, there was an agreement among commentators from the film industry, the broadcasting industry, and the popular press that the cinematic experience would remain distinguished from motion picture viewing on television. In their view, the reason was tied not to cinema's photographic basis or to its capacity of recording and reproduction, but rather to the psychological and social circumstances of mass spectatorship in a public setting. For example, a correspondent for *Exhibitors Trade Review* wrote in response to Jenkins's 1922 presentation of the prismatic ring that, as fascinating as the prospects of broadcasting films to the home might be, "the home cannot be made to supplant the picture theatre on any large scale if for no other reason than because its *entertainment psychology* is wrong."[84] In the correspondent's view, no domestic medium could re-create the essence of the cinematic experience because the latter involves crucial extrafilmic elements that cannot be reproduced on the small screen. "Most people attend the theatre as a means of escape from the familiar—sometimes too familiar—surroundings, of the home. They go to see the pictures chiefly, perhaps; but they also go to see the whole show, with its music, its lights and colors, its complete presentation atmosphere."[85] Likewise, cbs's William Paley remarked on the occasion of the collaboration between the radio network and Paramount in 1929 that, "man being a social creature, he likes to rub elbows with his fellow men. Emotional response in an audience is infectious. Laughs engender laughs, thrills sweep like electric currents through multitudes."[86] Given the distinct nature of collective reception, concluded Paley, movie theaters will continue to thrive as public gathering places regardless of the introduction of television.

At the same time, such an understanding of cinematic specificity as bound up with assumptions on the psychological and social nature of film spectatorship allowed others to come to markedly different conclusions about cinema's future. Robert Sherwood predicted in a 1929 essay that film theaters have "fulfilled their earthly mission as palaces of diversion," as they prove to be "an impractical institution in this age of transportation and communication."[87] Sherwood's view was neither anxious nor elegiac. For him, it was not only television but an entire new technological ecosystem that had rendered the motion picture theater obsolete. "As a matter of fact," he argues,

> in what we call our modern "community life," most of us are forced to congregate whether we like it or not. People must, of necessity, spend so much time in crowds—in streets, stores, trains and highways—that they are naturally anxious to escape from the turmoil in their leisure hours.... The automobile has made it easy for such people to break away, not only from their homes but from the cities and towns which are apt to be stiflingly narrow themselves. The airplane will make the escape still easier. The home is becoming a pleasanter place in which to live. Thanks to mechanical dishwashers, vacuum cleaners and similar boons, the home need no longer be associated with the anguish of drudgery and the horror of boredom. Television will add to its charms, by bringing into it everything that the theatre can offer, and much that the theatre has never been able to offer in the past.[88]

When experiments with the broadcasting of films began, it became clear that television was nowhere close to replacing the cinema experience. In March 1930, the Jenkins corporation announced "the first public broadcasting of film in the world" as part of a festive inauguration of Jenkins's television studio in Jersey City the following month.[89] The film scheduled to be broadcast was James Whale's *The Journey's End*, which had its New York theatrical première the next day and was supposed to be viewed exclusively on television sets placed in the studio itself. Despite the bleak forecasts about the competition with television, from the film industry's perspective the event marked the emergence of new promotional possibilities. Cinema trade journals regarded the broadcasting not only as the first airing of a film but also as the "first use of television as a medium of advertising motion pictures."[90] According to Koszarski, however, there is no clear indication that the film was ever broadcast.[91] Either way, given that at the time Jenkins's television receivers were only capable of reproducing fifteen frames per second with a picture definition of forty-eight lines per frame, the event was unlikely to have broken any ground from the media industry's viewpoint.

Indeed, with further experiments in broadcasting films, the critical focus shifted to the quality of the reproduction of the pictures on the new, distinct delivery mechanism. Such was the case with another broadcast that has been presented as the "first" transmission of a full-length motion picture, in March 1933. In this experimental broadcast, the Don Lee Broadcasting

System in Los Angeles transmitted *The Crooked Circle*, a World Wide Pictures production that had premiered six months earlier. Primarily intended as a test of the transmission equipment, the broadcast was carried out in the middle of the afternoon and without the film's soundtrack. Reportedly, there were only twelve television sets in the territory that could receive the transmission, of which one was made available for public viewing in a Los Angeles department store. Responses to the broadcast deemed it a disappointment. Due to the small size of the pictures and the low resolution of the eighty-line scanner, viewers found it hard to follow the story and read the credit titles and were able to identify the characters only when shown in close-up.[92] Don Lee stations continued experimenting with the transmission of films. For several years, the stations were supplied with new Paramount productions, and by December 1938 they had broadcast 11 million feet of film.[93] As far as intermedial comparisons go, commentators noted that these broadcasts resembled "looking at a magic lantern slide through a Venetian blind" more than a cinematic screening.[94] Evidently, if motion pictures were to be televised, they had to be designed for the medium. According to one British commentator, for example, the low resolution and stark contrast of mechanical television made it an ideal medium for carrying out artistic experiments in silent "shadow pictures," referring to post-*Caligari* German pictures from the late 1920s.[95] In any event, Hollywood filmmakers could not yet consider the mechanical television screen an apt outlet for motion pictures.

The transition to electronic systems in the second half of the 1930s allowed television broadcasters to present dramatically improved images that more closely matched the quality of small-gauge home movies. In 1939, RCA engineers developed a scanning apparatus that adapted the speed of electronic television scanners to twenty-four frames per second, the standard of sound films, thus making it possible to transmit motion pictures at the right speed.[96] Broadcasters wanted to acquire short films, considering them a cheap and convenient way to fill airtime, but by that point the film industry's sentiment toward television had changed. The major film studios grew concerned about the vast improvement in the viewing experience of domestic television and the mass marketing of receivers and consequently refused to sell pictures for television. As a result, broadcasters chiefly drew on French and British productions and on industrial and governmental short films.[97]

In early 1939, NBC's affiliation with RKO allowed for yet another "first" in moving image history—this time the first broadcast of a film especially adapted for the purpose of televising in the United States. The film chosen for adaptation was George Stevens's *Gunga Din*, which premiered in February of the same year. This spectacular adventure film was a somewhat counterintuitive choice given that, as one contemporary reviewer wrote, it was "the sort of movie that revives one's faith in the limitless scope and unique qualities of motion pictures" and specifically one that poses "a challenge to the radio and, yes, to television."[98] When the broadcast of the adaptation was announced, film exhibitors protested against what they saw as a collaboration of the studio with their business competitors. But in fact, the production of the television version originated as part of a large promotional campaign for the film and aired during a much-anticipated inaugural broadcast of NBC, following the live transmission from the World's Fair.[99]

NBC and RKO's strategies in reediting *Gunga Din* for television merit special attention. In this adaptation, they put into practice observations that were made throughout the experimental stage about the differences between cinema and television and about the possibilities for motion pictures to travel between them. According to descriptions in the trade press, the television adaptation functioned as an abridgment of the original film, covering the entire narrative using selected shots from the film over a running time of ten (or twenty, according to some reports) minutes compared with 116 minutes of the theatrical release. The selection of shots for the abridged version was made according to the perceived technical limitations of television screens. In the 1930s, television was considered "a close-up art" that was most suited to the reproduction of small-scale shorts in high contrast.[100] Television directors recognized the specificity of the medium's material support (to borrow yet another term from modernist art criticism) and developed a corresponding poetics of television. But motion picture films proved not to travel well from the big screen to the small, and the experience in broadcasting film footage indicated that long shots and low-contrast images did not appear with sufficient detail and clarity on the television screen. Accordingly, the television version of *Gunga Din* consisted of close-ups and medium shots from the film—specifically, following RCA engineers' recommendation, of shots taken in daylight and where action was concentrated in the center of the frame.

The adaptation's use of sound speaks of the continuous importance of the principles of Hollywood's classical style in this tentative stage of testing film's suitability to the television apparatus. In keeping with classical cinema's imperative of narrative intelligibility and coherence, the producers of the television adaptation opted to compensate for the omission of footage with a more extensive use of sound that would make the story run smoother and faster.[101] Hence, the televisual *Gunga Din* included additional sound effects and off-screen narration of events that were eliminated from the cut (including, strangely enough, the climactic battle scene), as well as descriptions of the characters' motivations. In several moments, reportedly, additional voice-over narration was included in order to fill in the space where the original version used long silences to build suspense.[102] In this respect, the adapted version may be seen as anticipating the network era's emphasis on television sound over image, as it effectively inverted the sound and image relations of the cinematic version.

An even more telling aspect of the adaptation is the studio's choice to reduce the running time and amplify the pace. The reason for this dramatic alteration was not the new medium's technical features (clearly, *Gunga Din* does not consist of 85 or 90 percent of unusable long shots). In shortening the picture to a version that sped up the action, RKO and NBC took into consideration the contemporary understanding of television spectatorship as a more strenuous activity compared with cinema spectatorship, regardless of the content of the images on the screen. Broadcasters recognized that audiences are unlikely to spend hours sitting close to a screen and focusing their eyes on a small flickering image while screening out domestic interferences and distractions. As NBC's television coordinator admitted, "Film has to be damned interesting to keep people absorbed even fifteen minutes."[103] Former RCA engineer Alfred Goldsmith suggested that it would be impossible for television viewers to maintain a similar level and duration of attention as in a theatrical space. In the theater, he noted, the absence of commercial breaks, the availability of air conditioning, the comfortable seats, and even the "suave but real discipline" maintained by the theater ushers helped keep the audience focused. The price of admission, too, "is a powerful deterrent to lack of interest," and moviegoers are likely to lose attention only in the case of a particularly poor film. Conversely, Goldsmith points out, "the customary surroundings of the home are not especially favorable for the creation of a world of illusion," since domestic manners "tend to be more 'free and easy' than is desirable for showman-like presentations."[104]

Critics of the late 1930s were similarly attentive to how the distinct environments of the home and the movie theater shape spectators' attention and emotional engagement in different manners. A perceptive article written by a USC cinema student in 1939 argued that whereas motion picture films allow for "prolonged emotional reaction of the theater's large audience," television programs will need to be shorter and faster paced, since "the emotional peaks of the small circle of home lookers will be neither as high nor as long as those of the cinema audience."[105] Critic Gilbert Seldes similarly believed that because television broadcasts were to be viewed by single individuals or very small groups, the tempo of the programming would need to be rapid. Contrary to the later "glance theory" of television, which persuasively suggests that television spectatorship is relatively relaxed and demands little concentration, Gilbert's experience with experimental era television led him to argue that the medium demands complete concentration and programs therefore have to be brief in order not to exhaust their viewers.[106] "The physical conditions of the moving-picture house will not be duplicated," he wrote. "At home we shall not be compelled to sit through a dull episode in silence, hoping for an exciting one to follow."[107] In light of these observations, it becomes evident that the condensed television-friendly version of *Gunga Din* was created not only to adjust the motion picture so that it would look good on the small screen of the new technological apparatus, but also to adapt it to a new and challenging environment that conditioned a distinct type of spectatorship. In this case, McLuhan's assertion about media always being the content of a newer media proves true, though with a caveat: as it turned out, film could indeed be absorbed by television—but only one reel at a time.

Musing on the particularities of television spectatorship led Seldes to speculate more broadly about its future intermedial influence on cinema. He foresaw that given that motion picture films were not suitable for television, the new medium would demand short and high-tempo motion pictures made expressly to be televised. The new televisual pictures, in turn, would affect both the practices of the film industry and the expectations of the audience, which would inevitably draw comparisons between the two forms of moving image media. Movies, Seldes argued, "will have to cut out their waste material" in order to meet the audiences' reformed expectations with respect to rhythm and brevity. For Seldes, the prospects of this scenario were positive. In his view, the adaptation to televisual style would energize the motion pictures, which had become "a little lethargic in their methods."[108] (Given that the average shot length of Hollywood pictures had doubled compared with the previous decade, it is easy to see why the critic thought that cinema of the 1930s was in need of being reenergized.) Television's impact on filmmaking became evident only much later, in the mid-1960s, when Hollywood started making films with small-screen presentation in mind. As David Bordwell has shown, the prospect of selling television broadcasting rights was one of the motivations that gave rise to Hollywood's "intensified continuity" style, which frequently employs tight framing and rapid editing.[109] Thus, intermedial influences go full circle: television, having first borrowed techniques from the cinema, developed its own distinctive stylistic traits, which in turn were borrowed by cinema.

My point here is not that Seldes accurately predicted future changes in film style, just as it is not that other critics were wrong in assuming that viewers would not sit in front of the screen for an entire evening. More important are the conditions that allowed for such predictions—namely, the fact that the initial experiments in broadcasting motion pictures or adapting them for television offered an early occasion for critics (and other commentators) to reflect about moving images in a broad intermedial manner and in historical perspective. These tentative efforts of relocating motion pictures to the television screen made clear, for the first time, that motion pictures may exist independently of the filmstrip and the darkened theater. In so doing, they allowed for an understanding of the very identity of cinema—not only ontologically, but also with respect to protocols of spectatorship and prevalent representational codes—as historically mutable and intertwined with other media.

Television in Films: Beyond Media Fantasies

Along with being television's commercial rival and setting technical standards for image quality, cinema of the 1920s and 1930s also played a role in documenting and narrativizing cultural responses to the emergence of television. In the United States alone no fewer than sixty films (and very possibly many others that await rediscovery) produced during the experimental era featured moving image transmission apparatus. Though the films chiefly speculated about media futures, moving image transmission technology was never strictly a science fiction motif. Filmgoers of the experimental era saw televisions in comedies, adventure films, westerns, musicals, thrillers, and dramas; in feature films, shorts, serials, and cartoons; in major studio productions and in B movies. They saw television apparatus used for entertainment, telecommunication, detection, and military operations, and operated by mass media institutions, tyrants, superheroes, soldiers, aliens, scientists, and singing cowboys.

American fiction films about television charted a vast array of media fantasies, taking the "interpretive flexibility" of the new medium to the extreme. Some films picked up on existing experiments with the deployment of moving image transmission. For example, in *Up the Ladder* (Edward Sloman, 1925) and *Hello Television* (Leslie Pearce, 1930), television devices appear as visual telephones; in *Exiled to Shanghai* (Nick Grinde, 1937) and *Five of a Kind* (Herbert Leeds, 1938), television images are projected in movie theaters, while *The Big Broadcast of 1936* (Norman Taurog, 1935) and the sponsored film *Thought for Food* (John Freese, 1933) depict television as a domestic broadcast medium. Televisual surveillance systems are featured in the cartoon *The Robot* (Dave Fleischer, 1932) and the horror classic *Werewolf of London* (Stuart Walker, 1935). In Charlie Chaplin's *Modern Times* (1936) the president of the factory supervises the workers via a closed-circuit television and even appears on a wall-mounted screen in their restrooms. Many other films took even greater freedom in imagining uses of television. In *Mystery Liner* (William Nigh, 1934) a television set is used for sending textual messages from a ship in midsea, in *The Phantom Empire* (Otto Brower and B. R. Eason, 1935) a mysterious underground empire is equipped with a television system, and in *Flash Gordon's Trip to Mars* (Ford Beebe and Robert Hill, 1938) passengers on a spaceship talk to distant planets via a televisual device.

The list can go on and on.[110] Clearly, media fantasies about television were produced and circulated by multiple channels—in the press, in literature, in technological and industry discourses, and in various graphic forms. And as with all media fantasies, popular speculations on the future possibilities of television responded to present social stakes and dominant political and ideological powers.[111] But cinema fantasized about moving image transmission in its own unique visual, narrative, and generic ways—which inevitably involved references to the nature of cinema itself. As such, although the filmic media fantasies partook in broader speculative discourses about television (and thereby more generally also about modernity and technologization), they merit consideration in film-specific terms. In the remaining pages of this chapter I discuss two B pictures that feature both image transmission and film apparatus as central elements in their plots. The two films narrate the intermedial encounters in form of metaphorical clashes between film and television. Thereby, I argue, the films can be read as allegories of the shifting status of cinema that seek to investigate the distinctions between the transmitted and the cinematographic in the context of the broad changes in the modern mediascape and, specifically, the American debates about the future of television in the 1930s.

Murder by Television (Clifford Sanforth, 1935), produced by poverty-row studio Cameo Pictures, is among the best-known examples of early filmic depictions of television, likely because it stars the ever-popular Bela Lugosi. Despite its ominous title, the film ("certainly Lugosi's worst," per the star's biographer)[112] by no means demonizes the medium of television and is far

4.5. The inaugural television broadcast, *Murder by Television*,
dir. Clifford Sanforth, 1935.

from making a technophobic statement. Instead, the terror elements in it
relate to institutional rivalry over the control of the new medium. *Murder
by Television* revolves around the efforts of several groups—including a
major television corporation and several foreign governments—to get hold
of a new state-of-the-art television technology. The inventor of the technology, Professor Houghland, refuses to sell it or even patent it. He sees
television as a utopian promise for a better world, insisting that it might
be "something more than just another form of amusement." Houghland
hosts a group of friends and professionals for a demonstration of his television system in his home laboratory, which doubles as an experimental
station that can broadcast to the entire United States without the use of
relays. When the demonstration starts, Houghland appears on the television screen, introducing a short musical performance that is followed by
the live transmission of images from France, England, China, and Africa
(figure 4.5). The montage of images recalls the subjects and aesthetics of
actualities from the era of early cinema; at the same time, typically for
early depictions of television, the images appear on the screen without any
explanation provided about who transmits them, or how. While describ-

ing the dispatches from Africa, Houghland suddenly grabs his chest and drops dead. The guests who have just witnessed the live transmission of the inventor's death rush to his laboratory. Arthur Perry (played by Lugosi) reaches Houghland's body first. He steals a copy of the television system's technical design and stashes it away.

This event starts a lengthy locked-room-mystery type of investigation, conducted by a police inspector who attended the demonstration and is convinced that the person responsible for Houghland's death and the theft of the technical documents (and apparently a television tube, too) is present in the house. During the investigation, the inspector learns that Perry was hired by the television corporation to help facilitate the purchase of Houghland's invention. But moments later, Perry—who has just become the prime suspect—is also found murdered. The twist in the plot is immediately followed by another: Lugosi's character returns to the scene, claiming that he is the real Perry, an officer in the Department of Justice, and that the murdered thief is his twin brother. A flashback that takes the film back to the moment when the evil twin's body is found confirms this claim. This time the discovery of the body is shown from a different camera angle, one that reveals the "real" Perry observing the event. When it is understood that the twin brother has represented himself as Perry in order to gain access to the television demonstration, Perry solves the mystery of Houghland's death, pointing at another guest in the demonstration, Dr. Scofield, as the murderer of both the inventor and the twin brother. This explanation is illustrated by another flashback, this time showing the twin brother taking the technical documents from the hiding place. In the film's final scene, Perry presents the investigator and the guests with evidence revealing that a movie camera was conveniently installed in the laboratory and thus "a permanent record of everything televised was made on film." The footage from the camera in the laboratory shows Scofield leaving his seat during the demonstration in order to make a telephone call. The telephone Scofield dialed activated another electric apparatus that radiated waves to Houghland's laboratory. "When these waves came in contact with those the professor's equipment was radiating," Perry explains, "it created interstellar frequency—which is the death ray."

Several scholars have addressed the different cultural meanings of *Murder by Television*'s depiction of the new medium. As it has been pointed out, by turning the television system into a murder weapon the film draws on the old theme of the scientist killed by his own invention.[113] At the same time, the film also expresses contemporary interwar anxieties about new technological weapons, creating a link between the anticipation of the new broadcasting medium to existing popular discourse of the death ray as a sinister offshoot of modern applications of electricity, X-rays, and radium.[114] Within the context of the dynamics of the 1930s media industries, the film has also been read as making a case for television as a powerful thought-control mechanism, posited at the heart of a struggle between capitalist corporations and the public nonprofit model.[115]

What is left out of such interpretations of *Murder by Television* is the equally fascinating way the film contrasts the futuristic story with a self-referential exploration of its own medium. The clunky plot resolution functions as something of a dramatization of a medium-specific argument regarding the nature of film and of television. Mirroring the rivalry between Perry and his evil twin, it sets up a binary opposition between the two media: the novel television technology turns into a murder weapon, whereas the film camera is used to solve the crime. Specifically, the resolution highlights the distinction between the functions of transmission and recording: the television system allows for instantaneous reproduction of images at a distance and for the radiation of the death ray, whereas the filmic record allows the reproduction of scenes captured in the past. This characteristic not only is thematized in the ultimate scene of *Murder by Television* but also plays a role in its narrative form, in particular in the two flashback scenes. Preceding the film's resolution, these scenes essentially do what Perry does in the presentation of the footage that was taken in the laboratory: they stop the ongoing flux of events and shed new light on past occurrences by depicting them from different perspectives. In other words, they do exactly what live television transmission cannot.

In its celebration of film's capacity to create and revisit visual records, *Murder by Television* revives a trope that was common in many early films (such as *Falsely Accused* [Wallace McCutcheon, 1908] and *The Evidence of the Film* [Edwin Thanhouser and Lawrence Marston, 1913]), which similarly assigned movie cameras the role of inscribing and reproducing reliable evidential records. According to film historians Stephen Bottomore and Tom Gunning, among others, the recurrence of this trope in the early cinema era represents self-reflexive efforts to come to terms with the properties of the new medium through an exploration of its association with themes of technologically mediated vision, voyeurism, and detection.[116] Four decades later, the emergence of television defamiliarized established notions about the media identity of cinema. The recurrence of the early cinema trope in a film like *Murder by Television* thus exemplifies how the mediascape of the

1930s necessitated a renewed exploration of its properties and a reassertion of its specificity.

Republic Pictures' *s.o.s. Tidal Wave* (John H. Auer, 1939) is another B movie that stages an intermedial clash between cinema and television. Released in early June 1939—seven months after the airing of Orson Welles's *War of the Worlds* radio broadcast and two months after the inauguration of NBC's television service—it exploits the popular concern with the influence of mass media that the radio broadcast had triggered, as well as the great public interest in the coming of the new medium. In essence, *s.o.s. Tidal Wave* takes what Jeffery Sconce has described as *War of the Worlds*'s expression of the "repressed potential for panic and disorder that lies just behind the normalizing functions of media technology" and casts it onto a story about a television program that causes mass panic.[117]

Even if the proximity of the infamous radio broadcast to the public introduction of television was purely coincidental, *The War of the Worlds* brought to the fore debates about the power of radio which, in turn, had bearings on the industrial competition over the control of television. Since the commercialization of television still depended on FCC approval, radio industry officials grew anxious about how the Welles scandal would affect the reputation and reliability of their medium. The radio networks accused newspapers of deliberately inflating reports on the responses to the broadcast in order to discredit the institution of radio, and instead portrayed the incident as validating the importance of the American system of commercial broadcasting. One radio trade magazine asked, if indeed "some real alarm resulted directly from the broadcast . . . what would happen if radio were ruled by a Government dictatorship?"[118] *s.o.s. Tidal Wave* tells precisely such a story of political abuse of the television. In this respect, it is best seen as an adaptation not of the *War of the Worlds* broadcast but rather of the press scandal that followed in its wake. Indeed, *Motion Picture Daily* considered *s.o.s. Tidal Wave* "something for the FCC to keep in mind when television newsreels become as commonplace."[119]

Set in a time when television is already commonplace, *s.o.s. Tidal Wave* tells the story of Jeff Shannon, a popular New York television reporter. Shannon initially prefers to avoid discussing political matters on his program, but changes his ways after the assassination of one of his colleagues. As Shannon learns, before his death the colleague had obtained incriminating evidence about the underworld connections of Clifford Farrow, a candidate in the coming mayoral elections. Shannon decides to go on the air on election day with filmed evidence taken by his late colleague and reveal the truth about Farrow. But his broadcast is soon interrupted when a warning about a hurricane that is sweeping the coasts of New York City appears on the screen. Before long, a competing television station announces that the storm has turned into an earthquake and airs a long series of images of New York buildings coming crashing down. Alongside these images, a terrified television announcer delivers apocalyptic warnings of an approaching tidal wave (which appropriate not only the simulated bulletins in the Welles's radio play but also the famous report of the Hindenburg crash): "Men and women of America . . . It is coming, it is here, an earthquake in New York. . . . It is indescribable, nothing can stop that. . . . It is too late now, there is no escape. . . . The city is doomed and the millions in it. Oh, the humanity!"

Mass panic breaks out as terrified people fill the city streets. In the meantime, Shannon watches the report on the television set in his office. While images of the collapse of the New York Stock Exchange building appear on the screen, he hears the ticking of the teletype apparatus which is receiving a message from the very same New York Exchange. Perplexed by the discrepancy between the information delivered by the television and the teletype, Shannon types a message back to the New York officer and promptly receives a confirmation that the building is intact. Shannon recognizes the conspiracy and rushes to Farrow's office, where he finds the politician and his associates faking the news report by televising a scene from a horror film off of a movie screen (figure 4.6). Shannon finds the can of the film used for the transmission and exclaims, "Here is your tidal wave—a movie!" But Farrow and his gang insist that the airing is intended to be nothing but harmless amusement and that "broadcasting a film is not a crime." Shannon takes over the transmission and announces that there is in fact no tidal wave coming and that the broadcast was fake. He reveals that Farrow transmitted images from a horror film and tells the viewers, "Go back to the polls; do your duty as citizens and vote."

This climactic scene of *s.o.s. Tidal Wave* establishes an unusually complex web of intermedial and intertextual references. Contemporary reviewers easily recognized that the scene alludes to the newspaper reports on the impact of Welles's radio play, itself an adaptation of H. G. Wells's novel. On the diegetic level, the scene depicts a transmission of a motion picture film under the guise of a live television broadcast (thereby presenting a film within a television broadcast within a film). As it happens, the low-budget *s.o.s. Tidal Wave* itself reappropriated the sequence of the destruction of New York from another motion picture, RKO's 1933 science fiction drama

4.6. A film projector in the television station, *s.o.s. Tidal Wave*, dir. John H. Auer, 1939.

Deluge. Finally, the protagonist becomes aware that the broadcast is fake only due to the intervention of actual "live" teletype transmission from the Stock Exchange. Correspondingly, at the end of the scene Shannon succeeds in restoring order—in the sense of both calming the city's panicking residents and reinstating the democratic process—only by separating the entanglement of the two media and stopping the feed of the filmed footage from the live television broadcast.

The happy ending of *s.o.s. Tidal Wave* reaffirms the true identity of the disaster footage by cutting to a close-up of the film can, making legible its label: "Rented from Horror Films Incorporated" (figure 4.7). As Lisa Gitelman suggests, labels on media products "necessarily take account of the product's intended ontology, of what the product *is*, frequently by specifying its origin, composition, and use."[120] The existence of the printed label is crucial here, since it is precisely a question of ambiguous intended ontology that is at stake in this scene. Unlike the case with *Murder by Television*, the earthquake scene in *s.o.s. Tidal Wave* confuses the supposed medium-specific distinction between the properties of cinema and the television. Rather than seeking an essence of television, *s.o.s. Tidal Wave* explores the dynamics

4.7. Close-up of the labeled reel of incriminating footage, *s.o.s. Tidal Wave*, dir. John H. Auer, 1939.

and consequences of remediation as it thematizes the changing status of moving images in different medial contexts. The depiction of the malicious manipulation of television broadcasting at the film's end relies on the notion that spectators cannot tell whether the image on-screen is prerecorded or simultaneously broadcasted.[121] Clearly, the sequence of the unnamed horror film that is televised in *s.o.s. Tidal Wave* would be a harmless work of entertainment when presented in its original cinematic context; only when it is reproduced on the television screen does the footage transform into panic-inducing material. In this way, *s.o.s. Tidal Wave* undermines the idea of liveness—and its associated notions of presence, urgency, immediacy, and actuality—as an ontological property of television. Instead, it shows that liveness is an effect of a particular set of media practices.

To conclude that in *s.o.s. Tidal Wave* the medium is the message would be a well-worn cliché (even if, to be fair, it was not a cliché in 1939). Yet it is worth emphasizing how the film expresses a view about the nature of liveness and television spectatorship. By setting its climactic scene around the airing of footage depicting a natural disaster, *s.o.s. Tidal Wave* perceptively points to what theorists identified decades later as live television's unique affinity with catastrophes. In particular, according to Mary Ann Doane's well-known argument, the interruption of regular programming for the unscripted (and indeed unscriptable) reporting of catastrophe produces the most emphatic manifestation of televisual liveness, for it "corroborates television's access to the momentary, the discontinuous, the real."[122] Quick to apply the lesson of the notorious *War of the Worlds* broadcast of a fictional catastrophe, *s.o.s. Tidal Wave* dramatizes this theoretical argument. By doing so, *s.o.s. Tidal Wave* indicates that cinema's and television's conditions of representation differ not only in matters of picture quality, command of attention, and the surrounding viewing environment. More fundamentally, as *s.o.s. Tidal Wave* suggests, the distinction lies in the social authority of the institutions of cinema and broadcasting and the spectatorial protocols associated with them.

5 "We Must Prepare!"

Dziga Vertov and the Avant-Garde
Reception of Television

On completing his best-known work, *Man with a Movie Camera* (1929), Dziga Vertov wrote an anticipatory statement regarding the film in hopes of publishing it in the Soviet party's daily newspaper, *Pravda*. In a letter to his friend and the *Pravda* critic Aleksander Fevralsky, Vertov noted that the publication or nonpublication of the statement would have a significant impact on the film's reception. For him, it was important to have an opportunity to explain to the public in advance some aspects of his unusual avant-garde film that "may not immediately be understood."[1] Vertov's statement described *Man with a Movie Camera* as "an experiment in cinematic transmission of visual phenomena without the help of intertitles . . . without the help of a script . . . without the help of theater . . . without actors, without sets, etc."[2] The film, Vertov continued, aimed to represent "an authentically international absolute language of cinema—*absolute kinography*—on the basis of its complete separation from the language of theater and literature." While Vertov repeated this claim in the film's opening titles, his statement goes on to indicate that nonetheless *Man with a Movie Camera* does have connections to another medium, as "on the other hand, the film . . . is already coming very close to the period of Radio-Eye."[3]

The term "Radio-Eye" refers to an emergent media form that Vertov conceived of during the early years of television's experimental phase and described as a "montage of visible-audible facts which are transmitted by radio."[4] Central to this conception of the televisual "Radio-Eye" was, of course, Vertov's notion of the Kino-Eye. In Vertov's film theory and practice, "Kino-Eye" stood for a radical approach to film as the representation of "life as it is," that is, real events caught unaware by the camera and organized by montage editing in a manner that aimed to make manifest otherwise hidden social and scientific aspects of reality. Just as Vertov considered Kino-Eye a filmic "deciphering of the visible world," he saw the Radio-Eye as an extension of this concept that would allow the deciphering of the visible and aural world by means of instantaneous television transmission. *Man with a Movie Camera*, therefore, was important for marking the pathbreaking transition from film to television—or, as Vertov put it, from Kino-Eye to Radio-Eye.

This chapter concerns Vertov's idea of the Radio-Eye as a manifestation of the 1920s avant-garde reception of television. Various histories of early cinema, phonography, and photography have demonstrated that modernist avant-garde movements thrive on the radical indeterminacies and transformative potentialities of new media technologies. Avant-garde artists saw new media forms not only as a promising site for aesthetic experimentation but also as an index of technical and scientific progress of art itself.[5] The height of the European avant-garde in the 1920s and 1930s coincided with television's experimental era, during which the commercial and mass culture identity of the new medium was not yet firmly in place and therefore no restrictive institutions and conventions existed. During that period, various artists and writers from avant-garde movements published proposals for radical uses of moving image transmission technologies.

The case of the avant-garde reception of television is by no means unique to the Soviet setting. In Italy, futurist F. T. Marinetti wrote about the potential for using television as part of innovative performances of "total theater." In these multisensory performances, Marinetti planned to have the spectators sit on mobile revolving chairs and to provide them with radios and television screens for close-up views of the multiple stages, where different scenes were to develop simultaneously.[6] Even more far-reaching was Marinetti's idea of the "Futurist theatre of the skies," a dramatic spectacle performed exclusively by airplanes, with huge television screens hanging from special airplanes so the spectators can see parts of the play that take place far out of sight.[7] In Hungary, artist László Moholy-Nagy also envisioned an avant-garde variation of television as a follow-up project for his Light-Space

Modulator, which featured in his film *Lichtspiel* (1930). He speculated about combining the modulator with a radio transmitter and turning it into a wireless "tele-projector" medium controlled at long distance.[8] In Germany, Dada artist Raoul Hausmann proposed the deployment of selenium on a technological device for the conversion of light to sound and vice versa, which he dubbed the Optophone and based on contemporary technological schemes for television.[9] Yet the case of Vertov's theorization on television in the Soviet Union is of particular interest, since his ideas were articulated in light of a cultural reception of broadcasting media which was markedly different from the American case that was discussed in the previous chapter, both politically and aesthetically. Furthermore, by considering how Vertov imagined the future of moving image transmission we also find evidence for how the coming of television intersected with one of the most famed projects in modernist cinema. Not unlike the case of Rudolf Arnheim, whose theoretical writings on television are discussed in the next chapter, Vertov is typically considered a filmmaker and thinker who is particularly committed to media-specific notions of cinema and its utopian possibilities. But as I argue in the following pages, by the late 1920s Vertov found the technical affordances of broadcasting media to be better suited for the purposes of his radical aesthetic and political project of using mass media as a means for promoting a revolutionary understanding of reality.

Soviet Wireless Utopias

The coming of radio and the first announcements about the realization of television technology were received in the Soviet Union in a context that can best be described as the intersection of two utopias: the utopia of the revolution and its consequences, and the utopian sense that accompanies the appearance of every new medium. The utopian mentality that characterized the postrevolutionary era related not only to the constitution of a new economy and politics but also to the creation of a new culture, new sciences, and new types of relationships among people. The revolution made the industrialization of the country one of its primary objectives, portraying Soviet technological and scientific advances as great promises for the future. This was particularly true regarding inventions in electric technology, which—as Lenin's famous formula "communism equals Soviets plus electrification" illustrates—were celebrated for their transformative and progressive nature. At the same time, Soviet views on radio were also associated with the utopian mode that typifies the reception of new media, which frequently involves a sense of "radical changes in representation, discourse, culture and sometimes society as a whole."[10] The emergence of radio in the 1920s stimulated the expression of such utopian views, which were shaped in turn by the specific historical situation of the Soviet culture.

The characteristics of radio technology were unique in the way they answered particular political and cultural concerns in the young Soviet Union. The Soviet government, desperately looking for ways to distribute propaganda and instructions over the enormous Soviet territory—spanning eleven time zones and populated by different national groups, among them a great number of illiterates—found radio a priceless tool of communication and political control. In 1920, despite the pressing postwar shortage of resources, the Soviet government initiated a plan for a broadcasting network. In a letter written in honor of the plan, Lenin presented another formula, according to which radio is "a newspaper minus paper and limits of distance."[11] The omission of paper was obviously not the reason to celebrate radio. It was the omission of written words from mass communication that put broadcasting on a high priority. The Soviet government had a monopoly over radio and dictated the political tone of its broadcasts of "highly instructive programs accessible to the masses."[12] Radio's mission, in the eyes of the government, was "to make Russia one in thought, in action, nationally. To unite every part of Russia . . . to break down isolation, remove difference of conduct, of speech, of thought and action."[13] As early as 1922, the world's most powerful radio transmitter was installed in Moscow.[14]

The transmission of Moscow's messages to every remote village in the union played a crucial role in informing the modernization of everyday life. Radio communication connected the rural periphery with the center, assisting in changing the lives and the worldviews of a huge population in need of immediate and simultaneous adaptation to the new principles of the revolution. In accordance with its social mission, 1920s Russian radio listening was often a collective experience. While many families in big Russian cities owned radio sets, public listening was common in workers' clubs and in central halls of peripheral villages.[15] In 1926, Leon Trotsky argued that since technological progress is necessary for the building of communism, radio—as a highly democratic product of the new phase of technology— might have been invented "especially to convince the bilious skeptics among us of the unlimited possibilities inherent in science and technology."[16] Emphasizing wireless technology's capacity to unify the center and periphery, he stated that it was more important to connect illiterate villagers to radio than to teach them how to read. In Trotsky's view, radio was also serving socialism by fighting religious prejudices: "What, indeed, does a 'voice from heaven' amount to, when there is being broadcast all over the country a voice from the Polytechnical museum?"[17]

Utopian views of radio also feature in various works of Soviet modernist artists of the 1920s. Vladimir Tatlin's famous unrealized architectural plan for the *Monument for the Third International* included the construction of a rotating radio station and the installation of radio antennas on top of the monument's 400-meter-high roof.[18] Russian futurist artists, who embraced new technologies as material for experimentation and a subject matter, were inspired to create a new kind of art that would take advantage of radio's possibilities. According to historian Richard Stites, "A whole array of electronic music inventions appeared in Soviet Russia in the 1920s designed to broaden the range of sonority and to broadcast on radio the wonders of urban noise, electricity, and revolutionary music."[19] Such futurist antibourgeois industrial machine music, highly suited to the radio, was considered progressive and even therapeutic. Avant-garde critic V. Kashnitsky even recommended that people record urban sounds and noises and transmit them to the countryside in order to "bring the life of the city to the darkness of the rural areas."[20]

In a similar fashion, futurist poet Velimir Khlebnikov in 1921 depicted a future in which human consciousness and mental life are constantly dependent on a radio network. "The radio of the future," Khlebnikov writes, "will open up a knowledge of countless tasks and will unite all mankind."[21] Ahead of the existing technology, the poem provides a proto-televisual metaphor of radio waves that "become letters on the dark screens of enormous books," in an intermedial construct that combines radio, film, and print media. "If previously radio was the ears of the world, now it is the eye which admits no distance," writes Khlebnikov, anticipating Vertov's description of the transition from radio to Radio-Eye as well as his utopian multisensual communication device, "now they have learned how to transmit the sensations of taste [and] even smell."[22] Poet and playwright Vladimir Mayakovsky also wrote of a futuristic form of radio in his 1929 play *The Bedbug*. In a scene that takes place in the utopian future of 1979, Mayakovsky describes a worldwide socialist vote where, "instead of human voters, radio loudspeakers equipped with arms like directional signals on an automobile" perform the voting from long distance.[23] Immediately after the voting, reporters from newspapers all over the world deliver the recent news using their portable radio apparatus.

In correlation to such views of radio, the Soviet cultural responses to the coming of television were also marked by far-reaching predictions. Decades before television sets appeared in Soviet households, they became common-place in Russian literary musings on the future. From L. S. Zlatopolsky's stories from the 1880s, where "radioscopes" are a part of the future cityscape, to Yevgeny Zamayatin's 1920 dystopian novel *We*, which portrayed a future Taylorist society typified by the ubiquity of televisual and wireless technologies, and until it became a science fiction cliché by the 1930s, television was considered the medium that would shape everyday life in the future, whereas film was a soon-to-be relic of the past.[24] In Aleksander Beliayev's 1928 science fiction novel *The Struggle in Space*, set in the futuristic city Radiopolis, a variety of televisual devices fulfill a range of functions from long-distance communication and transmission of archival films to display of news and medical imaging.[25] Following the literary trend, Soviet filmmakers also depicted futuristic television devices in science fiction scenarios: the aliens in *Aelita Queen of Mars* (Yakov Protazanov, 1924) use a modernist-looking screen apparatus to surveil Earth, and cosmonauts in *The Cosmic Voyage* (Vasilii Zhuravlyov, 1936) use a two-way television system to communicate with their home base while on their way to the moon.

Origins of the Radio-Eye

Vertov, therefore, encountered the reports about the technological realization of television already within an atmosphere that celebrated the powers and potentials of broadcasting media. In many of his films from the 1920s, Vertov included images of radio sets, antennas, loudspeakers, and headphones. In 1925 he dedicated the entire last installment of the *Kino-Pravda* newsreel to radio. Titled *Radio-Pravda*, the newsreel documents the purchase and installment of a wireless receiver in a village and provides explanations about its technical function. According to Yuri Tsivian, it is as if, symbolically, "Vertov wanted to pass on the baton to the younger medium."[26] In a scene from *A Sixth Part of the World* (1926), Vertov expresses radio's importance for the unification of the Soviet periphery and center by intercutting images of collective radio listening in a rural area, of irrigation canals in a field, and of an electric light bulb in a hut. The montage of those three sets of images implies that just as the canals bring water to the water-less steppes and the bulb lights the dark peasant hut, the radio modernizes the rural country by delivering information, instruction, and political messages from Moscow.

Well aware of how highly radio was valued by the Soviet government,

Vertov held that radio set the standard toward which film should aspire with respect to its potential political impact. In a 1923 plea for sufficient funding for his newsreel production, he proclaimed that given the opportunity, cinema could achieve a similar status and become "a new megaphone, a visual radio to the world."[27] Unsurprisingly, therefore, radio was also an inseparable part of Vertov's theoretical writings of film from their very beginnings. In the early 1920s, he introduced the concept of Radio-Ear, which—to paraphrase Thomas Edison—was conceived as an aural medium that does for the ear what the Kino-Eye does for the eye. Vertov described the Radio-Ear as a device of sound recording and transmission dedicated to the distribution of news and propaganda, which—just as his cinema aimed to do in visual terms—arranges and decodes the sonic reality. According to Vertov, the initial goal of Kinoks, his filmmaking collective, was to establish "a *visual* bond between the workers and the whole world," as well as to "organiz[e] what the workers *hear*."[28] Vertov never privileged vision over hearing; the Kino-Eye film practice was only a part of a larger project (or, rather, a methodical and cohesive battle plan) that ultimately aimed at the technological alteration of human perception, making it appropriate for the dazzling sensory challenges of modernity and exposing it, in a Marxist fashion, to otherwise unnoticeable connections between phenomena: "After the seen world, we attack the heard, tangible and other worlds."[29] When it first proved feasible that radio broadcasting could also incorporate pictures, Vertov embraced the new technical possibilities. Around the time Charles Francis Jenkins and John Logie Baird demonstrated the first prototypes of practical television apparatus, Vertov noted in an essay titled "Kino-Pravda and Radio-Pravda" that "technology is moving swiftly ahead, a method of broadcasting images by radio has already been invented. . . . In the near future man will be able to broadcast to the entire world the visual *and* auditory phenomena recorded by the radio-movie camera."[30]

It is likely that Vertov's first use of the term "Radio-Eye" was in a title of an essay which he submitted for publication in *Pravda*. Yet the newspaper published only an altered and retitled version of the essay, omitting any mention of the term "Radio-Eye."[31] A partial impression of the tone of the original article is available today in the form of a paragraph out of a youth-journal essay by Fevralsky, who quoted from Vertov's original unpublished text:

"Kino-Eye" is a union of science and newsreel for the sake of collective work against the kino-clergy, the work for the Communist decoding of the world and for the emancipation of the proletarian vision.

"Radio-Ear" is a union of science and radio-technology for the same goal—namely, the organization of workers' hearing, the decoding of the audible world.

"Radio-Eye" ("Kino-Eye" + "Radio-Ear") is a possibility of organized visual and audible perception of the entire world, the opportunity for the workers of all nations to jointly see, hear, and understand one another.

To the capitalist posse, which has captured the globe, "Radio-Eye" inevitably opposes the united proletarian class, joined together and organized through shared perception.[32]

Influenced by (and explicitly supportive of) Vertov, Fevralsky's essay presented an argument about the emergence of television within a Marxist-influenced sociological history of art. In Fevralsky's view, the formation of a communist society would change the status of art as an autonomous sphere, ultimately leading to art's dissolution into life, as one of many utilitarian activities. Television, in this context, exemplified the collapse of the boundaries that maintain the isolation of traditional art. Both an art form and a technological product, an aural (temporal) art and a visual (spatial) art, and an informational art and an agitational art, television's appearance marks the beginning of the end of the separation of the sphere of art, and a new stage in its technologization and transformation into industry. In this sense, the emergence of the new, still-unrealized medium was already seen as crucial in signifying the progression toward a communist utopia.

In his own writings, Vertov envisioned the Radio-Eye as *audible Kino-Eye transmitted by radio*," that is, as a dissemination platform for sound versions of Kino-Eye-type films.[33] He insisted that the emergent transmission medium must not be appropriated for the broadcasting of operas and dramas but rather—in the spirit of Lenin's statement on radio—for transmitting audiovisual propaganda "free of the limitations of space."[34] Just as radio for Lenin was newspaper minus paper, the Radio-Eye for Vertov was film minus celluloid. The possibility to transmit audiovisual works from one station to anywhere in the world would definitely have appealed to Vertov, a filmmaker who struggled throughout his career to find proper distribution for his films and who made films in order to address an international mass of workers, but whose films repeatedly met with very limited exposure. "The Issues of *Kino-Pravda*," he wrote in 1923, "are boycotted by film distributers, by the bourgeois and semibourgeois public," who prefer generic film melodramas to political newsreels.[35] In the face of such economic and cultural conditions, what the newly invented transmission apparatus promised was an ability to deliver such newsreel materials to viewers without the limitations posed by commercial-minded cultural gatekeepers and the disinterested upper classes.

Importantly, however, Vertov did not simply consider the Radio-Eye a visual radio that would enable the broadcasting of motion pictures. His intent was to utilize the new technology in a configuration of a two-way point-to-point communication system. In this sense, the Radio-Eye was conceived as similar to the telegraph and the telephone networks that provided the earliest models for imagining moving image transmission media in the nineteenth century. The Radio-Eye, in Vertov's words, could allow workers of all countries not only to "see and hear the whole world in an organized form" but also to "see, hear and understand *one another*."[36] By articulating his vision this way, Vertov prefigured Bertolt Brecht's famous call to transform radio from a broadcast medium into an "apparatus of communication" capable of reception as well as transmission. Writing in 1932, Brecht considered radio's capacity for distribution as incompatible with the function of communication. He envisioned a different technical and cultural configuration (one that in fact had been practiced by radio amateurs and the military) that would turn the medium into a "vast network of pipes" with a radically different political function: instead of isolating its listeners, such radio will bring them into a relationship with one another as a public.[37] Vertov, along similar lines, imagined the Radio-Eye as a networked communication system, free from the top-down control of media institutions, which would allow workers of all countries to partake in the exchange of audiovisual materials that, in the spirit of the Kino-Eye, depict and comment on political reality.

Radio-Eye, Intermediality, and Vertov's Cinema

By the end of the 1920s, Vertov announced that the members of the filmmaking collective were ready to concentrate on working in television. Instead of going by the name "Kinoks," they identified themselves as "Radioks." As Siegfried Zielinski puts it, Vertov "had left the contemporary dispositif of cinema far behind" in both his theory and praxis and embraced television.[38] Television apparatus was not yet available, but Vertov stated that the collective's theoretical and practical work "was in advance of our technical possibilities; they have long awaited the *overdue* (in relation to Kino-Eye) technical base for sound film and television."[39]

Although the enthusiastic manner in which Vertov embraced the new media technology appears to signify a radical break with his Kino-Eye experiments, Vertov did not regard film and television to be distinct media forms. Rather, for him they belonged to two different phases in the developmental trajectory of the same continuously transforming and historically mutable medium, similar to how sound film was a more advanced form of the medium of cinema. From this perspective, the coming of television marked not the appearance of a new medium, but rather a transition to "a new and higher stage in the development of nonacted films."[40] This transition, in turn, also confirmed Vertov's hypothesis that cinema was heading toward a sequence of future transformations that would steadily progress toward the end-of-media-history moment. First, he claimed, the audiovisual medium would be complemented with the capacity to transmit tangible and olfactory facts; then it would make possible "the filming unawares of human thoughts"; and finally, it would culminate in "the direct organization of thoughts (and consequently of the actions) of all humanity."[41]

Admittedly, with these comments Vertov departs from observations about current media changes and segues into what is today called imaginary media. Nevertheless, this media fantasy does shed most valuable light on Vertov's overall project. I propose thinking of the imaginary medium that can organize humanity's thought in line with what French film theorist André Bazin described as the "Myth of Total Cinema." In an article under the same name, Bazin claims that film history may be seen as progressing in reverse, with each technological development taking cinema closer to its origins, toward the guiding myth that inspired its invention. For Bazin, this myth is a fantasy of a reproduction of the world in its own image, "a perfect illusion of the outside world in sound, color, and relief," which cinema as we know it always falls short of achieving. "In short," Bazin provocatively argues, "cinema has not yet been invented."[42] Vertov, likewise, saw the cinema of his time as an incomplete manifestation of a future supreme form. Thus, even if Vertov repeatedly emphasizes that the movie camera's capacity of vision is superior to that of the human eye, he never considers the camera itself perfect.[43] For example, in his manifesto "Kinoks: A Revolution," Vertov states: "We cannot improve the making of our eyes, but we can *endlessly* perfect the camera."[44] Cinema, according to this logic, is essentially imperfect—and the coming of television signified an improvement on its present status.

Whereas Bazin conceives of cinema's guiding myth in light of an idealist approach to history, Vertov's materialism grounds his view of the present shortcomings and future possibilities of cinema in historical-specific political situations. In his 1926 essay "Kino-Eye," Vertov writes that although the cinematic apparatus was meant to improve human perception of the visible world, the movie camera "experienced a misfortune." Having been "invented at a time when there was no single country in which capital was not in power," cinema was doomed to be realized merely as a mass entertainment toy.[45] In Vertov's view, through its history, film was unable to fulfill its original potential. Even political nonfiction films that were made "as if the studios, the directors, Griffith, Los Angeles, had never existed" fell short of realizing the medium's promise.[46] As late as 1930, Vertov argues that "so far, not a single documentary or acted film has fully answered the political demands made on revolutionary cinema."[47] Elsewhere, he more closely anticipates Bazin's formulation, claiming that "in its present form, cinema *does not exist* and its main objectives have not been realized."[48]

This comment highlights the fact that although Vertov's theory and practice have become strongly identified with cinematic high modernism, his most fundamental commitment was not to the exploration of the intrinsic properties of film. Rather, Vertov's work was first and foremost guided by what he considered to be the political-perceptual objectives of cinema— namely, the ambition to "decode the world" in a Marxist fashion. In other words, Vertov was less interested in exploring the specificity of film as such than in using film as a means by which to reveal aspects of everyday reality that escape the naked eye and expose connections between natural and social phenomena.[49] Vertov also makes clear in several texts during the 1920s that film was not necessarily going to be the ultimate medium to deploy in service of his project. The emergence of image transmission technology—a media invention native of the postrevolutionary era—marked, therefore, a new stage in the history of cinema and an opportunity to realize the political demands and objectives that film had failed to meet. In particular, I wish to point out two traits of moving image transmission media which from Vertov's perspective were particularly suitable for realizing the revolutionary objectives, and which he had attempted to simulate in his films, creating Radio-Eye works *avant la lettre*.

The first trait is the instantaneous temporality of moving image transmission media. As Vertov repeatedly declares, his films aim at showing "life as it *is*"—which, not incidentally, is always written in the present tense. For Vertov's cinema is radically committed not only to nonfiction, nonacted films but also to materials of the now, the fleeting present that comprises the working class's immediate reality. According to the mission of his utilitarian cinema, the reality of the film must derive not only from the depiction of real events, but also from its relevance to the present lives of its spectators. Vertov goes as far as to dismiss the political merit of films that are based on real-life events from the past. This is illustrated in his famous dispute with Sergei Eisenstein, whose silent films *Strike* (1925), *Battleship Potemkin* (1925), and *October* (1928) were all based on historical events. Vertov considered his celebrated rival a filmmaker who "could not bring himself to face life head-on, and chose instead to act out a few historical scenes in a theatrical manner."[50] Here Vertov implicitly equates dealing with real life with dealing with present events. For him, the fact that a historical film is necessarily an acted and scripted restaging made it ideologically objectionable.[51] Vertov's own cinema, accordingly, expresses little interest in documentation of the past (with the notable exception of reusing historical footage of Lenin after the Soviet leader's death). Rather than recording the achievements of the revolution for posterity, Vertov principally wished to present viewers a more accurate view on the world in real time.[52]

It is precisely the importance of this aspect of "real-time" representation that explains Vertov's continuing dissatisfaction with film and attraction to television. As a recording medium of storage, film can only represent records of the past. Film has nothing to offer its spectators besides imprints of bygone time; in this sense, its suitability for the project of technologically mediating human perception of the world was, at best, compromised. From its very beginning, Vertov's film work attempted to push film toward simultaneous representation by diminishing the time lag between shooting and exhibiting. This is evident, for example, in his writings about the creation of "flash news bulletins"—a subcategory of documentary films that presents "events on the screen the *same day* they occur."[53] The ninth volume of *Kino-Pravda* (1922) documents the Kinoks' effort to shorten the time lag even more. It demonstrates them accomplishing the setting-up of a public film screening in a Moscow square within only eight minutes from receiving the request that had been delivered to them—as if they were a film-ambulance—over the telephone. Operating mobile equipment not only in the shooting of documentary footage but also in its exhibition allowed the Kinoks to depict events on the screen very close to the time they actually took place. Despite those efforts, the temporal lag that the medium of film imposes, however minimized, remains a fundamental characteristic of the medium. Television, conversely, is capable of transmitting images and sounds of events at virtually the same instance they occur. This capacity of moving image transmission technology for "liveness" made the imagined form of Radio-Eye appropriate for Vertov's insistence on instantaneous depiction of the present. In this sense, television appeared as a solution to film's fundamental ontological incapacity to represent history in the making.

But it was not only television's temporality that appealed to Vertov. Another aspect of moving image transmission media that seemed to him to complement the Kino-Eye project was the arrangement of audiovisual communication in a networked configuration. For Vertov, revolutionary cinema was distinguished from Hollywood-type film by virtue of being, like any other type of labor under communism, a truly collective effort. In his words, the Kino-Eye aimed at producing a "unified vision through millions of eyes."[54] Accordingly, his ambition was to involve in the Kino-Eye project an entire "army of kino-observers," consisting of numerous correspondents and amateur cinematographers spread across the entire Soviet Union (and ultimately the world), who would collaborate in the creation of what David Tomas describes as the cinematic "collectivization of the human sensorium."[55] As early as 1923, before making his first feature film, Vertov laid out an initial plan for the establishment of such a collective enterprise. He intended his own Kinoks group to be "a kind of ferment" that would collaborate with other groups of like-minded colleague and ultimately become a film experiment station that would instruct, supervise, and inventory the work of affiliated cameramen in the provinces.[56] In other words, what Vertov envisioned was a creation of a networked filmmaking operation. In this network, every filmmaking unit operates as a node and all nodes are connected to a central Moscow-based film repository where the documentary footage is edited and turned into new newsreel releases.

As Elizabeth Papazian notes, Vertov modeled the concept of the Kinoks network after the worker and peasant correspondent movement in the Soviet press. He planned that the filmmakers taking part in this network "would conduct surveillance of all aspects of 'life as it is' throughout the vast territory of the Soviet Union, organize and collect material, and disseminate information on a mass scale across language barriers."[57] The goal of establishing a full-scale network of filmmakers across the union was never met, let alone Vertov's intent to make the movie camera ubiquitous and make all workers of the union double as newsreel makers. But Vertov did experiment with this model, on a limited scale, in the production of *The Sixth Part of the World*. For this film, Vertov dispatched ten cameramen to shoot documentary footage across the Soviet Union, which allowed him to depict on the screen proletariats working simultaneously in different locations—

thus coming close to the ideal of allowing all workers of the world to see one another.[58]

Several commentators have noted that Vertov's utopian description of the network of Kinoks already came close to anticipating modern television practices.[59] Crucially, however, Vertov did not simply predict what broadcast television made possible in the following decades. He envisioned an alternative configuration of moving image transmission media, which in his view would push the very premise of the Kino-Eye project further. Specifically, the Radio-Eye meant to undo the centralized, hierarchical model of the Kinoks' cinematic network and was not "just an opportunity to transmit audio-visual documentary films by radio." Vertov envisioned the novel technology as one that would also enable filming at a distance by remote-controlled cameras and accumulating documentary audiovisual material from the Radio-Eye hub.[60] Thus, instead of having the central hub collecting all filmed footage, editing the newsreels, and distributing them, the Radio-Eye network offered more participatory and dialogical modes of communication. When logged in to the network of two-way transmission lines, all filmmakers (or, rather, Radioks) could draw on the sources available in the central hub in order create and exchange any number of works. Such a Radio-Eye network would fulfill Vertov's prophecy that moving image transmission media "can bring us still closer to our cherished basic goal— to unite all the workers scattered over the earth through a single consciousness, a single bond, a single collective will in the battle for communism."[61]

Vertov does not provide any further description of how the network of Radio-Eye transmission would operate. We can only speculate that it would include a central television experiment station, staffed not with archivists and editors of filmed footage but rather with switchboard operators (similar to those presented working at an inhuman pace in *Man with a Movie Camera* [figure 5.1]), who would facilitate the instantaneous exchange of audiovisual materials between the Radioks around the world. More than being an improvement of the cinematic apparatus, a networked system of this sort would radically revolutionize cinema's modes of production and spectatorship. It would eliminate the distinction between film viewers and producers and do away with the centralized institutions of filmmaking and film distribution. In this respect, Vertov's vision of a new advanced stage in cinema history consisted not only of an imaginary technological formation but also of a radical reformation of the very ability of the masses to participate in the administration of media flows.

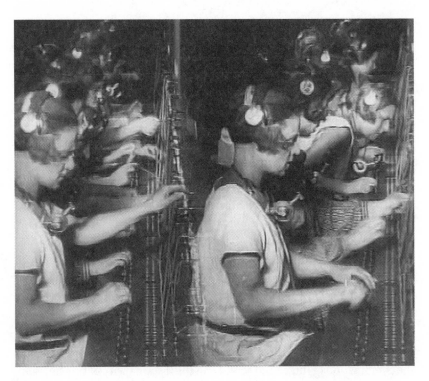

5.1. Operators at a switchboard in *Man with a Movie Camera*, dir. Dziga Vertov, 1929.

Man with a Movie Camera and the Simulation of Television

In his 1925 essay "Kino-Pravda and Radio-Pravda," which represents one of Vertov's earliest responses to the coming of television, the revolutionary filmmaker declares, "We must prepare to turn these inventions of the capitalist world to its own destruction."[62] "Preparation" is a key notion in Vertov's relation to new media technologies. Having stated that the revolutionary potential of cinema had been compromised by the West, Vertov realized in typical avant-garde fashion that the Soviets must fulfill the promise of television before it fell prey to capitalism and suffered a "misfortune" similar to that of the movie camera. In his view, the belated arrival of available televisual technology was lagging behind the cultural readiness for it. (His claim that the technology was "overdue" thus contradicts technological determinism; the material realization of the Radio-Eye was late to meet its historical era.)[63] However, following the initial breakthroughs in the development of television around the mid-1920s came a period of several years of postponement, so the Kinoks were able to spend this period "preparing themselves for meeting in full armor the transition . . . to work in the context of Radio-Eye."[64] By the 1929 release of *Man with a Movie Camera*, the Kinoks announced that they were prepared and eager to utilize televisual media for the purposes of the revolution before the West could appropriate it for art and entertainment. They turned the cinema of the late silent era into a training ground for work in television.

Man with a Movie Camera became best known as an exemplary work of cinematic self-reflexivity, given its depiction of the process of shooting, editing, projecting, and viewing a film. Art theorist Rosalind Krauss referred to it as "perhaps the most medium-specific film in the history of cinema."[65] But at the same time, *Man with a Movie Camera* could also be seen as a fundamentally intermedial work, one that reflects its makers' fascination with the prospects of television. Vertov's own statement regarding the film argues that while *Man with a Movie Camera* is still a work of silent cinema, it comes "very close to the period of Radio-Eye," for it is constructed "in the direction from Kino-Eye to Radio-Eye." In other words, it simulates in several instances the devices of the yet-unavailable television technology, namely the combination of image and sound and the instantaneity of transmission.

The use of one medium to simulate the properties of another comes across as a sharp violation of modernism's feted aesthetic principle of medium specificity. However, as I noted above, even if Vertov's work became a model for high-modernist cinematic aesthetics, he distanced himself from all matters related to art and would have been hostile to the very notion of aesthetic theory that revolves around the autonomy of the arts. Indifferent to the notion of the purity of his medium, Vertov regarded his later film *Enthusiasm* (1930) as a filmed symphony and the *Kino-Pravda* newsreels as filmed newspapers. Therefore, when Vertov states in the beginning of *Man with a Movie Camera* that the film is free from the influence of theater, he does not do so in order to highlight the autonomy of the cinematic medium; rather, he emphasizes the distinction between this documentary and single-authored fictional works in the tradition of bourgeois art. In *Man with a Movie Camera*, the intermedial aspiration is highlighted already in the very beginning, when the film's opening title declares that what we are about to watch is a segment from a cameraman's diary. Soon afterward, Vertov also includes the note that "this film presents an experiment in the cinematic communication of visible events." The Russian word передачи, which Vertov uses here and is commonly translated in the film's English-titled releases as "communication," also denotes "rendering," "delivery," "transmission," and today also "broadcast." Vertov, in this latter sense, declares at the outset that the film deploys the tools of the cinema in order to experiment with the possibilities of visual transmission.

One property of television that Vertov attempts to simulate in *Man with a Movie Camera* is the combination of sound and image—a possibility that was a novelty in film at the time, but appeared as an inherent property of the newly emerging transmission medium. In his statement, Vertov argues that his silent film is constructed as "a visible-audible-film-thing." This effect is achieved in two ways. First, *Man with a Movie Camera* employs numerous techniques in an attempt to convey sound solely through images—for instance, in shots that superimpose images of musical instruments (and of Vertov's own left ear) on top of images of radio loudspeakers, and in the sequences that depict the movie theater orchestra or a spoon and bottles tapping. Second, the film also anticipates sound in its very structure. According to Vertov, it was "edited not only in visual but also in noise, sound terms"—taking into account not only how the shots refer to one another visually, but also according to the sounds their objects convey.[66] Likewise, the omission of intertitles also gives the film a form that resembles titleless sound film, where spoken words replace writing. *Man with a Movie Camera*, in short, is constructed as if it actually had a soundtrack.

Film scholars Gilles Delavaud and Jean-Paul Fargier have demonstrated in different contexts that *Man with a Movie Camera* also features attempts at similarly simulating the effect of televisual simultaneous transmission.[67] To be sure, the challenge of depicting simultaneously occurring events was not new to the cinema of the late 1920s. Responding to the demand for complex narrative forms, early narrative films developed new storytelling techniques for clear and effective representations of multiple actions that happen at the same time in different places. Chief among those was the method of parallel editing, an alternation between shots that depict multiple simultaneous events in a continuous manner.[68] Vertov utilizes this technique of parallel editing in many instances throughout *Man with a Movie Camera* precisely in order to achieve such an effect. Years later he explained, "In anticipation of television it should be clear that such 'vision-at-a-distance' is possible in film-montage."[69]

Clearly, however, the impression this editing technique creates applies only to different actions or events that occur at the same time within the film's diegesis; it does not create the effect of "live" televisual simultaneity, in the sense of depicting events virtually at the same time of their actual occurrence. Vertov's solution to this shortcoming, paradoxically, was to turn to cinematic self-reflexivity. In the opening scene of the film, we see a projectionist preparing for the screening of a film labeled *Man with a Movie Camera*—the very film we are watching at the moment. The remainder of the film then depicts the different stages of its own making (in Vertov's description, "The film's passage from camera through laboratory and editing room to screen—will be included, by montage, in the film's beginning, middle and end").[70] Consider in this light the effect that is created in the film's climactic final scene. In that scene, Vertov rapidly cuts back and forth between images of an audience seated in a movie theater looking at a projected image on the screen and shots from various scenes that appeared at earlier points in the film. The scene begins with cross-cutting between a sequence of stop-motion animation and reaction shots of individual audience members, thus establishing the sense of simultaneity—that is, we see the audience while they are watching the images. The spatial and temporal relations, however, become more complex as the scene progresses. Close to the film's end, Vertov alternates between three sequences, cutting between images of a family sitting in a carriage, the cameraman shooting the family from a moving vehicle, and an audience watching pictures of both the family and the cameraman projected on the screen in the movie theater (figures 5.2–5.5). Interwoven in this fashion, the images of the film's shooting and exhibition are represented as if they take place in the same instant. Combined with the fact that the film that is being exhibited to the on-screen audience is *Man with a Movie Camera* itself, the effect this sequence creates comes very close to the impression of "live" televisual instantaneity: the depicted events are being caught on camera and presented to us (and the on-screen audience) at the same time they occur.

By striving to emulate instantaneous audiovisual transmission with the means of silent cinema, *Man with a Movie Camera* exemplifies Walter Benjamin's observation that "the history of every art form has critical periods in which the particular form strains after effects which can be easily achieved only with a changed technical standard—that is to say, in a new art form."[71] Vertov's exemplary work of cinematic high modernism strives not only to free the cinema from foreign influences of theater and literature, but also to reach beyond what cinematic technology could achieve. In the midst of a period of vast changes in the mediascape, *Man with a Movie Camera* was made with one eye on its own means of production and another already looking ahead at future media technologies. Vertov recognized the limited potential of film to fully realize the goals of decoding "life as it *is*" and was

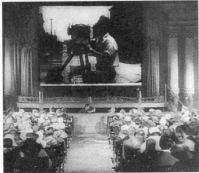

Figures 5.2–5.5. Scenes simultaneously captured in the street and shown on the screen in *Man with a Movie Camera*, dir. Dziga Vertov, 1929.

eager to start working with the new incarnation of audiovisual media. A crowning achievement of silent cinema, *Man with a Movie Camera* is in this sense also a compromise: it showcases cinematic compositional methods that emerged out of an attempt to move away from film and resemble televisual effects. During the decades-long delay in the arrival of available television technology, Vertov had to settle for a medium that could at least give him an opportunity to be prepared for the new highly anticipated technology, before capitalist powers corrupted its potential.

Aftermath and Legacies of Revolutionary Television

In August 1930, Vertov gave a speech at the first All Union Conference on Sound Cinema, which was dedicated to current challenges of the transition to sound. Typically ahead of his time, Vertov took the opportunity to propose a five-year plan to establish "a powerful audio-visual-sound-recording and radio-transmitting station."[72] For Vertov, the Soviet film industry had to orient itself not only toward the coming of sound but also toward "the long distance transmission of sound films." As he insisted, the delay in the realization of image transmission technologies offered the Soviets an opportunity to compete against the United States in the development of television stations and thereby, in his words, "not only catch up with the West but also overtake it."[73]

However, despite Vertov's urgent call to expedite the development of a Soviet television system, Soviet officials had decided to rely on Western television technology. In May 1930, the Moscow-based technical-scientific administration of the People's Commissariat of Post and Telegraph contacted the Jenkins Corporation in New Jersey and asked to acquire a model of the latest Jenkins television system, stating that the Commissariat "intends to make an extensive use of the Television system in USSR."[74] The following years, several Russian laboratories engaged in the development of television transmission capabilities. A Moscow station operated test broadcasting, and a Research Institute for Television was founded in Leningrad.[75] But by the middle of the decade, the Soviet Union ordered $2 million worth of television equipment from the Radio Corporation of America in a transaction that, after being approved by the United States government and military, materialized in 1937.[76] In June 1938, experimental broadcasts started in Moscow, relying mostly on airing existing motion picture materials and serving about one hundred receivers in various public and domestic settings.[77] As in

THE CONFLICT ON THE ETHER WAVES—AN ENGLISH VIEW

5.6. Russian, Italian, and Soviet television sets. Illustration from *New York Times*, September 13, 1936.

the case of the rest of Europe and the United States, it was only after the end of World War II that Russian television became a mass medium.

Vertov's conception of the Radio-Eye never materialized. When it became possible to experiment with television transmission, the avant-garde was no longer in vogue in the Soviet Union. The unilateral broadcasting model suited the purposes of the political order better than the distributed network of interconnected channels of communication that Vertov imagined. A *New York Times* cartoon from 1936 captured well how political currents ended up guiding the development of European mass media in the interwar era (figure 5.6). Depicting German, Italian, and Soviet television screens, each shaped like the symbols of their respective autocratic political parties, the cartoon gives an early figurative expression to the notion that broadcasting takes the form of dominant political powers (although it is worth noting that in the 1930s both the Soviet Union and Germany were licensing American television technologies from RCA). The television sets in the cartoon neither show the masses nor face the masses. Instead, they all face one another as they display Stalin, Hitler, and Mussolini simultaneously declaring increases in military power while cornering a female incarnation of Europe—the sole actual human to appear in the cartoon outside a screen. The mass media here glorify dictators and create nothing but a feedback loop of international hostility—a far cry from what Vertov had envisioned for the future of television.

After the coming of sound, Vertov's writings engaged less frequently with the prospect of moving image transmission media. His use of the term "Radio-Eye" in that period referred to talking films rather than to television. Nevertheless, the ideas that Vertov put forth about the prospects of an open and inclusive transmission network that would enable the masses to partake in the circulation of audiovisual media and promote social change have proved to have a long-lasting relevance in later debates about the modern mediascape. In 1970, Hans Magnus Enzensberger declared that electronic media would counter the centralized and unilateral nature of cinema and television by "making possible mass participation in a social and socialized productive process."[78] Shortly afterward, the *Guerrilla Television* manifesto described how the newly available portable and affordable video technology could be deployed for activist grassroots media production. In the spirit of the contemporary counterculture movement, the manifesto referred to such video practice as an "anticipatory intelligence network."[79] Sharing these sentiments, many commentators who have witnessed the proliferation of digital audiovisual technologies and the ubiquity of the World Wide Web in the 1990s and early 2000s saw in them a utopian promise to counter centralized mass culture and make it more inclusive and participatory.[80] Each of these moments of media transition seems to have reenergized the ongoing discourse about the possibility to reshape the mediascape and undo the hierarchies of the established culture industries—a discourse that may be traced as far back as the earliest days of television and to Vertov's utopian anticipation of a postcinematic, postrevolutionary era.

6　Thinking across Media

Classical Film Theory's Encounter with Television

In the previous chapters, I have shown how television's characteristics and possibilities were debated in technical, industrial, regulatory, political, and popular-culture discourses between the mid-1920s and late 1930s. In this final chapter, my aim is to show how during the same period, the future of television also concerned debates in what has come to constitute the canon of classical film theory. Drawing on the work of German critic and perceptual psychologist Rudolf Arnheim, this chapter will show how classical film theory's engagement with television constitutes the first attempts at theorizing the medium of television while also opening up possibilities for rereading the heritage of film theory from an intermedial perspective.

Classical film theory is most commonly described as a historical project that was concerned with coming to terms with the new phenomenon of cinema by striving toward the formulation of essentialist claims on its nature. It is identified with what D. N. Rodowick recently termed "the aesthetic discourse" on film: a diverse body of works that poses questions about the medium's aesthetic value and singularity as an art form, seeks to define its medium-specific properties, and prescribes how cinema's unique means of expression should be best put to use.[1] Typically, this concern with the new and the indeterminate on one hand and specificity on the other has been understood as distinguishing classical film theories from the concern of contemporary film theorists. Whereas thinkers from the first decades of the twentieth century engaged questions about the essence and distinguishing features of cinema, the mediascape of the turn of the millennium rather raised questions about transformations in cinema's ontology, cultural role, and the nature of its relation with other media.

But as I show in the following pages, the emergence of television in the late 1920s and 1930s necessitated that film theorists engage with very similar questions to the ones film scholars have later encountered with the proliferation of digital media. As Rodowick has noted elsewhere, "Periods of technological change are always interesting for film theory because the films themselves tend to stage its primary question: *What is cinema?*"[2] Rodowick maintains that the emergence of professional film studies coincided with the periods in which cinema was facing fierce competition from other media, namely from television broadcasting in the 1950s and video technologies of the 1980s. This leads him to suggest that "perhaps the drive to understand film and cinema was fueled in direct proportion to its economic displacement and physical disappearance."[3] Similarly, Mary Ann Doane remarks that "it is as though the object of theory were to delineate more precisely the contours of an object at the moment of its historical demise."[4] In light of these claims, I wish to argue that just as the introduction of digital technologies has triggered current efforts to revisit some of the foundational (though not yet theoretically exhausted) aspects of the cinema, so too did the recognition of the imminent appearance of television affect film theory in the 1920s and 1930s.[5] The emergence of moving image transmission technologies did not only signal the starting point of television history. To paraphrase Friedrich Kittler, the coming of television also ended cinema's thirty-year monopoly in the field of moving images and thereby transformed the entire ecology of visual media. Given this media-historical context, we may assume that even if the primary objective of classical film theory has been the pursuit of the essence of the medium, the identity of cinema could no longer be considered fixed and absolute—but proved to be deeply historical and contingent on its place in the media ecology.

Arnheim was by no means the sole classical film theorist who wrote about television. During the 1950s, André Bazin published many television criticism pieces that attempted to define a "provisional essence" of the medium and assess its impact on society and on the cinema.[6] Unsurprisingly, Bazin understood the nature of television to be rooted in its capacity for liveness—that is, in opposition to the cinematic capacity to mummify time that was central in his theorizing of the ontology of film. Siegfried Kra-cauer, too, dedicated a section to the new medium's impact on cinema in his 1960 book *Theory of Film*, arguably the last major work in classical film theory. For Thomas Elsaesser, the growing cultural significance of television in the 1950s may have been one of the reasons for writing *Theory of Film*, as Kracauer was seeking "to try and define the cinema one last time" before it lost its dominant position among the media.[7] Yet Kracauer's passages about television are chiefly concerned the similarities between the two media. De-spite grounding his theory in the photographic basis of cinema, Kracauer proclaims that television and the cinema "share certain essential charac-teristics" and therefore television "affords at least some of the satisfactions which make, or made, so many people crave the movies."[8]

A number of other film theorists, however, in the 1920s and 1930s had al-ready addressed the coming of television. Most of these writings are largely forgotten and have been left out of the canonical body of film theory. None-theless, they merit excavating and revisiting in the context of current de-bates on intermediality. Obviously, these engagements with television were not based on observations of actual television programs. Rather, the early theorists who commented on the emergent medium offered speculations about its future possibilities and attempted to define its place in relation to cinema and within various historical lineages of media technologies and art forms.

Walter Benjamin mentions television in a 1928 essay as the most recent development in the historical sequence of "techniques of the observer"—practical and mechanized media forms that do not qualify as "art" in the traditional sense—thereby putting the new medium in line with optical de-vices such as the magic lantern and dioramas.[9] Elsewhere, Benjamin men-tions television in his working notes for the essay "The Storyteller," which traces changes in the transmission of memory and narrative form between oral traditions, the novel, the short story, and the press. In these notes, Ben-jamin evokes television alongside the gramophone as examples of modern media technologies that threaten to bring about the demise of traditional linear narration.[10] These passing comments do not amount to a substantial engagement with television, but they do invite speculations about the ab-sence of any mention of television in Benjamin's "The Work of Art in the Age of Its Technological Reproducibility," which focuses precisely on ques-tions related to the emergence of new visual media technologies. Not only was this essay first published just fifteen months after the inauguration of German television services; it also opens with a quote from a Paul Valéry text that foresees a future in which the delivery of audiovisual material to the home is as common as the supply of water, gas, and electricity.

Sergei Eisenstein, too, had a long and continuous interest in television, which culminated in his unpublished project on the general history of cinema. In his notes for the general history, Eisenstein describes the new medium as belonging to a more advanced stage in the historical development of cinema, while also positing it within a much longer transhistorical and transcultural lineage that originates in the ancient Dionysian rituals.[11] As early as 1929, however, Eisenstein made a brief but evocative mention of television in an addendum written for the German translation of his essay "Perspectives," in which he lays out his theory of an intellectual cinema. With the concept of intellectual cinema, Eisenstein set out to do no less than invent a new mode of cinema with formal characteristics and a social mission appropriate for the postcapitalist age. In this context, television (alongside radio and the theory of relativity) embodies that standard to which, Eisenstein claims, the new mode of cinema should aspire.[12] As Eisenstein claims, only a cinema capable of conveying philosophical ideas in form of visual images will prove worthy of existing among these scientific and technological achievements of the twentieth century.

But it is in Arnheim's oeuvre that we find the most substantial body of work on television in the context of film theory. Trained in the school of Gestalt psychology, Arnheim became interested in making use of principles of visual perception in theoretical work on visual arts, and in the mid-1920s started working as a film critic in Berlin. Like other critics of his generation, he approached film as an intriguing new experiment in aesthetic and visual expression that could result in the formation of a new art. Arnheim's well-known book of film theory, *Film als Kunst* (*Film as Art*), was published in 1932. In 1936 it was followed by *Radio*, a pioneering book-length study of the aesthetic possibilities of sound broadcasting, which also delved into the medium's political significance. Arnheim dedicated the final chapters of both his film and radio books to the emergence of television, a topic he continued to explore in several other articles he published during the same decade. In the remainder of this chapter, I discuss Arnheim's arguments about the promises and threats of television in the context of his own theory of film and in relation to more recent theoretical engagement with questions of media change and media convergence. I will show not only that Arnheim was early in identifying issues regarding the aesthetic possibilities and the political significance of television, but also that his engagement with the new medium led him to extend his theoretical project by way of developing claims regarding mass media spectatorship and intermediality.

The Art and Politics of Television

Arnheim's theory of film concerned the ways in which cinema may be qualified as an art form. His primary goal in *Film as Art* was to identify cinema-specific means of expression, on the one hand establishing that cinema is not merely a tool for mechanical reproduction, and on the other hand distinguishing it from other arts. Focusing on the particular material properties of the filmstrip and the movie camera, Arnheim emphasizes instances in which film falls short of perfectly reproducing reality (namely, by rendering the real world monochromatic, two-dimensional, and silent) and sees these shortcoming as allowing for possibilities for aesthetic expression. A strong proponent of media purity, Arnheim objected to advances in color and sound film. In his view, the significance of cinema was in its exclusive use of visual representation, implying that the novel cinematic techniques took away from the medium's artistic potential by bringing cinematic representation too close to reality.

Applying the same criteria in his assessment of the possibilities of television, Arnheim quickly and unambiguously denied that the new medium had any artistic potential. Although it would be easy to assume that, in light of his previous work on film, Arnheim would similarly seek to define television's aesthetic possibilities in accordance with the unique technical affordances of moving image transmission technologies, Arnheim does not follow this path. In fact, he does not regard the distinction between filmic recording and televisual transmission as significant in defining artistic properties. What concerned him more was the fact that television featured a combination of sound and moving images—two means of expression that were already manifested in their pure forms in silent film and in radio. Therefore, according to Arnheim, television lacked medium-specific expressive qualities and had to rely on the dramaturgic principle of other media forms. In various instances he referred to television as "Radio-Film," as both "a marriage" and "struggle" between radio and film, and as "a hybrid creature, born of the movies, the radio, and the theatre."[13] Additionally, Arnheim anticipated that television broadcasters would sacrifice the ability to utilize the aesthetic device of montage, since in live transmission they would not be able to select the best shots and arrange them in an artistically meaningful order. For these reasons, Arnheim deemed television purely a means of transmission without an aesthetic value of its own. As such, he considered television not a part of the lineage of artistic media but rather a relative of the car and the airplane.[14]

As Arnheim removes the question of art from the consideration of television, he instead goes on to theorize about aspects that go beyond his typical concern with artistic values. In his account, the loss in aesthetic potential is matched by a gain in the television's documentary capacity. Thus, he notes that rather than creating new artistic possibilities, television's combination of sight and sound and its capacity for live transmission would allow it to present its viewers with new ways of experiencing the world. In Arnheim's words, "Television will not only portray the world as the film does . . . but it will make this portrayal all the more fascinating because instead of seeing the mere records, we shall be able to *participate* in distant events the moment of their happening."[15] However, Arnheim's distinction between seeing (in cinema) and participating (in television) should not be read in the same sense as that used today in the context of interactive media. Rather, what Arnheim invokes is a subjective feeling of immersion, of being-there, and perhaps most importantly of a lack of mediation that he associates with live television. He continues with a long list of things we may see and hear on television—which include the central square of neighboring towns, political speeches, cultural events, athletic matches, scholarly lectures, landscapes, aerial views, railway collisions, deep-sea fish, factories, and the polar ice—and concludes that "the great world itself lives its life in our room" without the detour of the verbal description or other language barriers.[16] Television in this respect held the promise of promoting peace, since, Arnheim maintains, the ability to see and hear people in foreign countries will remind us of our commonalities. Three years before the outbreak of World War II, Arnheim writes, "Is it not essential for the creation of a war-spirit to have a certain distorted caricature of one's idea of the foreign nation; is it not essential to forget that beyond the trenches are men like ourselves living in the same way?"[17]

Not only does Arnheim claim that television lacks aesthetic possibilities; he also describes how the new medium might put other artistic media in peril. The coming of television, in his view, threatened not only the artistic integrity of cinema as the advent of sound and color did, but also the very existence of cinema. "Within measurable time," he wrote in *Film*, "films will be broadcast from a central projecting station by wireless, so that the same film will be performed in hundreds of theatres simultaneously, or may even be listened-in to in private houses."[18] According to his prediction, once television technology became available to producers, the traditional method of filming, printing, and distributing reels of film would become economically nonviable compared with the transmission of a single live performance from a studio to millions of receivers at once. Under such conditions, Arnheim warned, the film industry would cease to exist. The motivation of television broadcasters to cater to as broad an audience as possible would lead them to aim at lower artistic standards than those of film, in order to satisfy viewers who seek "distraction and amusement" in the form of "raw, pointless viewing."[19] In *Radio*, Arnheim similarly suggests that the identity of the purely aural medium was facing a similar fate in its competition with television. Although radio broadcasts in the Weimar Republic were typified by high cultural value and offered a variety of educational programming, Arnheim doubted that radio could continue developing in its pure form alongside television. He feared that visual broadcasting "will make short shrift of the special new means of expression and representation that [radio] broadcasting has given us" and declared that television will destroy radio's aesthetic character "even more radically than the sound film destroyed silent film."[20]

As Arnheim makes clear, the challenges that television posed to cinema's and radio's artistic potential had political significance. In *Film*, he predicts that the consolidation of all moving image production into a single transmission station would eliminate the "multiplicity of local and provincial stimuli and opportunities for evolution" that are vital for the cultural development of the nation and instead usher in a "thoroughgoing standardization of all forms of culture."[21] This understanding of the power of television broadcasting as analogous to totalitarian control over social institutions demonstrates the extent to which the political currents of the late Weimar period influenced Arnheim's media theory. Arnheim, in other words, projects onto his account of the concurrent process of technological media change a political concern with the impending centralization of power, silencing of creative voices, and standardization of culture. These concerns turned out to be justified when the Nazi party came to power in Germany and banned Arnheim's book just months after its publication. Soon after, as part of the efforts toward the centralization of culture, the Nazi government launched the first regular television service in the world. It is very appropriate, therefore, that Arnheim concludes *Film* by stating: "The future of film depends on the future of economics and politics. . . . What will happen to film depends upon what happens to ourselves."[22]

In the summer of 1933 Arnheim left Germany and settled in Italy, where racial laws had not yet been applied. Upon his arrival in Rome, he received an appointment as a writer and editor at the International Institute of Educational Cinematography. Among his responsibilities at the institute was the preparation of a wide-ranging encyclopedia on cinema, which was never realized but allowed him to pursue his work on film and television.[23] As Zoë Druick has shown, the institute's work had to mediate a variety of political philosophies.[24] On the one hand, it was created by the League of Nations in order to promote international political communication through the study and making of educational and documentary films. On the other, funding for the institute came from the Italian government, and its presidents were all figures in the Fascist regime, whose interest was in improving Italy's image abroad.

Thus, while Arnheim insisted that the institute enjoyed the spirit of international objectivity, the political commentary in Arnheim's Italian writings should be read in the context of such an ambivalent position. In February 1935, Arnheim's essay "Seeing Afar Off" (which was later published in an abbreviated form in Film as Art, under the title "A Forecast of Television") appeared in a special volume that the institute's official journal, Intercine, dedicated to television. As opposed to the fear of the monopolization of media that Arnheim expresses in his writings in Germany, "Seeing Afar Off" concludes with a plea to the modern state to exercise its authority and put television to positive use. There Arnheim writes that the monopolization of intellectual life "does not only lead to standardization in the negative sense of the word, but assists at the same time that unification of popular culture which today is so much desired by every government that can interpret the spirit of the time."[25] In the closing of the essay, Arnheim maintains that the state should utilize the advantages of television in order to reawaken communal feelings and save the creative powers of individuals from being "weakened by the division of labor." In accordance with the institute's stated purpose, Arnheim calls for a productive use of television, saying, "The state should allocate the beautiful new reception apparatus to its proper place, to convert passivity to activity so that what the treasures of the electric wave bring into the house don't rot like a dead capital but would be useful."[26]

These passages from "Seeing Afar Off" appear to derive from Arnheim's observations regarding the control of radio and cinema in the 1930s. According to Arnheim, radio programs have greater intellectual and educational value than the cinema, since while the film studios are managed by profit-driven producers "of execrable taste and minimum culture," radio service in most countries (including Germany) is under the influence of governments who use it for educational ends and do not give in to public taste. In Arnheim's view, the cultural significance of television was going to be determined by the outcome of the struggle between the values it inherited from cinema and values it inherited from radio. The possibility that the new technology would follow the model of radio and be under the control of the state was therefore preferable in his view to television being privately owned and becoming a new arm of the entertainment world. Nonetheless, as the exclusion of the essay's concluding section from its 1957 republication indicates, the hope that television could offer an alternative to mindless entertainment media was not realized, even long after the appearance of television.

Television Spectatorship and the Cult of the Image

Alongside the discussions of the technical affordances and institutional control of television, Arnheim's early writings on television also develop a theory of spectatorship. Here Arnheim departs from the topics that marked his work on cinema. Whereas Arnheim's film theory engages with questions of spectatorship as they pertain to the perception of formal and compositional qualities of film, his discussion of television spectatorship is grounded in social- and historical-specific concepts. Although television holds the promise of enhancing human sensory capacity, he writes, its value will only be determined by what viewers will make of it.

Principal in Arnheim's view of television is the belief that given the medium's capacity to transmit raw, unedited, multisensory information of the world, television would alter its spectators' relation to reality. By getting a better sense of the multiple events that take place simultaneously in the world, spectators of the future would become aware that their place in the world is "only one point among many," a notion that Arnheim hoped would make them "more modest and less egocentric."[27] In this claim, Arnheim seems to anticipate Marshall McLuhan's influential "global village" argument about the decentralizing effect of electronic media and its power to create a global collective consciousness and restore a universal feeling of tribalism that modern life has annihilated. Ascribing such a utopian transformative power to the instantaneous nature of television broadcasts, Arnheim proposes (as McLuhan would again later on) that in the case of television it is not the content of television transmission that has a unifying effect on its viewers, but the experience of the technological capacities of the apparatus itself. Yet Arnheim does not base this claim on a technologically deterministic view. He goes on to qualify his observation, noting that in and of itself, the "television apparatus does not suffice for obtaining this result. It offers us the material of extending our experience, even for acquiring a new conception of the world, but we must utilize this material."[28]

Arnheim's main concern was that instead of educating its viewers, television will become a new instrument of "the cult of sensory stimulation" (or, as the 1933 translation put it, "the cult of perception through sensory channels").[29] In the spirit of numerous other critics of modern culture, Arnheim considered the cult of sensory stimulation as a social tendency typical of the era of technological media. Whereas Arnheim notes that in the modern age our conception of the world is "much more concrete, ample, immediate, and finer" compared with that of previous generations, he insists that "the cultivation of sensory perception implies a corresponding retrograde movement for the spoken and written word. . . . The easier and more accessible the means of perception become, the firmer becomes fixed in us the dangerous illusion that seeing means knowing."[30] True knowledge of the world, according to Arnheim, is not readily available to the senses; it can only be obtained by the spirit and by abstract concepts. Similar to his compatriot Siegfried Kracauer's statement that "the world itself has taken on a photographic face," Arnheim acknowledges that social reality presents itself as ready available for visual reproduction; at the same time, he notes that "our world today is a bad actor" that does not reveal its true essence.[31] Arnheim maintains that since raw visual sensation requires analysis and interpretation, television will be beneficial only to viewers who are accustomed to independent and critical thought. Hence, in order for television to make the world not only visible but also comprehensible, it should shift the balance from the visual to the aural and accompany the transmitted images with a voiceover commentary. As he writes in *Radio*, "Let [television] give us a voice that can speak of the general when we see a picture of the particular, and of causes while we are observing effects."[32]

Arnheim was keenly aware that mass audiences would find in television broadcasts an appealing substitute for conversing, reading, and other intellectual means of acquiring concepts, and therefore the new medium could become a threat to those capacities for communication and education. In this respect, his view of human faculties is similar to his view of media technologies and art forms, where the more convenient and immediately available means supersede and marginalize their rivals. "But when it becomes sufficient to move the finger in order to indicate," he writes, "it may come about that the lips will grow mute, the hand that writes or draws will be arrested, and the spirit will perish."[33] Accordingly, Arnheim predicted that despite the medium's utopian possibilities, the television viewer of the future may become a culturally impoverished, antisocial consumer of spectacles who is content with the televisual simulation of the presence of others. Indeed, domestic radio listening already atomized the consumption of culture, but as Arnheim predicts, television would "compensate the lack of bodily presence even better" and set an even higher barrier between individual and community.[34] He describes a thousand-year-long evolutionary process of isolation and separation, which starts with people gathered around the bivouac fire and ends with the figure of the grotesque and lonely television viewer who cannot even applaud in the end of a performance "without making himself ridiculous."[35]

Overall, Arnheim's perspective on the possible impact of television recalls the deeply ambivalent critical positions that Benjamin took with respect to the possibilities of cinema and Kracauer took with respect to photography. In the revised version of his television essay in *Film as Art*, Arnheim concludes that "television is a new, hard test of our wisdom. If we succeed in mastering the new medium it will enrich us. But it can also put our mind to sleep."[36] It is worthwhile probing deeper into the terms Arnheim uses in this formulation. The meaning of "enrich" in this context is relatively clear: television's ability to function as an educational device, to provide documentary information, to facilitate global exchange of cultural products, and to allow an understanding of the richness and complexity of the world are all valued by Arnheim as enlightening effects. By contrast, Arnheim's assertion that television could "put our mind to sleep" refers to how the ease of communication by modern means may weaken the human powers of expression and creativity. This concept explicitly connects Arnheim's ideas on television to the theories he developed about the role of art and its relation to the mind in the context of his works in the fields of psychology and art. As Ara Merjian notes in his insightful discussion of Arnheim's film and art theory, for Arnheim "art is a tool, a method of learning about the world so as to more easily inhabit it. . . . Viewing art is a form of necessary mental and perceptual exercise."[37] According to Arnheim, visual perception involves interpretation and organization of raw sensory material into meaningful forms. Works of art, likewise, embody a procedure of interpretation of raw materials from reality, although on a higher order. Artists express and organize in their works particular subject matters in a manner that captures something universally significant about reality. The encounter with such works of visual art thus demands from the viewer an intensified act of interpretation. In this way, art challenges and coaches the viewer's mental capacities by making perceivable principles of organization and meaning of reality that the viewer otherwise would remain unaware of. Hence, the art experience actively and productively intensifies the capacities of the mind. In other words, it is the opposite of putting the mind to sleep.

Arnheim thus considers television not only as lacking artistic means of expression, but also as countering the effects of art in a manner that runs the risk of numbing the mind. This is not to say, of course, that every non-artistic object has such an effect. The dichotomy between "enrich" and "put us to sleep" does not correspond to the dichotomy between aesthetic and nonaesthetic. Even at its best, television cannot acquire artistic value, but as we have seen, it may have positive social and educational effects by other means. However, since Arnheim believed that "without the flourishing of visual expression no culture can function productively," television's power to supersede radio and film art and replace them with a ubiquitous offering of audiovisual materials with no aesthetic value appeared to him to be a threat to the mental capacities of individuals as well as to culture as a whole.[38] According to Arnheim's formulation, the future of television is still to be determined; however, its potential threats supersede its possible gains.

These observations on the power of new media technologies to put the mental capacities of their users to sleep anticipate ideas that have become (and remained) fundamental in later media theory. Namely, both Walter Benjamin and Marshall McLuhan present expansive and complex conceptions of the notion of numbness in their discussions of technology's negative effects on the human body and psyche. Benjamin writes in his famous "On Some Motifs in Baudelaire" that the numbing of the senses, the faculty of memory, and the cognitive system is the human psyche's strategy to survive the perpetual shocks of technological stimuli imposed on the individual by the modern city, factory, or battleground. This strategy, in turn, results in a sense of alienation and a blocking of the sense of experience which, for Benjamin, typifies modern life.[39] McLuhan, who famously regarded media as "extensions of man" that amplify the capacities of human organs, senses, and nerves, described the effect of the human nervous system's self-protection from the extended sensation that technology brings upon the body as a state of narcosis and numbness. According to McLuhan, since electric media technology extends and amplifies the human mental capacities, a corresponding protective reaction could result in the numbing of the central nervous system itself.[40]

Thus, while Arnheim argues from the perspective of Gestalt psychology, his discussion of the impact of television reaches a conclusion very similar to those of the discussions of new technologies by Benjamin (who is in this case indebted to a Freudian approach) and McLuhan (who was influenced by midcentury studies of the nervous system). Arnheim differs from these influential thinkers when he prescribes a way to remedy or avoid the numbing effect of television. By contrast to Benjamin and McLuhan's theories, which advocate not a resistance to technology but acceptance and openness to the incorporation of technology as a strategy to survive its potential negative effects, Arnheim holds that engagement with media technology must be governed and restricted in order to properly benefit from its advantages and minimize its threats.

A key to what Arnheim means by "mastering the new medium" can be found in his article "Disciplining the Gramophone, Radio, Telephone, and Television," which first appeared in the Italian magazine *Sapere* in December 1937. In his article, Arnheim forcefully rejects the ideology of progress, marshalling against it a variant of his medium-specificity argument. "Every new development, be it material or of the mind, is to some degree dangerous because it tends toward uncontrolled generalization," he writes. "It is therefore necessary, for practical reasons among others, to define the boundaries within which a new medium can yield benefits that couldn't be attained without it, and the limits beyond which it remains inferior to traditional means."[41] For Arnheim, the danger lies not in the new technological devices themselves but in modern society's uncontrolled tendency to see new technologies as capable of answering every need. Hence, the notion of discipline in the article's title refers to self-control and the restriction of the use of new devices, two qualities that Arnheim sees as fundamental for heightening the new media's positive effects and eliminating their negative ones. He invokes the figure of the Sorcerer's Apprentice to argue that the modern user of technology "runs the risk of losing sovereignty over the great minds that have been placed in his service unless he exercises his will against the seductions of inertia and passivity."[42] The efficiency of modern communication technologies thus depends on economical use. For Arnheim, it is appropriate to employ new technologies only when traditional means—either human or technological—prove insufficient. Clearly, although the article deals with multiple media forms, it is written with the coming of television in mind as Arnheim attempts to make use of the few years left before television sets appear in the public's living rooms to advocate for the need to discipline the use of the new technology before its negative consequences take effect.

Arnheim's early writings about the emergence of television and its relationship with film and radio reveal a more dynamic and flexible conception of what constitutes a medium than we are accustomed to associate with his positions. In his film theory, Arnheim famously insists that the proper aesthetic use of cinema may be determined according to its unique formal properties, which, in turn, derive from the physical properties of the apparatus. This view has been criticized as essentialist, for it assumes that each medium has a fixed inherent nature, much in the spirit of the notion of medium specificity in modernist art theory.[43] In this closing section of the chapter, I explore how Arnheim's theoretical engagements with television challenge the assumption that for him the possibilities and limitations of a given medium are defined solely according to its material basis, as well as that for him media forms are inherently distinct from one another due to their different material properties.

Given that Arnheim addresses the coming of television in the context of discussing future developments of both film and radio, a good question to pose at the outset is whether television constitutes a new autonomous medium in Arnheim's view. Arnheim does not explicitly address this question in his film theory book. However, in the book's original edition, the section that concerns television appears in the chapter titled "The Faultless Film" (or "The Complete Film" in the later edition), where Arnheim discusses sound film as well as well color and stereoscopic film—all of which are considered not as new media forms per se but, rather, as technical developments of cinema. Even more suggestive in this respect is the discussion about television in the concluding chapter of *Radio*, where Arnheim claims, "With the coming of picture, broadcasting loses its peculiarity as a new medium of expression and becomes purely a medium of dissemination."[44] As this passage suggests, moving image transmission technology is not a new media form in its own right. Although it allows for new methods of audiovisual representation and dissemination, Arnheim considers it merely a new variation of radio. With this claim, Arnheim appears to contradict the common understanding of what a medium is according to classical film theory; despite the fundamental material differences between the technologies of radio and television, it refers to them as different manifestations of the same medium.

The notion that a single medium may exist in different material variations appears in Arnheim's *Film* in the context of the coming of sound. In this text, Arnheim questions whether sound cinema is a new medium—

which, in his view, depends on whether or not it is governed by its own aesthetic laws. Instead of an essentialist, fixed notion of what constitutes a medium, he presents an understanding of media by way of a spatial analogy, which recalls the Lessingian notion of the realms and borders of different art forms. Lessing's *Laocoön*—famously, one of the foremost influences on Arnheim—notes that "painting and poetry should be like two just and friendly neighbors, neither of whom indeed is allowed to take unseemly liberties in the heart of the other's domain, but who exercise mutual forbearance on the borders."[45] Arnheim similarly claims that every artistic medium is a sphere consisting of a center, periphery, and outer boundaries. "It is not the boundaries of a sphere of art that are important, but its center," he writes. "At its edges it may encroach upon other domains." However, Arnheim adds, "there is something a little doubtful about these intermediate positions. Great artists strive towards the center of their subject. . . . They work in perfectly clean media."[46] According to this view, silent film is the center—the ideal, purest form—of the sphere of cinema. Sound films, conversely, are closer to the boundaries of the sphere of cinema, where the medium overlaps with the sphere of theater.

This formulation also sheds light on Arnheim's view of television. It suggests that, much as with the distinction between silent and sound film, the distinction between radio and television should not be defined according to their material properties. Rather, the two technologies appear to be two manifestations of the medium of broadcasting. Like cinema, broadcasting may take a "pure" aural form or a "hybrid" audiovisual form and still remain the same medium; like all media, the identity of broadcasting is thus neither coherent nor fixed. Within the sphere of broadcasting, radio defines the center due to its reliance on pure aural means of expression. The hybrid form of television, on the other hand, is considered to be farther away in the periphery of broadcasting, where its overlap with the boundaries of cinema brings together moving images with sound.

Well aware that television was about to impact the entire modern mediascape, Arnheim knew that his theoretical project had to take into consideration not only how television would assume a position among other media, but also how its appearance necessitated a redefinition of the relations among other media. This, again, involves a revision of ideas from his theory of film. Like other classical film theorists from Vachel Lindsay to Bazin, Arnheim elaborated in his canonical writings about the factors that distinguish film from theater. He points out, for instance, the differences between the effect of the actual space and the presence of real flesh-and-blood performers in the theater and the cinematic two-dimensional, colorless representation of performers and spaces. Likewise, he singles out the device of cinematic montage, which grants film a greater degree of temporal and spatial liberty than that of the theater.[47] The encounter with television, however, made Arnheim refine his view on the distinction between media. In a 1937 magazine article on the future of television, he wrote about NBC's television studio in New York, where a multicamera system allowed points of view to be shifted between several cameras during a live transmission of a performance and thus enabled television to emulate (although only to a limited degree) the aesthetic possibilities of filmic montage. Arnheim greatly valued this technique. For him, the "simple transmission" of a performance, in the sense of a linear direct broadcasting without the ability to shift between different points of view, "would not be enough to distinguish a television show from a normal theatre production." As he remarks, "It would be theatre electrically transmitted through space, but still theatre!"[48]

By suggesting that a theater performance remains "still theatre" even when it is reproduced electronically on the small screen, Arnheim devalues the extent to which material properties distinguish between media. Rather than adhering to rigid ontological definitions, he acknowledges that the identity of a medium is influenced by intermedial relations and historical mutations. This does not mean, however, that Arnheim has abandoned the notion of medium specificity altogether. While in his view the ability of television to transmit materials that originate in other media has weakened the bond between a work of art and its medium, television's capacity to reproduce films and theatrical works allows for a productive development of his theory of medium specificity. As he argues in *Radio*, the distinctions between the properties of theater and film "will either vanish before the screen of the television apparatus, or will have to be founded on more essential and inner differences."[49] In other words, Arnheim argues that rather than threatening the validity of medium specificity, televisual remediation brings to light even finer diagnoses regarding the specific features of various media. In this case, television transmission proves that the physical properties of a film or a theater performance, which are customarily seen as central in Arnheim's focus on distinctions between art forms, are mere "external facts." What is of greater importance for Arnheim is, rather, the "inner" expressive principles of each medium. In his view, direct televisual transmission of films and theatrical productions kept their respective expressive means and dramaturgical principles intact *despite* the mediation of the distinct material delivery system. In this way, the spatiotemporal continuity and the centrality that is given to the spoken word may be seen as the essential qualities of theater, while the shifts between different viewpoints, times, and spaces may typify film more accurately than its material support. In Arnheim's view, therefore, television's ability to transmit both films and stage performances would enable the inspection of the aesthetic characteristics of cinema and theater separately from their respective material bases. Hence, whereas television was deprived of unique expressive means, it could allow for the truly essential artistic qualities of other artistic forms to more fully reveal themselves.

In recent years we have witnessed a certain "return to classical film theory," with numerous scholarly projects that aim at reevaluating the heritage of this body of thought against the backdrop of today's postcinema culture.[50] Most often, the canon of classical film theory is approached in this context as the locus of ontological essentialist arguments about the moving image, which are either troubled or thrown into sharp relief by the present situation. But as I have attempted to show in this chapter, we have a good reason to read classical film theory in a different light. Revisiting Arnheim's early writings on television makes apparent that although his legacy within the tradition of film theory is most strongly associated with a rigorous, essentialist insistence on medium specificity, his texts on the coming of television acknowledge that film has responded to changes in the modern mediascape. Given how the specter of the advent of television and the consequent threat to the future of film loom over Arnheim's major works on cinema, it could be argued that his theoretical project was motivated not by a will to provide fixed notions regarding the nature of film, but by a concern with the dynamics of its transformation and possible disappearance. By considering television as the next step in the development of both cinema and broadcasting, and by predicting that television will bring about the consolidation of all film production and distribution activities, Arnheim departs from what is typically seen as the concern of classical theory and offers a pioneering attempt at theorizing intermediality and media convergence. Arnheim's work thus demonstrates the extent to which the project of classical film theory was indeed flexible, dynamic, and responsive to the altering mediascape out of which it originated. Just as important, it also validates that television has played a vital part in shaping our understanding of cinema from its very beginning.

CONCLUSION

In 2012, at a television studies conference, I presented some materials from early chapters of this book. For the sake of historical accuracy, when I discussed nineteenth-century technological schemes for moving image transmission devices I referred to them not as television, but as "what we today call television." The paper that preceded mine on the same panel concerned new forms of mobile and streaming media, to which the presenter referred as online variants of "what we, for the time being, call television." This unplanned correspondence in the choice of words brought to the fore the contingent nature of television's very identity. It seems to suggest, furthermore, that the long history of moving image transmission media can be read as a palindrome of sorts. Whether we read it from the 1870s forward or from the present moment backward, we encounter the story of multiple newly invented technologies of connectivity that gradually solidify around a relatively stable dominant mass media form for a few decades, then splinters once more into a multiplicity of configurations. Likewise, both ends of the processes of solidifying and fragmenting television's media identity are accompanied by heated cultural debates, typified by far-reaching declarations about the alteration of the entire mediascape. For example, ideas from the early 2000s about a single "black box" device that would allegedly unite and perform all of our media tasks find a parallel in the nineteenth-century description of imaginary televisual media forms that bring together the properties of telegraph, telephone, phonograph, and the moving image (as exemplified, for instance, in the "cinema-phono-telegraphique" communication device depicted in figure 3.1).

Likewise, if this book considered the late nineteenth century as marking the point of the simultaneous emergence of cinema and television, the early 2000s saw an inflation in declarations about their simultaneous end, or even death, and the coming of a postcinema, posttelevision era.[1] For a powerful illustration of the current confusion about the status of moving image media, we need to look no further than debates about whether or not motion pictures that were released online by streaming services could qualify for international film festival competitions and Academy Awards. As one Academy of Motion Pictures Arts and Sciences governor confessed in 2017, "We've got to define what is a movie."[2] Almost eight decades after Hollywood and the broadcasting industry first debated the identity of television, its distinctions from cinema, and its potential to eclipse film culture, the concern with the boundaries of each moving image medium now introduces itself once more.

To be sure, I am not referring to these recurrences in order to make a snarky, well-worn, media-historical argument along the lines of "This is actually not new" or "All of this has already taken place before." I believe there is a good reason why there is such a great concern about cinema losing its identity or its place in our culture at the present moment even though a viable commercial alternative to cinematic moving images has been in existence since the inauguration of television broadcasts in the mid-twentieth century. This reason, in my mind, has everything to do with the creation of the acknowledged, autonomous, and distinctive media identity that this book has explored. If today there is a sense that digital media is transforming (or, as some scholars would claim, killing, absorbing, or relocating) cinema, it is because the new image technologies are seen not as occupying their own distinct cultural space but as threatening the boundaries of what we define as cinema. This notion, in turn, reveals something about the unequivocal success of creating a sense of televisual specificity during the experimental era. By the late 1940s, television emerged as a medium with its own distinct traits. As such, while the young medium of television certainly was perceived as a competitor to the cinema, it did not appear to be stepping on its proverbial toes or violating cinema's integrity as a distinctive form in its own right. By contrast, today's very terms of understanding digital moving images are still intertwined with those of cinema—and as such they have the power to trouble the existing conceptions of ontology and specificity.

Consider, for example, the differences between the scholarly discourse about cinema's encounter with television and with digital moving images. Within the field of cinema studies, early debates about the emergence of digital media often focused on how the new audiovisual technologies challenged the most fundamental notions of the ontology of cinema—the truth claim of the photographic image, its complex temporality, and the specificity of its material properties. Such concerns were frequently cast into questions of how the digital breaks from the notion of filmic indexicality, thereby altering the very nature of cinematic signification.[3] But as Thomas Elsaesser observes, long before the emergence of digital technologies, television had also "broken with the indexicality of the photographic image, without however provoking a similar crisis."[4] Television was never chiefly theorized in academic debates in light of the supposed essence of its material basis. Instead, Elsaesser points out, it is understood according to its ideological function, institutional structure, and textual-cultural struggles for meaning. In this way, television "put[s] the digital 'in perspective.'"[5]

As I have shown throughout this book, many of the earliest commentators who witnessed the emergence of the new medium were in fact deeply engaged with questions regarding the distinctions between the transmitted moving image and photographic media. Time and again, the early writings about image transmission speculated on the nature of its correspondence with the human body, its affiliation with surrounding media forms, and, particularly, its relation to the real. Such broad ontological concerns, however, were pushed to the margins of debates about television by the beginning of the broadcast era. The cultural, industrial, and economic factors that came to identify television technology with the broadcasting model have effectively reframed the terms in which television was understood. Critical engagements with the medium, therefore, started revolving around a set of cultural traits that became identified as unique to broadcast television as a media institution. Today, with the end of the dominance of the (domestic, nation-bound) broadcasting model and with the digitization simultaneously of both filmic and televisual media, the integrity of the respective media institutions and their autonomous identity are challenged. As a result, questions about the prospects of image transmission technologies absorbing or outright replacing cinema are now resurfacing after having been initially introduced in the 1920s and 1930s, thereby proving themselves to be recurring media archaeological *topoi* that span historical eras in different formulations.[6]

Similarly, changing our perspective on the historiography of television may shed new light on current debates within television studies. In recent years, television scholars have been exploring the technological, aesthetic, regulatory, and textual transformation in the present "postnetwork era"—an era during which the dominance of nationwide broadcasting networks is being challenged by a variety of novel television delivery formats.[7] The concept of postnetwork television has proved productive in providing new perspectives on some of the fundamental claims about the medium's specificity, which were conceived predominantly in light of broadcasting practices (for example, in theories that pointed at the temporality of liveness, the arrangement of programming flow, or domestic distracted spectatorship as constitutive of the medium's identity).[8] Yet seeing that the broadcasting model itself is a medial configuration that appeared fairly late in the history of moving image transmission allows us to think of the current transformations in television in a different fashion. If we take into consideration the fifty-year era of "prebroadcast" television, during which moving image transmission was understood chiefly as an extension of telegraph and telephone networks, it transpires that what we are witnessing today is not only the end of the dominant model of broadcast television, but part of a longer ongoing trajectory of shifts in configurations of moving image transmission media. In the late nineteenth century, the initial imaginary forms of moving image transmission media resembled the structure of other telecommunication networks, wherein numerous interconnected wires could link a virtually infinite number of points by allowing two-way point-to-point instantaneous communication across an unlimited breadth of space. By the mid-twentieth century, the dominant concept of moving image transmission media had altered and became associated with a configuration modeled after radio broadcasting networks and their one-directional communication from single points to numerous scattered receivers. Presently, "postnetwork" television practices have become increasingly embedded in yet another kind of network, one that facilitates flows of data via satellites, the internet, and other interconnected digital devices and allows for a range of media experiences, from "microcasting" to dialogical two-way image transmission.

Tracing these transitions between the networked connectivity modalities that typified the conception of moving image transmission media in different moments allows us to map the history of television onto widescale changes in the culture and mediascape of modernity. As this book has shown, the earliest imaginary forms of moving image transmission media appeared at a time when electrical telecommunication networks came to play a crucial role in coordinating flows of people, capital, and information in correspondence to the new economic, political, and cultural demands of late nineteenth-century modernization. Telegraphy and telephony appeared as both symptoms of and support mechanisms for the modern concern with speed, territorial expansion, and aspiration to "annihilate space and time." By contrast, the rise of the broadcasting model at the time of the large-scale realization of television services corresponded to the distinct economic and political context of the interwar era. Unlike the decentralized global networks of the telegraph, the centralized and hierarchical broadcasting networks emerged as national enterprises, both politically and economically, which aimed at the creation of mass audiences on the basis of a synchronized and unified media experience. The most recent forms of television services, in turn, correspond to the needs and possibilities of our contemporary cultural moment of global neoliberal economy and new forms of social control, in which our own networked society organizes itself according to powerful and flexible systems of interconnected economic relationships, data flows, and cultural exchanges. As such, they take a new form of distributed ubiquitous networks, modeled by (and frequently absorbed within) the internet. With this brief historical sketch, importantly, I do not intend to offer a reductive telos of technological development. Communication structures, after all, "do not live by themselves." As Manuel Castells argues, "They always express, in a contradictory and conflictive pattern, the interests, values, and projects of the actors who produce the structure while being conditioned by it."[9]

And so, if today we are under the impression that what we are witnessing is but one more moment in a series of countless "deaths of cinema" and that history (or at least media history) inevitably repeats itself, I should end with a plea that we not lose sight of the historical-specific circumstances of media change.

NOTES

Introduction

1. "The Nice Congress," *Intercine* 7, no. 4 (April 1935): 193. About the international assembly, see also "Radio and Cinema in Europe to Cooperate on Television," *Broadcasting*, May 15, 1935, 54.

2. William Uricchio, "Storage, Simultaneity and the Media Technologies of Modernity," in *Allegories of Communication: Intermedial Concerns from Cinema to the Digital*, ed. John Fullerton and Jan Olsson (Eastleigh, UK: John Libbey, 2004), 132.

3. See, for example, C. W. Ceram, *Archaeology of the Cinema* (London: Thames and Hudson, 1965); Deac Rossell, *Living Pictures: The Origins of the Movies* (Albany: State University of New York Press, 1998); Laurent Mannoni, *The Great Art of Light and Shadow: Archeology of the Cinema*, trans. Richard Crangle (Exeter: University of Exeter Press, 2000).

4. For research on early cinema's relation to the telephone, the telegraph, and the railway, see Tom Gunning, "Heard over the Phone: *The Lonely Villa* and the De Lorde Tradition of Terrified Communication," *Screen* 32, no. 2 (Summer 1991); Paul Young, "Media on Display: A Telegraphic History of Early American Cinema," in *New Media 1740–1915*, ed. Lisa Gitelman and Geoffrey B. Pingree (Cambridge, MA: MIT Press, 2003), 229–264; Lynne Kirby, *Parallel Tracks: The Railroad and Silent Cinema* (Durham, NC: Duke University Press, 1997).

5. On the cultural and institutional origins of television broadcasting see William Boddy, *Fifties Television: The Industry and Its Critics* (Urbana: University of Illinois Press, 1992); Lynn Spigel, *Make Room for TV: Television and the Family Ideal in Postwar America* (Chicago: University of Chicago Press, 1992); and Philip Sewell's detailed discussion of notions of quality and control in prebroadcast American television in *Television in the Age of Radio: Modernity, Imagination,*

and the Making of a Medium (New Brunswick, NJ: Rutgers University Press, 2014). For a perspective outside the field of television studies, Joseph H. Udelson's *The Great Television Race: A History of the American Television Industry, 1925–1941* (Tuscaloosa: University of Alabama Press, 1982) provides a thorough institutional history of the American television industry.

6. See, for example, VIEW *Journal of European Television History and Culture* 4, no. 7 (September 2015), a special volume on archaeologies of television; Luke Stadel, "Television as a Sound Medium, 1922–1994" (PhD diss., Northwestern University, 2015); Mireille Berton and Anne-Katrin Weber, eds., *La télévision du téléphonoscope à Youtube: Pour une archéologie de l'audiovision* (Lausanne: Antipodes, 2009).

7. See Albert Abramson, *The History of Television, 1880 to 1941* (Jefferson, NC: McFarland, 1987); Russell W. Burns, *Television: An International History of the Formative Years* (London: Institution of Electrical Engineers, 1998); George Shiers, *Early Television: A Bibliographic Guide to 1940* (New York: Garland, 1997); and André Lange's remarkably rich online database of primary sources on television, https://www.histv .net/.

8. Leo Charney and Vanessa R. Schwartz, introduction to *Cinema and the Invention of Modern Life*, ed. Charney and Schwartz (Berkeley: University of California Press, 1995), 1.

9. For an overview of central issues and contributions for the debates in this area, see Ben Singer, *Melodrama and Modernity: Early Sensational Cinema and Its Contexts* (New York: Columbia University Press, 2001).

10. Tom Gunning, "The Whole Town's Gawking: Early Cinema and the Visual Experience of Modernity," *Yale Journal of Criticism* 7, no. 2 (1994): 193–194; Mary Ann Doane, *The Emergence of Cinematic Time: Modernity, Contingency, the Archive* (Cambridge, MA: Harvard University Press, 2002), 62; Miriam Bratu Hansen, *Cinema and Experience: Siegfried Kracauer, Walter Benjamin, and Theodor W. Adorno* (Berkeley: University of California Press, 2012); Ann Friedberg, *Window Shopping: Cinema and the Postmodern* (Berkeley: University of California Press, 1993).

11. Tom Gunning, "Modernity and Cinema: A Culture of Shocks and Flows," in *Cinema and Modernity*, ed. Murray Pomerance (New Brunswick, NJ: Rutgers University Press, 2006), 302, 297.

12. See, for instance, Peter Kramer, "The Lure of the Big Picture: Film, Television and Hollywood," in *Big Picture, Small Screen: The Relations between Film and Television*, ed. John Hill and Martin McLoone (Luton, UK: John Libbey, 1996), 9–46; Erkki Huhtamo, "Seeing at a Distance: Towards an Archaeology of the Small Screen," in *Art@Science*, ed. Christa Sommerer and Laurent Mignonneau (Vienna: Springer, 1998), 262–278; David Hendy, "Television's Prehistory: Radio," in *The Television History Book*, ed. Michele Hilmes (London: BFI, 2008), 4–7; and Michael Z. Newman, *Video Revolutions: On the History of a Medium* (New York: Columbia University Press, 2014).

13. Harold A. Innis, *Empire and Communications*, ed. David Godfrey (Toronto: Press Porcépic, 1986), 5.

14. William Uricchio, "Storage, Simultaneity, and the Media Technologies of Modernity" and "Cinema as Detour? Towards a Reconsideration of Moving Image Tech-

nology in the Late 19th Century," in *Der Film in der Geschichte*, ed. Knut Hickethier, Eggo Müller, and Rainer Rother (Berlin: Edition Sigma, 1997), 19–25.

15. Siegfried Zielinski, *Audiovisions: Cinema and Television as Entr'actes in History*, trans. Gloria Custance (Amsterdam: Amsterdam University Press, 1999), 59.

16. Zielinski, *Audiovisions*, 14.

17. John Durham Peters, *The Marvelous Clouds: Toward a Philosophy of Elemental Media* (Chicago: University of Chicago Press, 2015), 306–307.

18. Peters, *The Marvelous Clouds*, 309.

19. Anne-Katrin Weber, "Recording on Film, Transmitting by Signals: The Intermediate Film System and Television's Hybridity in the Interwar Period," *Grey Room* 56 (Summer 2014): 27.

20. See André Gaudreault, *From Plato to Lumière: Narration and Monstration in Literature and Cinema*, trans. Timothy Barnard (Toronto: University of Toronto Press, 2009), 151–164, and *Film and Attraction: From Kinematography to Cinema*, trans. Timothy Barnard (Urbana: University of Illinois Press, 2011).

21. André Gaudreault and Philippe Marion, "A Medium Is Always Born Twice . . . ," *Early Popular Visual Culture* 3, no. 1 (May 2005): 3–15.

22. André Bazin, "The Myth of Total Cinema," in *What Is Cinema?*, vol. 1, trans. Hugh Gray (Berkeley: University of California Press, 1967), 21.

23. On the concept of discursive invention, see Erkki Huhtamo, "From Kaleidoscomaniac to Cybernerd: Towards an Archeology of the Media," in *ISEA '94*, ed. Minna Tarkka (Helsinki: University of Art and Design, 1994), 130–135.

24. Charles Musser, *The Emergence of Cinema: The American Screen to 1907* (New York: Scribner's, 1990), 55–89.

25. Miriam Bratu Hansen, "America, Paris, the Alps: Kracauer (and Benjamin) on Cinema and Modernity," in Charney and Schwartz, *Cinema and the Invention of Modern Life*, 363.

26. Wolfgang Ernst, *Digital Memory and the Archive*, ed. Jussi Parikka (Minneapolis: University of Minnesota Press, 2013), 165.

27. Lisa Gitelman, *Always Already New: Media, History, and the Data of Culture* (Cambridge, MA: MIT Press, 2006), 8.

28. "Television History in Making Here," *Sound Waves* 1, no. 4 (October 1928): 7; Merlin Hall Aylesworth, "The Magic Carpet of Television," *Liberty*, November 21, 1931, 23.

1. Ancient Affiliates

1. "The Electroscope: Is This Marvel to Be the Next Achievement of Modern Science?," *New York Sun*, March 29, 1877, 2, reproduced in https://www.histv.net /electroscope-1878.

2. François Albera, "First Discourses on Film and the Construction of a 'Cinematic Episteme,'" in *A Companion to Early Cinema*, ed. André Gaudreault, Nicolas Dulac, and Santiago Hidalgo (Malden, MA: Wiley-Blackwell, 2012), 126, emphasis in the original.

3. Adriano De Paiva, "A telephonia, a telegraphia e a telescopia," *O Instituto* 25

(March 1878). The English version of this text appeared in De Paiva's *La télescopie électrique basée sur l'emploi du selenium* (Porto: José da Silva, 1880), 45; the latter brochure is fully reproduced in https://www.histv.net/la-telescopie-electrique-1.

4. De Paiva, *La télescopie électrique*, 45.

5. "The Diaphote: A Remarkable Invention by Dr. H. E. Licks," *Daily Times* (Bethlehem, Pennsylvania), February 10, 1880; reproduced in https://www.histv.net /diaphote-10-2-1880.

6. Lisa Gitelman, *Scripts, Grooves, and Writing Machines: Representing Technology in the Edison Era* (Stanford, CA: Stanford University Press, 1999), 86.

7. George du Maurier, "Edison's Telephonoscope," *Punch Almanac for 1879*, December 9, 1878; "Conversations for the Times," *Fun*, July 3, 1889, 6, reproduced in Stephen Herbert, ed., *A History of Early Television*, vol. 1 (London: Routledge, 2004), 21; "Sight May Be Transmitted," *St. Louis Post-Dispatch*, September 7, 1896, 3.

8. William Uricchio, "Television's First Seventy-Five Years: The Interpretive Flexibility of a Medium in Transition," in *The Oxford Handbook of Film and Media Studies*, ed. Robert Kolker (Oxford: Oxford University Press, 2008), 289.

9. Alexander Graham Bell, Improvement in telegraphy, US Patent No. 174465 A, dated March 7, 1876; "The Telephone," *New York Times*, March 4, 1877; George Bartlett Prescott, *The Speaking Telephone, Talking Phonograph, and Other Novelties* (New York: D. Appleton and Co., 1878), 146–147.

10. John Cammack, "Phonograph," *English Mechanic*, December 14, 1877. Reproduced in https://www.histv.net/cammack-1877.

11. "Ocean Telephone," *Daily Astorian*, September 30, 1882, 1.

12. "The Electroscope: Is This Marvel to Be the Next Achievement of Modern Science?," *Milan Exchange*, July 12, 1877, 2; "Future of Electric Invention," *New York Times,* April 16, 1881, 3.

13. Albert Robida, *The Twentieth Century* (Middletown, CT: Wesleyan University Press, 2004), 30.

14. See introduction to Anthony Enns and Shelley Trower, eds., *Vibratory Modernism* (New York: Palgrave, 2013); Gillian Beer, *Open Fields: Science in Cultural Encounter* (New York: Oxford University Press, 1996), 295–318.

15. See, for example, "The Probability of Future Long Distance Vision," *San Francisco Call*, July 26, 1896, 28.

16. "Seeing by Electricity," *Hickman Courier*, June 16, 1893, 4.

17. George Shiers, "Historical Notes on Television before 1900," SMPTE *Journal* 86, no. 3 (March 1977), esp. 135–136.

18. On the range of professional backgrounds of the pioneers of cinema see Deac Rossell, *Living Pictures: The Origins of the Movies* (Albany: State University of New York Press, 1998), 4.

19. Charles Francis Jenkins, "Transmitting Pictures by Electricity," *Electrical Engineer*, July 25, 1894, 62–63.

20. Charles Francis Jenkins, *Animated Pictures: An Exposition of the Historical Development of Chronophotography, Its Present Scientific Applications and Future Possibilities* (Washington, DC: Press of H. L. McQueen, 1898).

21. Henry Middleton, "Seeing by Telegraph: To the Editor of the Times," *The*

Times (London), April 24, 1880, 12. Middleton writes, "These images can be either viewed directly or by reflected light (after the fashion of the Japanese mirrors and projection on a screen), or by suitable apparatus they can be retained as photograph, a thermograph or chemicograph." Shelford Bidwell claimed in 1881 that he transmitted "simple designs in black and white painted upon and projected by a magic lantern." See Russell W. Burns, *Television: An International History of the Formative Years* (London: Institution of Electrical Engineers, 1998), 57.

22. See Constantin Senlecq, "The Telectroscope," *The Times* (London), January 27, 1879, 4–5, reproduced in https://www.histv.net/the-times-21-1-1879; John Perry and W. E. Ayrton, "Seeing by Electricity," *Nature*, April 22, 1880, 589, reproduced in https://www.histv.net/perry-ayrton-april-1880; Noah Amstutz, "Visual Telegraphy," *Electricity* 6 (February 28, 1894): 77–80. W. E. Sawyer reported on his efforts in "rendering visible objects at a distance through a single telegraphic wire" in a letter published in *Scientific American*, June 12, 1880.

23. "The Electroscope: Is This Marvel to Be the Next Achievement of Modern Science?"

24. "Science's Latest Marvel," *Northern Tribune*, June 17, 1883, 3.

25. "Televue: A New Device Which Enables Telephone Users to See Each Other," *Brooklyn Daily Eagle*, May 21, 1905, 26.

26. André Gaudreault, "The Diversity of Cinematographic Connections in the Intermedial Context of the Turn of the 20th Century," in *Visual Delights: Essay on the Popular and Projected Image in the 19th Century*, ed. Simon Popple and Vanessa Toulmin (Trowbridge, UK: Flicks Books, 2000), 9.

27. See, for instance, James Carey, "Technology and Ideology: The Case of the Telegraph," in *Communication as Culture: Essays on Media and Society* (New York: Routledge, 2009), 155–177; Roland Wenzlhuemer, *Connecting the Nineteenth-Century World: The Telegraph and Globalization* (Cambridge: Cambridge University Press, 2013).

28. See Giusy Pisano, "The Théâtrophone, an Anachronistic Hybrid Experiment or One of the First Immobile Traveler Devices?," in *A Companion to Early Cinema*, ed. André Gaudreault, Nicolas Dulac, and Santiago Hidalgo (Malden, MA: Wiley-Blackwell, 2012), 80–98; Carolyn Marvin, *When Old Technologies Were New* (Oxford: Oxford University Press, 1988), 63–108; and Ithiel de Sola Pool, *Forecasting the Telephone: A Retrospective Technology Assessment of the Telephone* (Norwood, NJ: Ablex, 1983), 97–98.

29. On the notion of new media appearing as extensions of other media, see André Gaudreault and Philippe Marion, "A Medium Is Always Born Twice . . . ," *Early Popular Visual Culture* 3, no. 1 (May 2005): 3–15.

30. David Nye, *Electrifying America: Social Meanings of a New Technology* (Cambridge, MA: MIT Press, 1990), 1.

31. Nye, *Electrifying America*, x.

32. Kristen Whissel, "Electricity," in *The Encyclopedia of Early Cinema*, ed. Richard Abel (New York: Routledge, 2004), 217–219.

33. James W. Carey and John J. Quirk, "The Mythos of the Electronic Revolution: Part II," *American Scholar* 39, no. 3 (Summer 1970): 396.

34. Marvin, *When Old Technologies Were New*, 208.

35. On technological imaginary see, for instance, Patrice Flichy, *Understanding Technological Innovation: A Socio-Technical Approach*, trans. Liz Carey-Libbrecht (Cheltenham, UK: Edward Elgar, 2007).

36. For example, Ayrton and Perry noted their indebtedness to the aforementioned *Punch* cartoon in "Seeing by Electricity," and Mark Twain wrote a fictional story about the real inventor Jan Szczepanik in his "From the London Times of 1904," in *The Writings of Mark Twain*, vol. 22 (New York: Harper and Brothers, 1899), 276–292.

37. Kristen Whissel, *Picturing American Modernity: Traffic, Technology, and the Silent Cinema* (Durham, NC: Duke University Press, 2008); Marvin, *When Old Technologies Were New*; Tom Gunning, "The Birth of Film out of the Spirit of Modernity," in *Masterpieces of Modernist Cinema*, ed. Ted Perry (Bloomington: Indiana University Press, 2006), 13–40.

38. W. K. L. Dickson and Antonia Dickson, *History of the Kinetograph, Kinetoscope and Kinetophonograph* (New York: Albert Bunn, 1895), 6.

39. For a thorough discussion of transformations of spatiotemporal experience in modernity see Stephen Kern, *The Culture of Time and Space, 1880–1918* (Cambridge, MA: Harvard University Press, 1983).

40. Richard R. John, *Network Nation: Inventing American Telecommunications* (Cambridge, MA: Belknap Press of Harvard University Press, 2010), 11–12.

41. Quoted in Wenzlhuemer, *Connecting the Nineteenth-Century World*, 38.

42. Wolfgang Schivelbusch, *The Railway Journey: The Industrialization of Time and Space in the Nineteenth Century* (Berkeley: University of California Press, 1986), 35.

43. Patrice Flichy, *Dynamics of Modern Communication: The Shaping and Impact of New Communication Technologies*, trans. Liz Libbrecht (London: Sage, 1995), 38.

44. Quoted in Tom Standage, *The Victorian Internet* (New York: Walker and Co., 1998), 102.

45. Kirby, *Parallel Tracks*, 51. See also Carlene Stephens, "'The Most Reliable Time': William Bond, the New England Railroads, and Time Awareness in 19th-Century America," *Technology and Culture* 30, no. 1 (January 1989): 1–24.

46. Kern, *The Culture of Time and Space*.

47. See Marvin, *When Old Technologies Were New*, and Daniel J. Czitrom, *Media and the American Mind: From Morse to McLuhan* (Chapel Hill: University of North Carolina Press, 1982), 3–29.

48. Laura Otis, *Networking: Communicating with Bodies and Machines in the Nineteenth Century* (Ann Arbor: University of Michigan Press, 2001), offers a comprehensive study of this metaphor.

49. Michael Angelo Garvey, *The Silent Revolution, or, The Future Effects of Steam and Electricity upon the Condition of Mankind* (London: William and Frederick G. Cash, 1852), 7, 104.

50. "Annihilating Time and Space," *Washington Post*, June 15, 1913, MS2.

51. George du Maurier, "Edison's Telephonoscope," *Punch Almanac for 1879*, December 9, 1878.

52. On the spatial relations established in this illustration, see Anne-Katrin Weber,

"Audio-Visionen um 1880: Zum Beispiel George Du Mauriers Edison's Telephonoscope," in *Medien in Raum und Zeit: Maßverhältnisse des Medialen*, ed. Ingo Köster and Kai Schubert (Bielefeld, Germany: Transcript, 2009), 293–312. See also Ivy Roberts, "Edison's Telephonoscope: The Visual Telephone and the Satire of Electric Light Mania," *Early Popular Visual Culture* 15, no. 1 (2017): 1–25.

53. Carey, "Technology and Ideology," 160.

54. Quoted in Brian Winston, *Media Technology and Society: A History. From the Telegraph to the Internet* (New York: Routledge, 1998), 243–244.

55. Manuel Castells, *The Internet Galaxy: Reflections on the Internet, Business, and Society* (New York: Oxford University Press, 2001), 1.

56. Tom Gunning, "Systematizing the Electric Message: Narrative Form, Gender and Modernity in *The Lonedale Operator*," in *American Cinema's Transitional Era*, ed. Charlie Keil and Shelley Stamp (Berkeley: University of California Press, 2004), 28.

57. Standage, *The Victorian Internet*, 58–59.

58. De Paiva, *La télescopie électrique*, 47–48.

59. See Adam Roberts, *The History of Science Fiction* (Basingstoke, UK: Palgrave Macmillan, 2006), 91.

60. Marvin, *When Old Technologies Were New*, 7–8.

61. For a treatment of these themes see Neil Harris, "Utopian Fiction and Its Discontents," in *Cultural Excursions: Marketing Appetites and Cultural Tastes in Modern America* (Chicago: University of Chicago Press, 1990), 150–173. Other sources I have consulted in the search for televisual apparatus in nineteenth-century literature include Everett F. Bleiler and Richard J. Bleiler, *Science-Fiction, the Early Years* (Kent, Ohio: Kent State University Press, 1990); James Osler Bailey, *Pilgrims through Space and Time: Trends and Patterns in Scientific and Utopian Fiction* (New York: Argus Books, 1947); Jean Pfaelzer, *The Utopian Novel in America, 1886–1896: The Politics of Form* (Pittsburgh: University of Pittsburgh Press, 1984); Kenneth M. Roemer, *The Obsolete Necessity: America in Utopian Writings, 1888–1900* (Kent, Ohio: Kent State University Press, 1976); see also Tom Willaert, "How Literature Imagined Television, 1880–1950," *Orbis Litterarum* 72, no. 6 (2017): 591–610.

62. See, for example, Jules Verne, "In the Year 2889," in *Collected Works of Jules Verne* (Charleston, SC: Bibliobazaar, 2007), 69–84. On the influence of Robida on the story, see Arthur B. Evans, "The 'New' Jules Verne," *Science Fiction Studies* 22, no. 1 (March 1995): 35–46.

63. Verne, "In the Year 2889," 69.

64. "A.D. 10,000—What Man Is Destined to Accomplish on This Planet," *Wichita Daily Eagle*, July 11, 1893, 6.

65. Edward Bellamy, *Equality* (New York: Appleton and Co., 1913), 205.

66. Bellamy, *Equality*, 389.

67. Bellamy, *Equality*, 348.

68. William N. Harben, *The Land of Changing Sun* (1894; repr., Middlesex, UK: Echo Library, 2007). A comparable image transmission surveillance system is featured in H. G. Wells, *When the Sleeper Wakes* (London: Harper and Brothers, 1899).

69. Michel Foucault, *Discipline and Punish: The Birth of the Prison*, trans. Alan Sheridan (New York: Vintage, 1977), 208–209.

70. Twain, "From the London Times of 1904"; for useful commentary on the story in the context of nineteenth-century science and technology, see Otis, *Networking*, 192–194.

71. Dolf Sterngerger, quoted in Schivelbusch, *The Railway Journey*, 62.

72. Chris Otter, *The Victorian Eye: A Political History of Light and Vision in Britain, 1800–1910* (Chicago: University of Chicago Press, 2008), 7.

73. Edward A. Robinson and George A. Wall, *The Disk: A Tale of Two Passions* (Boston: Cupples, Upham and Co., 1884), 18.

74. Robinson and Wall, *The Disk*, 65–66.

75. Robinson and Wall, *The Disk*, 68.

76. Marshall McLuhan, *Understanding Media: The Extensions of Man* (Cambridge, MA: MIT Press, 1994), 8.

77. McLuhan, *Understanding Media*, 52, 8.

78. Karl Marx and Friedrich Engels, *The Communist Manifesto: A Modern Edition*, trans. Samuel Moore (London: Verso, 2012), 38.

79. Manuel Castells, "An Introduction to the Information Age," *City* 2, no. 7 (1997): 12–13.

80. Wendy Hui Kyong Chun, "Crisis, Crisis, Crisis, or Sovereignty and Network," *Theory, Culture and Society* 28, no. 6 (2011): 91–112.

81. Jonathan Crary, *24/7: Late Capitalism and the Ends of Sleep* (London: Verso, 2013), 30.

82. Crary, *24/7*, 3–4.

83. Crary, *24/7*, 9.

84. Steven Shaviro, *Connected, or What It Means to Live in the Network Society* (Minneapolis: University of Minnesota Press, 2003), xi.

85. McLuhan, *Understanding Media*, 52.

86. Ben Singer, *Melodrama and Modernity* (New York: Columbia University Press, 2001), 26.

87. Mary Ann Doane, *The Emergence of Cinematic Time: Modernity, Contingency, the Archive* (Cambridge, MA: Harvard University Press, 2002), 82.

88. *La Poste*, December 30, 1895, quoted in Doane, *The Emergence of Cinematic Time*, 62.

89. Bolesław Matuszewski, "A New Source of History: The Creation of a Depository for Historical Cinematography" (1898), trans. Laura U. Marks and Diane Koszarski, *Film History* 7, no. 3 (Autumn 1995): 322–324. For further discussion of cinema and the notion of the annihilating space and time, see Kirby, *Parallel Tracks*, chap. 1.

90. William Uricchio, "Storage, Simultaneity and the Media Technologies of Modernity," in *Allegories of Communication: Intermedial Concerns from Cinema to the Digital*, ed. John Fullerton and Jan Olsson (Eastleigh, UK: John Libbey, 2004), 125, 127–128, emphasis added. Likewise, Thomas Elsaesser remarked that "the late nineteenth century did not expect the cinema: rather, the imagination of the 1880s and 1890s was fired by impatience for devices of simultaneity and instantaneity." See "Louis Lumière: The Cinema's First Virtualist," in *Cinema Futures: Cain, Abel or Cable?*, ed. Elsaesser and Kay Hoffmann (Amsterdam: Amsterdam University Press, 1998), 48.

91. See Friedrich Kittler, *Gramophone, Film, Typewriter*, trans. Geoffrey Winthrop-Young and Michael Wutz (Stanford, CA: Stanford University Press, 1999); Lisa Gitelman, *Scripts, Grooves, and Writing Machines: Representing Technology in the Edison Era*.

92. Doane, *The Emergence of Cinematic Time*, 82, emphasis added.

93. Tom Gunning, "An Aesthetic of Astonishment: Early Film and the (In)Credulous Spectator," *Art and Text* 34 (1989): 40.

94. Gunning, "An Aesthetic of Astonishment," 40.

95. Ben Singer, "The Ambimodernity of Early Cinema," in *Film 1900: Technology, Perception, Culture*, ed. Annemone Ligensa and Klaus Kreimeier (Eastleigh, UK: John Libbey, 2009), 39–40, emphasis in the original.

96. Gunning, "An Aesthetic of Astonishment," 40, emphasis added.

97. Tom Gunning, "The Whole Town's Gawking: Early Cinema and the Visual Experience of Modernity," *Yale Journal of Criticism* 7, no. 2 (1994): 193–194.

98. Tom Gunning, "Modernity and Cinema: A Culture of Shocks and Flows," in *Cinema and Modernity*, ed. Murray Pomerance (New Brunswick, NJ: Rutgers University Press, 2006), 309.

99. Gunning, "The Whole Town's Gawking," 194.

100. Miriam Bratu Hansen, *Cinema and Experience: Siegfried Kracauer, Walter Benjamin, and Theodor W. Adorno* (Berkeley: University of California Press, 2012), 132–146.

101. Samuel Jones, *The New Right: A Plea for Fair Play through a More Just Social Order* (New York: Eastern Book Concern, 1899), 443, emphasis added.

102. "May Send Moving Pictures by Wire," *Daily Capital Journal*, March 7, 1913, 6.

2. Prolonged Optic Nerves

Several sections of chapter 2 develop ideas that appeared in "L'histoire des débuts de la télévision et les théories modernes de la vision," in *Télévision: Le moment experimental, 1935–1955*, ed. Gilles Delavaud and Denis Maréchal (Rennes: Apogée, 2011).

1. "Eye Taken from Boy Aided Television," *New York Times*, February 11, 1928, 4. Baird mentioned this experiment earlier in his article "Television," *Experimental Wireless* (December 1926): 736.

2. Albert Abramson, *The History of Television, 1880 to 1941* (Jefferson, NC: McFarland, 1987), 84.

3. John Logie Baird, *Television and Me: The Memoirs of John Logie Baird*, ed. Malcolm Baird (Edinburgh: Mercat, 2004), 56.

4. Monika Elsner, Thomas Müller, and Peter M. Spangenberg, "The Early History of German Television: The Slow Development of a Fast Medium," *Historical Journal of Film, Radio and Television* 10, no. 2 (1990): 207; Philip Sewell, *Television in the Age of Radio: Modernity, Imagination, and the Making of a Medium* (New Brunswick, NJ: Rutgers University Press, 2014), 33.

5. Jonathan Crary, *Techniques of the Observer: On Vision and Modernity in the Nineteenth Century* (Cambridge, MA: MIT Press, 1990).

6. "Seeing by Electricity," *Coventry Herald*, March 14, 1890, 7.

7. Sungook Hong, "Marconi and the Maxwellians: The Origins of Wireless Telegraphy Revisited," *Technology and Culture* 35 (1994): 717–749.

8. Oliver Lodge, "Electrical Radiation from Conducting Spheres, and Electric Eye, and a Suggestion Regarding Vision," *Nature*, March 20, 1890, 462–462; "The British Association," *The Times* (London), August 15, 1894, 121.

9. Oliver Lodge, *The Ether of Space* (New York: Harper and Brothers, 1909), 10.

10. Oliver Lodge, *Signaling across Space without Wires: Being a Description of the Works of Hertz and His Successors* (London: Electrician Printing and Publishing, 1900), 29–32. See also Lodge, "Electric Theory of Vision," *Engineering*, September 21, 1894, 383–384.

11. Iwan Rhys Morus, "The Measure of Man: Technologizing the Victorian Body," *History of Science* 37 (1999): 278.

12. H. G. Wells, "The Story of Davidson's Eyes," in *Thirty Strange Stories* (New York: Harper and Brothers, 1898), 306. The story has also been published under the title "The Remarkable Case of Davidson's Eyes."

13. Wells, "The Story of Davidson's Eyes," 291.

14. Laura Otis, "The Metaphoric Circuit: Organic and Technological Communication in the Nineteenth Century," *Journal of the History of Ideas* 63, no. 1 (2002): 105, 107. See also Iwan Rhys Morus, "The Nervous System of Britain: Space, Time and the Electric Telegraph in the Victorian Age," *British Journal for the History of Science* 3, no. 4 (December 2000): 455–475.

15. Timothy Lenoir, "Helmholtz and the Materialities of Communication," *Osiris* 9 (1994): 186.

16. Quoted in Otis, "The Metaphoric Circuit," 113. For an appearance of such ideas in the popular discourse, see "Every Man a Magnetic Telegraph," *The Sun*, July 18, 1856, 2.

17. See Crary, *Techniques of the Observer*, 90–91.

18. Lenoir, "Helmholtz and the Materialities of Communication," 186.

19. Jonathan Sterne, *The Audible Past: Cultural Origins of Sound Reproduction* (Durham, NC: Duke University Press, 2003), 62.

20. "On the Action of Light on Selenium," *Nature*, March 23, 1876, 407–408.

21. Frances Terpak, "Objects and Contexts: The Eye, Natural and Artificial," in *Devices of Wonder: From the World in a Box to Images on a Screen*, ed. Terpak and Barbara Stafford (Los Angeles: Getty Publications, 2001), 143–147.

22. Geoffrey Batchen, *Burning with Desire: The Conception of Photography* (Cambridge, MA: MIT Press, 1999), 81–82.

23. John Durham Peters, "Helmholtz, Edison, and Sound History," in *Memory Bytes: History, Technology, and Digital Culture*, ed. Lauren Rabinovitz and Abraham Geil (Durham, NC: Duke University Press, 2004), 178.

24. "Siemens's Sensitive Artificial Eye," *Scientific American*, December 9, 1876, 374.

25. "On the Action of Light on Selenium," 408.

26. Hermann von Helmholtz, "The Recent Progress of the Theory of Vision," in *Popular Lectures on Scientific Subjects* (New York: D. Appleton and Co., 1897), 197.

27. See Anson Rabinbach, *The Human Motor: Energy, Fatigue, and the Origins of Modernity* (Berkeley: University of California Press, 1992).

28. Mary Ann Doane, *The Emergence of Cinematic Time: Modernity, Contingency, the Archive* (Cambridge, MA: Harvard University Press, 2002), 81.

29. See George Shiers, *Early Television: A Bibliographic Guide to 1940* (New York: Garland, 1997), x; Russell W. Burns, *Television: An International History of the Formative Years* (London: Institution of Electrical Engineers, 1998), 35.

30. John Swift, *Adventure in Vision: The First Twenty-Five Years of Television* (London: John Lehmann, 1950), 19. For an earlier version of this notion, see Alfred Dinsdale, *Television: Seeing by Wireless* (London: W. S. Caines, 1926), 17.

31. Adriano De Paiva, *La télescopie électrique basée sur l'emploi du selenium* (Porto: José da Silva, 1880), 46–48; reproduced in https://www.histv.net/la-telescopie-electrique-0.

32. "A New Metal That Sees and Hears," *St. Louis Post-Dispatch*, November 7, 1909, B5.

33. Burns, *Television*, 41. See also, in the same chapter, Burns's description of the systems proposed by Carey, Redmond, Middleton, Jenkins, and Ayrton and Perry.

34. Denis Redmond, "Seeing by Electricity," *English Mechanic and World of Science*, February 7, 1897, 540, reproduced in https://www.histv.net/redmond-1879.

35. Henry Middleton, "Seeing by Telegraph: To the Editor of the Times," *The Times* (London), April 24, 1880, 12, reproduced in https://www.histv.net/middleton-1880.

36. "Seeing by Electricity," *The Electrician*, March 7, 1890, 448–450. See also the contemporaneous assertion about the electrical television was an imitation of the sense of sight in Raphael Eduard Liesegang, *Das Phototel: Beitrage zum Problem des electrischen Fernsehens* (Dusseldorf: E. Liesegang, 1891), iv, quoted in Stefan Andriopoulos, "Psychic Television," *Critical Inquiry* 31 (Spring 2005): 632.

37. "Glasgow Listens to Sound of Faces," *New York Times*, February 4, 1927, 6. See also John Mills, *Through Electrical Eyes* (New York: Bell Telephone Laboratories, 1928).

38. Von Helmholtz, "The Recent Progress of the Theory of Vision," 208, 211, 210.

39. This summary draws on Jutta Schickore's historical account in "Locating Rods and Cones: Microscopic Investigations of the Retina in Mid-Nineteenth-Century Berlin and Wurzburg," *Science in Context* 13, no. 1 (2000): 137–152.

40. Crary, *Techniques of the Observer*, 129.

41. Crary, *Techniques of the Observer*, 129, emphasis added.

42. "Seeing by Electricity," 450.

43. It is worth noting that Charles Francis Jenkins continued experimenting with the multicell scheme as late as the 1930s in attempts to construct a television screen for daylight viewing, but this model never became commercial. In 2010 an installation work by the artist Gebhard Sengmüller consisted of such an apparatus that employed a grid of 2,500 photoconductors, connected by the same number of wires to a receiver made of 2,500 light bulbs. See Jussi Parikka, *What Is Media Archaeology?* (Cambridge: Polity, 2012), 41–43.

44. Rosing, in an essay written for the French journal *Excelsior* circa 1910. Quoted in Burns, *Television*, 121.

45. Alden P. Armagnac, "Human-Eye Camera Opens New Way to Television," *Popular Science Monthly* (September 1933): 12, 11.

46. Mills, *Through Electrical Eyes*, esp. 21, emphasis added.

47. Sigmund Freud, *Civilization and Its Discontents*, trans. James Strachey (New York: Norton, 1961), 43, 37; Marshall McLuhan, *Understanding Media: The Exten-

sions of Man (Cambridge, MA: MIT Press, 1994); Friedrich Kittler, *Discourse Networks 1800/1900* (Stanford, CA: Stanford University Press, 1990), 231.

48. James Lastra, *Sound Technology and American Cinema: Perception, Representation, Modernity* (New York: Columbia University Press, 2000), 21.

49. For a notable exception, see Jonathan Sterne's discussion of the "human telephone" in *The Audible Past*, 81–83.

50. For examples and further discussion of this metaphor in early cinema and the avant-garde, see Thomas Elsaesser and Malte Hagener, *Film Theory: An Introduction through the Senses* (London: Routledge, 2009), 84–89. For an in-depth discussion of the camera as eye metaphor see William C. Wees, "The Camera-Eye: Dialectics of a Metaphor," in *Light Moving in Time: Studies in the Visual Aesthetics of Avant-Garde Film* (Berkeley: University of California Press, 1992), 11–31.

51. Cleveland Moffett, "An Interview with Professor Alexander Graham Bell," *McClure's* (June 1893): 42–32.

52. "Machine Enables the Blind to See," *Cincinnati Enquirer*, September 30, 1899, 11.

53. "Seeing by Electricity," *New York Times*, March 10, 1901, 21.

54. "Now a Teleautophote: It May Bring Sight to the Blind through Electricity," *New York Times*, November 12, 1906, 6.

55. On the double logic of prostheses see Hal Foster, "Prosthetic Gods," *Modernism/Modernity* 4, no. 2 (1997): 5–38; Mark Seltzer, *Bodies and Machines* (New York: Routledge, 1992).

56. "The Telephote," *Telegraphic Journal and Electrical Review*, August 16, 1889, 186, reproduced in www.histv.net/courtonne-scottish-leader.

57. Oliver Wendell Holmes, "Sun-Painting and Sun-Sculpture," *Atlantic Monthly* 8 (July 1861): 14–15, quoted in Rosalind Krauss, "Photography's Discursive Spaces: Landscape/View," *Art Journal* 42, no. 4 (Winter 1982): 314.

58. Edward Bellamy, *Equality* (New York: D. Appleton and Co., 1897), 204.

59. Bellamy, *Equality*, 157.

60. Bellamy, *Equality*, 204.

61. Bellamy, *Equality*, 205.

62. McLuhan, *Understanding Media*, 18.

63. McLuhan, *Understanding Media*, 42–43.

64. F. T. Marinetti, "Extended Man and the Kingdom of the Machine," quoted in Stephen Kern, *The Culture of Time and Space, 1880–1918* (Cambridge, MA: Harvard University Press, 1983), 122.

65. For a discussion of this metaphor in its historical context, see Lynn Spigel, *Make Room for TV: Television and the Family Ideal in Postwar America* (Chicago: University of Chicago Press, 1992), 99–135.

3. Happy Combinations

1. For the place of television in the periodization of film history see, for example, the section "Cinema in the Age of Television" in *The Oxford History of World Cinema*, ed. Geoffrey Nowell-Smith (Oxford: Oxford University Press, 1996), 466–496, or the

section titled "The Television Era: 1950–1977" in Douglas Gomery and Clara Pafort-Overduin, *Movie History: A Survey*, 2nd ed. (New York: Routledge, 2011), 230–357.

2. See William Uricchio, "Storage, Simultaneity and the Media Technologies of Modernity," in *Allegories of Communication: Intermedial Concerns from Cinema to the Digital*, ed. John Fullerton and Jan Olsson (Eastleigh, UK: J. Libbey, 2004), 123–138. For application of such distinction in the context of technological history, see Albert Abramson, *The History of Television, 1880 to 1941* (London: McFarland, 1987), 3.

3. "Next Please!," *Electrical Engineer*, March 11, 1898, 304.

4. "Wonderful Edison," *Rochester Daily Republican*, September 13, 1889, 4. Later that year, Edison claimed, "I am studying on a device for a telephone, so that you can see the man you are talking to. I am almost sure I can make it a scientific success, but I doubt it will ever be a commercial one." See "What Mr. Edison Noticed in Europe," *Scientific American*, October 19, 1889, 249.

5. "Edison's Conjury—Wonders Which He Has in Store for Musicians and Sports," *The Sun*, May 13, 1891, 1.

6. *World's Columbian Exposition Illustrated* (May 1891), 23. See also Gordon Hendricks, *The Edison Motion Picture Myth* (Berkeley: University of California Press, 1961), 104–105.

7. See "Edison and the Kinetograph," *Montreal Daily Star*, April 20, 1895, reprinted in *Film History* 11, no. 4 (1999): 407.

8. Hendricks, *The Edison Motion Picture Myth*, 103–104.

9. Paul Spehr, *The Man Who Made Movies: W. K. L. Dickson* (New Barnet, UK: John Libbey, 2008), 174.

10. See Hendricks, *The Edison Motion Picture Myth*, 113, citing from *New York Sun*, May 20, 1891.

11. "Edison's Conjury—Wonders Which He Has in Store for Musicians and Sports," 1.

12. Walter L. Welch and Leah Brodbeck Stenzel Burt, *From Tinfoil to Stereo: The Acoustic Years of the Recording Industry, 1877–1929* (Gainesville: University Press of Florida, 1994), 13. See also John Durham Peters, "Technology and Ideology: The Case of the Telegraph Revisited," in *Thinking with James Carey: Essays on Communications, Transportation, History*, ed. Jeremy Packer and Craig Robertson (New York: Peter Lang, 2006), 144–145.

13. Thomas Edison, "The Perfected Phonograph," *North American Review* 146, no. 379 (June 1888): 643.

14. Peters, "Technology and Ideology," 144.

15. To quote Friedrich Kittler, whose influential media theory emphasizes the phonograph's capacity to store information that falls outside the grid of language: "The phonograph cannot deny its telegraphic origin." See *Gramophone, Film, Typewriter* (Stanford, CA: Stanford University Press, 1999), 35.

16. "Telephonic Repeater," US Patent No. 340,707, dated April 27, 1886; Thomas A. Edison, "The Phonograph and Its Future," *North American Review* 126, no. 262 (May–June 1878): 535.

17. Edison, "The Perfected Phonograph," 647, 649.

18. Edison, "The Phonograph and Its Future," 534, emphasis added.

19. It is worth noting that during the last years of the nineteenth century, Edison expressed different views about the prospects of moving image transmission. In 1894 he argued that contemporary efforts to fabricate devices for seeing by electricity were impractical, while four years later he claimed that the technology was feasible but that he did not see great value in it. See "Mr. Edison as a Prophet," *Washington Post*, October 28, 1894, 17; "Edison Has Faith in the Telectroscope," *Chicago Tribune*, April 4, 1898, 7.

20. "Notes on Current Science, Invention, and Discovery," *Leisure Hour* (August 1891): 712.

21. "The Kinetograph," *London Standard*, August 20, 1891, 2.

22. "Kinetoscope Pictures on the Screen," *Photographic News* 40, no. 3 (January 17, 1896): 33, emphasis added.

23. Uricchio, "Storage, Simultaneity and the Media Technologies of Modernity."

24. Uricchio, "Ways of Seeing: The New Vision of Early Non-fiction Film," in *Uncharted Territory: Essays on Nonfiction Film*, ed. Daan Hertogs and Nico de Klerk (Amsterdam: Stichting Nederlands Filmmuseum, 1997), esp. 128–131.

25. Jonathan Auerbach, *Body Shots: Early Cinema's Incarnations* (Berkeley: University of California Press, 2007), 15–41; Paul Young, "Media on Display: A Telegraphic History of Early American Cinema," in *New Media, 1740–1915*, ed. Lisa Gitelman and Geoffrey B. Pingree (Cambridge, MA: MIT Press, 2003), 229–264.

26. Quoted in Charles Musser, *The Emergence of Cinema: The American Screen to 1907* (New York: Scribner's, 1990), 275.

27. "The Kinetograph," *Wichita Daily Eagle*, April 25, 1893, 4, spelling modified and emphasis added.

28. "Seeing by Electricity," *English Mechanic and World of Science*, August 28, 1891, 15.

29. For Edison's design see Musser, *The Emergence of Cinema*, 63–64. Notably, August's model adds the projection mechanism that does not exist in Edison's model.

30. See Siegfried Zielinski, *Deep Time of the Media: Toward an Archaeology of Hearing and Seeing by Technical Means*, trans. Gloria Custance (Cambridge, MA: MIT Press, 2006), 3.

31. By comparison, in the veteran Cooke and Wheatstone's telegraph system the electric current sent from the transmitter moved needles that were attached to a board in the receiving apparatus, so that they pointed at corresponding letters on the board. On the advantages of the Morse telegraph see Richard R. John, *Network Nation: Inventing American Telecommunications* (Cambridge, MA: Harvard University Press, 2010), 29.

32. "Movies Sent by Telegraph," *Los Angeles Times*, August 27, 1914, II6.

33. "$30,264 to Wireless 8 Feet of Newsreel," *Motion Picture Herald*, November 3, 1934, 10.

34. John Logie Baird, *Television and Me: The Memoirs of John Logie Baird*, ed. Malcolm Baird (Edinburgh: Mercat, 2004), 64.

35. Anne-Katrin Weber, "Recording on Film, Transmitting by Signals: The Inter-

mediate Film System and Television's Hybridity in the Interwar Period," *Grey Room* 56 (Summer 2014): 10.

36. George Shiers, "Historical Notes on Television before 1900," SMPTE *Journal* 86, no. 3 (March 1977): 133.

37. See Russell W. Burns, *Television: An International History of the Formative Years* (London: Institution of Electrical Engineers, 1998), 97–98. On Szczepanik see also the article "Seeing by Wire," with an introduction by Richard Brown, *Early Popular Visual Culture* 6, no. 3 (November 2008): 305–312.

38. "Flashing Pictures around the World," *San Francisco Call*, April 3, 1898, 25; "New Scientific Star," *Chicago Daily Tribune*, May 1, 1898, 29; "A Hungarian Edison," *Manchester Courier and Lancashire General Advertiser*, August 30, 1901, 4; Mark Twain, "The Austrian Edison Keeping School Again," *Century Illustrated Monthly Magazine* (August 1898): 630.

39. "New Scientific Star," 29.

40. "Distance Seer to Be a Feature of Paris Fair," *Chicago Tribune*, December 3, 1899, 53.

41. "Paris Exhibition," *Glasgow Herald*, April 12, 1900, 4.

42. "The Telelectroscope," *San Francisco Call*, April 19, 1898, 6.

43. "Flashing Pictures around the World," 25.

44. Theodore Waters, "Wonders of the Telelectroscope," *Courier Journal*, April 3, 1898, B2; "Der elektrische Fernseher," *Neues Wiener Tageblatt*, March 17, 1898, 3, translated to English in https://www.histv.net/szczepanik-neues-wiener-taglblatt.

45. British Patent No. 5031, dated February 24, 1897; "New Scientific Star," *Chicago Tribune*, May 1, 1898, 29.

46. "Flashing Pictures around the World," 25, emphasis added.

47. Mary Ann Doane, *The Emergence of Cinematic Time: Modernity, Contingency, the Archive* (Cambridge, MA: Harvard University Press, 2002), 24.

48. "Gossip of the Day," *Yorkshire Evening Post*, March 10, 1898, 2.

49. Doane, *The Emergence of Cinematic Time*, 159.

50. According to Mimi White, liveness functioned as "television's alibi for truth and objectivity" and "served to characterize fundamental differences (ontological and/or ideological) between film and television as distinctive media." See "The Attractions of Television: Reconsidering Liveness," in *Mediaspace: Place, Scale, and Culture in a Media Age*, ed. Nick Couldry and Anna McCarthy (London: Routledge, 2004), 76.

51. Gilbert Seldes, *Writing for Television* (New York: Doubleday, 1952), 32, quoted in William Boddy, *Fifties Television: The Industry and Its Critics* (Urbana: University of Illinois Press, 1990), 80–81.

52. "Sending Photographs by Telegraph," *New York Times*, February 24, 1907, SM7. See also "Telegraphing Pictures," *Review of Reviews* 35, no. 210 (June 1907): 632; "Scientific Miscellany," *Amador Ledger*, July 5, 1907, 1.

53. "Photographs by Telegraph: Television Next?," *New York Times*, November 24, 1907, SM7.

54. "Seeing by Telephone the Latest," *St. Louis Post-Dispatch*, October 28, 1906, 3.

See also W. E. Brindley, "See the Person Whom You Phone," *Talking Machine World* 11, no. 5 (May 15, 1905): 15; "The 'Televue,'" *New York Times*, October 9, 1906, 6.

55. "The Televue," *Los Angeles Herald*, February 17, 1907, P7.

56. See Thomas Elsaesser, "Early Film History and Multi-media: An Archaeology of Possible Futures?," in *New Media, Old Media: A History and Theory Reader*, ed. Wendy Hui Kyong Chun and Thomas Keenan (London: Routledge, 2006), 21.

57. See André Gaudreault and Philippe Marion, "A Medium Is Always Born Twice . . . ," *Early Popular Visual Culture* 3, no. 1 (May 2005): 3–15.

58. On this period as the beginning of the transition era see Charlie Keil and Shelley Stamp, eds., *American Cinema's Transitional Era: Audiences, Institutions, Practices* (Berkeley: University of California Press, 2004). In *Film and Attraction: From Kinematography to Cinema*, trans. Timothy Barnard (Urbana: University of Illinois Press, 2011), André Gaudreault noted that the years 1907–1908 were crucial in "setting in motion" the process of the institutionalization of cinema.

59. Doane, *The Emergence of Cinematic Time*, 160–161. André Gaudreault, too, notes that early narrative films foregrounded temporal elements, in "Temporality and Narrativity in Early Cinema, 1895–1908," in *Film before Griffith*, ed. John Fell (Berkeley: University of California Press, 1983), 311–329.

60. Doane, *The Emergence of Cinematic Time*, 23.

61. I am indebted to Jan Olsson and Trond Lundemo for bringing *Dr. Ams Tram Grams Kikkert* to my attention. I have not been able to determine whether this film, which was distributed in Sweden in 1915, is the same film originally released as *Le merveilleux telecinematoscope*. On imaginary televisions in early cinema, see also Wanda Strauven, "The Imagination of Wireless Distribution," in *Networks of Entertainment: Early Film Distribution 1895–1915*, ed. Frank Kessler and Nanna Verhoeff (New Barnet, UK: John Libbey, 2007), 295–303.

62. Jay David Bolter and Richard Grusin, *Remediation: Understanding New Media* (Cambridge, MA: MIT Press, 1999), 45.

63. See "Typesetting Next by Wireless Waves," *New York Times*, April 29, 1908, 1, and "Knudsen's Process of Transmitting Pictures by Wireless Telegraphy," *Scientific American*, June 6, 1908, 412.

64. Stephen Bottomore, "'Devant le cinématographe': The Cinema in French Fiction 1896–1914," *KINtop* 13 (2005): 92–110.

65. Importantly, the shock that Max experiences differs from other troubling encounters with novel modern technologies, as popularized in numerous stories about the railway and the cinema: it is not the seeing at a distance device itself that distresses Max, but rather the way it exposes him to the shock of witnessing the unexpected scene.

66. Mary Ann Doane, "Information, Crisis, Catastrophe," in *New Media, Old Media: A History and Theory Reader*, ed. Wendy Hui Kyong Chun and Thomas Keenan (New York: Routledge, 2006), 251.

67. Anton Kaes, "War—Film—Trauma," in *Modernität und Trauma: Beiträge zum Zeitenbruch des Ersten Weltkrieges*, ed. Inka Mülder-Bach (Vienna: Edition Parabasen, 2000), 121–130.

4. Cinema's Radio Double

1. For an account of Jenkins's work on television, see Donald G. Godfrey, *C. Francis Jenkins, Pioneer of Film and Television* (Urbana: University of Illinois Press, 2014), 95–167.

2. Hugo Gernsback, "Radio Vision," *Radio News* (December 1923): 681, 823–824.

3. C. Francis Jenkins, "Prismatic Rings," *Transactions of the Society for Motion Picture Engineers* 14 (1922): 70.

4. Jenkins, "Prismatic Rings," 70.

5. Jonathan Sterne, *The Audible Past: Cultural Origins of Sound Reproduction* (Durham, NC: Duke University Press, 2003), chap. 4.

6. André Gaudreault and Philippe Marion, "A Medium Is Always Born Twice . . . ," *Early Popular Visual Culture* 3, no. 1 (May 2005): 3–5. Charles Musser, more recently, offered a valuable contrasting account of the failure of the stereopticon, a nineteenth-century photographic slide projector, to develop as "a sufficiently distinctive practice" and gain recognition as an individuated medium distinct from its affiliate media institutions of magic lantern projection, photography, and the illustrated lecture. See "Stereopticon and Cinema: Media Form or Platform?," in *Cine-Dispositives: Essays in Epistemology across Media*, ed. François Albera and Maria Tortajada (Amsterdam: Amsterdam University Press, 2014), 129–159.

7. Philip Sewell, *Television in the Age of Radio: Modernity, Imagination, and the Making of a Medium* (New Brunswick, NJ: Rutgers University Press, 2014), 24.

8. See Lisa Gitelman, "How Users Define New Media: A History of the Amusement Phonograph," in *Rethinking Media Change: The Aesthetics of Transition*, ed. David Thorburn and Henry Jenkins (Cambridge, MA: MIT Press, 2003), 61–80; Susan J. Douglas, *Inventing American Broadcasting, 1899–1922* (Baltimore: Johns Hopkins University Press, 1987); and André Gaudreault, *Film and Attraction: From Kinematography to Cinema*, trans. Timothy Barnard (Urbana: University of Illinois Press, 2011).

9. See "Television Show Goes Out but Coast Fans Mum If They Get It," *Variety*, September 26, 1933, 1. For a different argument about the cultural significance of the activity of early television amateurs see Sewell, *Television in the Age of Radio*, chap. 2.

10. The histories of early television in Europe comprise a large and diverse body of scholarship. On the German case, see William Uricchio, "Television as History: Representations of German Television Broadcasting, 1935–1944," in *Framing the Past: The Historiography of German Cinema and Television*, ed. Bruce A. Murray and Christopher J. Wickham (Carbondale: Southern Illinois University Press, 1992), 167–196, and Klaus Winker, *Fernsehen unterm Hakenkreuz: Organisation, Programm, Personal* (Cologne: Böhlau, 1994). On the British, see Russell W. Burns, *British Television: The Formative Years* (London: Peregrinus, 1986), and Jason Jacobs, *The Intimate Screen: Early British Television Drama* (Oxford: Oxford University Press, 2000); on the Italian, see Diego Verdegiglio, *La TV di Mussolini: Sperimentazioni televisive nel ventennio fascista* (Rome: Cooper & Castelvecchi, 2003). For a more recent transnational perspective, see Anne-Katrin Weber, "Television before TV: A Transnational History of an Experimental Medium on Display, 1928–1939" (PhD diss., Université de Lausanne, 2014).

11. William Uricchio, "Contextualizing the Broadcast Era: Nation, Commerce, and Constraint," *Annals of the American Academy of Political and Social Science* 625 (September 2009): 62.

12. See Amanda Lotz, *The Television Will Be Revolutionized* (New York: NYU Press, 2007).

13. Waldermar Kaempffert, "Seeing by Wire and Radio Opens New Highways in the Field of Communication—Practical Use of the Invention Described," *New York Times*, April 17, 1927, XX5. See also Richard Koszarski, *Hollywood on the Hudson: Film and Television in New York from Griffith to Sarnoff* (New Brunswick, NJ: Rutgers University Press, 2008), 410.

14. Douglas Gomery, "Theatre Television: The Missing Link of Technological Change in the U.S. Motion Picture Industry," *Velvet Light Trap* 21 (1985): 54–61.

15. See James N. Miller, "The Latest in Television," *Popular Mechanics* (September 1929): 472–476; Russell W. Burns, *John Logie Baird: Television Pioneer* (London: Institution of Engineering and Technology, 2000), 111–122.

16. Patrice Flichy, *Dynamics of Modern Communication: The Shaping and Impact of New Communication Technologies*, trans. Liz Libbrecht (London: Sage, 1995), 71. See also Lynn Spigel, *Make Room for TV: Television and the Family Ideal in Postwar America* (Chicago: University of Chicago Press, 1992), 26–35.

17. For early history of broadcasting see, for example, Douglas, *Inventing American Broadcasting*. For an account of the emergence of the American System of Broadcasting, see Michele Hilmes, "NBC and the Network Idea: Defining the 'American System,'" in *NBC: America's Network*, ed. Hilmes (Berkeley: University of California Press, 2007), 7–24.

18. "Public Must Wait for Television," *New York Times*, August 14, 1928, 27.

19. Edwin Schallert, "Television's Effect on Film Revealed by Expert," *Los Angeles Times*, February 24, 1935, A2.

20. Quoted in David Sarnoff, *Pioneering in Television: Prophecy and Fulfillment* (New York: Radio Corporation of America, 1946), 10.

21. David Sarnoff, "Radio-Vision Era Is Dawning," *New York Times*, May 31, 1931, XX9.

22. Sewell, *Television in the Age of Radio*, 93–127.

23. David Sarnoff, "In Television Sarnoff Sees a New Culture," *New York Times*, July 13, 1930, 115.

24. For early discourses about film as a democratic art, see Miriam Hansen, *Babel and Babylon: Spectatorship in American Silent Film* (Cambridge, MA: Harvard University Press, 1991), 77, 193.

25. Sarnoff, "Radio-Vision Era Is Dawning," 9.

26. Sarnoff, "Radio-Vision Era Is Dawning," 9.

27. William leBaron, "Third Dimension, Large Screen, Color," *Film Daily*, May 24, 1929, 4. See also "After Talkies Come What?," *Los Angeles Times*, June 9, 1929, 15, 28; Eric Smoodin, "Motion Pictures and Television, 1930–1945: A Pre-history of the Relations between the Two Media," *Journal of the University Film and Video Association* 34, no. 3 (Summer 1982): 4.

28. Paul Rotha, *The Film Till Now: A Survey of the Cinema* (New York: Jonathan Cape and Harrison Smith, 1930), 35.

29. "Far Off Speakers Seen as Well as Heard Here in Test of Television," *New York Times*, April 8, 1927, 1, quoted in Garth Jowett, "Dangling the Dream? The Presentation of Television to the American Public, 1928–1952," *Historical Journal of Film, Radio, and Television* 14, no. 2 (1994): 125.

30. C. Francis Jenkins, "Transmission of Movies by Radio," *Transactions of the Society of Motion Picture Engineers* 36 (1929): 915.

31. "'Mummy Case,' Television's Equivalent of 'Great Train Robbery,' Shown in N.Y.," *Variety*, May 25, 1938, 1.

32. See, for example, "Motion Pictures by Radio Invented by C. F. Jenkins," *Motion Picture Herald*, June 27, 1925, 42. The Motion Picture Producers and Distributors of America Digital Archive includes a letter addressed to Will Hays from August 21, 1928, with a brief report about the status of television development; see mppda .flinders.edu.au.

33. A letter from William Fox Studios to Jenkins Laboratories dated December 11, 1928, is included in the George H. Clark Collection, National Museum of American History, series 5, box 42.

34. "Radio Men Regard Television as Ally," *New York Times*, January 15, 1928, 5.

35. "Loew Circuit in Deal for Jenkins Television Movies," *Exhibitors Daily Review*, December 13, 1928, 1–2.

36. "Hollywood in High Gear," *New York Times*, June 22, 1930, X2.

37. R. E. Sherwood, "Hollywood's Lost Enthusiasm and Its Other Laments," *Hollywood Spectator*, July 18, 1931, 14.

38. Sherwood, "Hollywood's Lost Enthusiasm and Its Other Laments," 14.

39. Michele Hilmes, *Hollywood and Broadcasting: From Radio to Cable* (Urbana: University of Illinois Press, 1999), 26; Richard B. Jewell, "Hollywood and Radio: Competition and Partnership in the 1930s," *Historical Journal of Film, Radio and Television* 4, no. 2 (1984): 126. On RKO see "Radio Corp. and General Electric Acquire Interest in FBO," *Motion Picture News*, January 7, 1928, 17.

40. "Dodging That Big, Bad Television," *New York Times*, April 12, 1936, 4.

41. Ross Melnick, *American Showman: Samuel "Roxy" Rothafel and the Birth of the Entertainment Industry, 1908–1935* (New York: Columbia University Press, 2012), 307.

42. "Warner Buy Interest in Film, Radio Patents," *Film Daily*, April 23, 1930, 1; "Laemmle Eyes Television," *Film Daily*, May 3, 1932, 2.

43. Quoted in Hilmes, *Hollywood and Broadcasting*, 50.

44. Koszarski, *Hollywood on the Hudson*, 428.

45. William Boddy, *Fifties Television: The Industry and Its Critics* (Urbana: University of Illinois Press, 1990), 17. See also Jowett, "Dangling the Dream?," 128–129.

46. Edgar H. Felix, *Television: Its Methods and Uses* (New York: McGraw-Hill, 1931), 223.

47. See Robert H. Stern, "Regulatory Influences upon Television's Development: Early Years under the Federal Radio Commission," *American Journal of Economics and Sociology* 22 (April 1963): 347–362.

48. See Boddy, *Fifties Television*, 56; Christopher Anderson, "Television and Hollywood in the 1940s," in *Boom and Bust: American Cinema in the 1940s*, ed. Thomas Schatz (New York: Scribner's, 1997), 425.

49. "Television Seen as Boon to Films," *Los Angeles Times*, April 7, 1937, 16.

50. Robert Robins, "Television: One View of Its Development and Control," *Vital Speeches*, July 15, 1936, 663–664.

51. "Film Industry Advised to Grab Television," *Broadcasting*, June 15, 1937, 7, 30–31.

52. "Pix Biz Chilly on Tele," *Variety*, July 14, 1937, 3.

53. For a comprehensive history of early two-way television, see Luke Stadel, "Television as a Sound Medium, 1922–1994" (PhD diss., Northwestern University, 2015), 50–97.

54. "New Cable for Television," *Broadcasting*, June 1, 1935, 24; "AT&T System Not to Enter Television," *Broadcasting*, August 1, 1935, 39.

55. Sewell, *Television in the Age of Radio*, 111.

56. Max Horkheimer and Theodor Adorno, *Dialectic of Enlightenment*, trans. Edmund Jephcott (Stanford, CA: Stanford University Press, 2002), 95.

57. On the ideological and economic foundations of broadcasting, see James Schwoch, "Selling the Sight/Site of Sound: Broadcast Advertising and the Transition from Radio to Television," *Cinema Journal* 30, no. 1 (Fall 1990): 55–66; Thomas Streeter, *Selling the Air: A Critique of the Policy of Commercial Broadcasting in the United States* (Chicago: University of Chicago Press, 1996); and Robert McChesney, *Telecommunications, Mass Media, and Democracy: The Battle for the Control of U.S. Broadcasting, 1928–1935* (Oxford: Oxford University Press, 1993).

58. Stern, "Regulatory Influences upon Television's Development," 356–357.

59. Fourth Annual Report of the FRC—1930, quoted in "The Evolution of Television: 1927–1943," 215.

60. For theoretical discussions of the concepts of television liveness in different historical moments, see Jane Feuer, "The Concept of Live Television: Ontology as Ideology," in *Regarding Television*, ed. E. Ann Kaplan (Frederick, MD: University Publications of America, 1983), 12–22; Mark Williams, "History in a Flash: Notes on the Myth of TV Liveness," in *Collecting Visible Evidence*, ed. Jane Gaines and Michael Renov (Minneapolis: University of Minnesota Press, 1999), 292–312; and Elana Levine, "Distinguishing Television: The Changing Meanings of Television Liveness," *Media, Culture and Society* 30, no. 3 (2008): 393–409.

61. Boddy, *Fifties Television*, 81–82.

62. Robert Vianello, "The Power Politics of 'Live' Television," *Journal of Film and Video* 38 (Summer 1985): 26–40.

63. Second Annual Report of the FRC—1928, appendix M, quoted in "The Evolution of Television: 1927–1943," 208.

64. Quoted in Koszarski, *Hollywood on the Hudson*, 416. On the affinity between television liveness and disaster, see Mary Ann Doane, "Information, Crisis, Catastrophe," in *New Media, Old Media: A History and Theory Reader*, ed. Wendy Hui Kyong Chun and Thomas Keenan (New York: Routledge, 2006), 251–264.

65. "A Silhouette Studio," *Journals of the Society of Motion Picture Engineers* 15 (September 1930): 381–384.

66. William Paley, "Radio and the Movies Join Hands," *Nation's Business* (October 1929): 22. On the early television broadcasts of CBS see Koszarski, *Hollywood on the Hudson*, 425–431, 456–460.

67. Sarnoff, "In Television Sarnoff Sees a New Culture," 115.

68. Quoted in Alexander Russo, "Defensive Transcriptions: Radio Networks, Sound-on-Disc Recording, and the Meaning of Live Broadcasting," *Velvet Light Trap* 54 (Fall 2004): 7.

69. Russo, "Defensive Transcriptions," 6.

70. *Second Annual Report of the Federal Radio Commission to the Congress of the United States* (1928), 155.

71. Sewell, *Television in the Age of Radio*, 135.

72. Quoted in Joseph H. Udelson, *The Great Television Race: A History of the American Television Industry, 1925–1941* (Tuscaloosa: University of Alabama Press, 1982), 94.

73. Orrin E. Dunlap, "Seeing Nationally: Transcontinental Television Is Called Formidable Task of Engineering," *New York Times*, June 13, 1937, 182. See also Jonathan Sterne, "Television under Construction: American Television and the Problem of Distribution, 1926–62," *Media, Culture and Society* 21 (1992): 503–530.

74. "Television vs. Theatre," *Variety*, May 3, 1939, 30.

75. "Television vs. Theatre," 30.

76. An argument could be made about earlier optical devices such as the mutoscope or the kinora having already dissociated motion pictures from film. However, given the format of these devices, they were only capable of carrying scenes of several seconds each, and as such they were not able to properly "absorb" complete motion pictures.

77. Jay David Bolter and Richard Grusin, *Remediation: Understanding New Media* (Cambridge, MA: MIT Press, 1999).

78. C. H. W. Nason, "Characteristics of Television Signals," *Radio Broadcast* (April 1930): 318.

79. See, for example, "Television to Develop Own Art Form after Borrowing First from Movies," *Broadcasting*, June 15, 1937, 30.

80. Alexander Galloway, *The Interface Effect* (Cambridge: Polity, 2012), 20.

81. On the notion of postcinema see Anne Friedberg, "The End of Cinema: Multimedia and Technological Change," in *Reinventing Film Studies*, ed. Christine Gledhill and Linda Williams (London: Arnold, 2000), 438–452; André Gaudreault and Philippe Marion, *The End of Cinema? A Medium in Crisis in the Digital Age*, trans. Timothy Barnard (New York: Columbia University Press, 2015); and John Belton, "If Film Is Dead, What Is Cinema?," *Screen* 55, no. 4 (Winter 2014): 460–470.

82. Francesco Casetti, *The Lumière Galaxy: Seven Keywords for the Cinema to Come* (New York: Columbia University Press, 2015).

83. Casetti, *The Lumière Galaxy*, 29.

84. L. W. Boynton, "The Theatre vs. the Home," *Exhibitors Trade Review*, October 28, 1922, 1386, emphasis added.

85. Boynton, "The Theatre vs. the Home," 1386.

86. William S. Paley, "Radio and the Movies Join Hands," 21–22.

87. R. E. Sherwood, "Beyond the Talkies—Television," *Scribner's Magazine*, July 1929, 7.

88. Sherwood, "Beyond the Talkies," 7–8.

89. "Television Broadcast of 'Journey's End' to Be Attempted April 7 in Jersey," *Variety*, March 19, 1930, 67.

90. "Tiffany to Use Television in Advertising Its Product," *Exhibitors Daily Review*, March 21, 1930, 1.

91. Koszarski, *Hollywood on the Hudson*, 419.

92. "Crooked Circle in Television Test," *Hollywood Reporter*, March 23, 1933, 2; "Television Trial a Disappointment," *Hollywood Reporter*, March 24, 1933, 4.

93. Koszarski, *Hollywood on the Hudson*, 439; "11,000,000 Feet of Film Telecast on West Coast," *Film Daily*, April 24, 1939, 8.

94. "Tele-Broadcasting of Films Now Being Undertaken Here," *Los Angeles Times*, May 27, 1934, 3.

95. Shaw Desmond, "Television and the Films," *Television*, September 1928, 287.

96. "New Adaptor Opens Way for Tele Use of Day's Films," *Film Daily*, April 24, 1939, 1, 8.

97. "Films for Television," *Motion Picture Herald*, July 1, 1939, 9; "Television Films," *Motion Picture Herald*, July 8, 1939, 9; "Majors Cold to Television's Plea for Pix Use," *Film Daily*, April 25, 1939, 1, 3.

98. "Gunga Din Rousing Adventure Show Will Click Big," *Independent Exhibitors Film Bulletin*, February 25, 1939, 5.

99. David Pierce, "'Senile Celluloid': Independent Exhibitors, the Major Studios and the Fight over Feature Films on Television, 1939–1956," *Film History* 10, no. 2 (1998): 141.

100. *Academy of Motion Picture Arts and Sciences Technical Bulletin* (November 1938): 7.

101. "First Regular Daily Broadcasts of Television Few Weeks Away," *Motion Picture Herald*, March 11, 1939, 35; "Television 'Din' for the Fair," *Boxoffice*, March 25, 1939, 22.

102. "Television 'Din' for the Fair," 22.

103. "Shorts Called Television's Need," *Motion Picture Herald*, April 1, 1939, 61.

104. "An Authority on Television," *Harrison's Report*, October 12, 1935, 164.

105. John Western, "Television Girds for Battle," *Public Opinion Quarterly* 3, no. 4 (October 1939): 557.

106. The idea of television glance as opposed to the gaze of the film spectator comes from John Ellis, *Visible Fictions: Cinema, Television, Video* (London: Routledge and Kegan Paul, 1982).

107. Gilbert Seldes, "The 'Errors' of Television," *Atlantic* 159, no. 5 (May 1937): 535.

108. Seldes, "The 'Errors' of Television," 539.

109. David Bordwell, *The Way Hollywood Tells It: Story and Style in Modern Movies* (Berkeley: University of California Press, 2006), 148.

110. Imaginary forms of television appeared not only in American films but all over international production. For a comprehensive international annotated film-

ography of early television in films, see Richard Koszarski and Doron Galili, "Television in the Cinema before 1939: An International Annotated Database," *Journal of E-Media Studies* 5, no. 1 (2016), http://journals.dartmouth.edu/cgi-bin/WebObjects /Journals.woa/xmlpage/4/article/471. See also Richard Koszarski, "Coming Next Week: Images of Television in Pre-war Motion Pictures," *Film History* 10, no. 2 (1998): 128–140, and Jane Stokes, *On Screen Rivals: Cinema and Television in the United States and Britain* (New York: St. Martin's, 2000). For a discussion of Hollywood's "videophobic fantasies" on television see Paul Young, *The Cinema Dreams Its Rivals: Media Fantasy Films from Radio to the Internet* (Minneapolis: University of Minnesota Press, 2005), 137–191.

111. Carolyn Marvin, *When Old Technologies Were New* (New York: Oxford University Press, 1988).

112. Arthur Lenning, *The Immortal Count: The Life and Films of Bela Lugosi* (Lexington: University Press of Kentucky, 2003), 221.

113. Stokes, *On Screen Rivals*, 147.

114. William J. Fanning Jr., "The Historical Death Ray and Science Fiction in the 1920s and 1930s," *Science Fiction Studies* 37 (2010): 254.

115. Toby Miller, *Television Studies: The Basics* (London: Routledge, 2009), 3.

116. Stephen Bottomore, "'Devant le cinématographe': The Cinema in French Fiction 1896–1914," *KINtop* 13 (2005): 92–110; Tom Gunning, "Tracing the Individual Body: Photography, Detectives, and Early Cinema," in *Cinema and the Invention of Modern Life*, ed. Leo Charney and Vanessa R. Schwartz (Berkeley: University of California Press, 1995), 15–45.

117. Jeffrey Sconce, *Haunted Media: Electronic Presence from Telegraphy to Television* (Durham, NC: Duke University Press, 2000), 117.

118. "Press and Public Divided in Reaction to Mars Program," *Broadcasting*, November 15, 1938, 15; "Well, Wells, Welles," *Broadcasting*, November 15, 1938, 40.

119. "S.O.S. Tidal Wave," *Motion Picture Daily*, May 29, 1939, 5.

120. Lisa Gitelman, *Scripts, Grooves, and Writing Machines: Representing Technology in the Edison Era* (Stanford, CA: Stanford University Press, 2000), 151, emphasis in the original.

121. On this notion, see also Feuer, "The Concept of Live Television."

122. Doane, "Information, Crisis, Catastrophe," 262.

5. "We Must Prepare!"

1. A letter from Dziga Vertov to Aleksander Fevralsky, November 8, 1928, first published by Fevralsky in *Iskusstvo kino* 12 (1965): 71–73. Translated and reprinted as "*Man with the Movie Camera*: Absolute Kinography and Radio-Eye," in *Lines of Resistance: Dziga Vertov and the 1920s*, ed. Yuri Tsivian (Pordenone, Italy: Le Giornate del Cinema Muto, 2004), 318. Citations will come from the version in Tsivian, *Lines of Resistance*.

2. Vertov, "*Man with the Movie Camera*, Absolute Kinography and Radio-Eye," 318.

3. Vertov, "*Man with the Movie Camera*, Absolute Kinography and Radio-Eye," 319.

4. Vertov, "*Man with the Movie Camera*: Absolute Kinography and Radio-Eye," 319.

5. Renato Poggioli, *The Theory of the Avant-Garde*, trans. Gerald Fitzgerald (New York: Harper and Row, 1968), 136.

6. F. T. Marinetti, "Total Theatre: Its Architecture and Technology," in *Critical Writings*, ed. Gunter Berghaus, trans. Doug Thompson (New York: Farrar, Straus and Giroux, 2006), 400–407.

7. F. T. Marinetti, "A Futurist Theatre of the Skies Enhanced by Radio and Television," in *Critical Writings*, 408–409.

8. László Moholy-Nagy, "Light-Space Modulator for an Electric Stage," in *Moholy-Nagy*, ed. Krisztina Passuth (New York: Thames and Hudson, 1985), 310. On Moholy-Nagy's art and telecommunications see also Eduardo Kac, *Telepresence and Bio-Art: Networking Humans, Rabbits, and Robots* (Ann Arbor: University of Michigan Press, 2005), 16–24.

9. See Jacques Donguy, "Machine Head: Raoul Hausmann and the Optophone," *Leonardo* 34, no. 3 (June 2001): 217–220; Doron Galili, "Postmediales Wissen um 1900: Zur Medienarchäologie des Fernsehens," *Montage AV* 25, no. 2 (2016): 181–200. For further discussions of avant-garde artists and transmission media, see Alfonso Puyal, *Arte y radiovisión: Experiencias de los movimientos históricos de vanguardia con la televisión* (Madrid: Editorial Complutense, 2009).

10. Philip Rosen, *Change Mummified: Cinema, Historicity, Theory* (Minneapolis: University of Minnesota Press, 2001), 303.

11. Brian McNair, *Glasnost, Perestroika, and the Soviet Media* (London: Routledge, 1991), 47–48; Vertov quotes the phrase in "Kino-Pravda and Radio-Pravda," *Pravda*, July 12, 1925, translated and reprinted in *Kino-Eye: The Writings of Dziga Vertov*, ed. Annette Michelson (Berkeley: University of California Press, 1984), 56.

12. Huntly Carter, *The New Spirit in the Russian Theatre, 1917–28* (New York: Brentano's, 1929), 294.

13. Carter, *The New Spirit in the Russian Theatre*, 294.

14. Eli Noam, *Television in Europe* (Oxford: Oxford University Press, 1991), 276.

15. Carter, *The New Spirit in the Russian Theatre*, 292. Mass radio listening is illustrated in a number of Vertov's films. His *Radio-Pravda* newsreel shows peasants purchasing and installing a radio in their village, and in *Man with a Movie Camera* there is a scene of radio playing in a workers' club. *A Sixth Part of the World* (1926) and *The Eleventh Year* (1928) depict outdoor public listening to radio reports in montage sequences in which Vertov cuts between images of individuals and groups and close-ups of loudspeakers.

16. Leon Trotsky, "Radio, Science, Technology and Society" (1926), *Semiotext(e)* 16 (1993): 241.

17. Trotsky, "Radio, Science, Technology and Society," 247.

18. Annette Michelson, introduction to Vertov, *Kino-Eye*, xxxii–xxxiii; Maria Gough, "Switched On: Notes on Radio, Automata, and the Bright Red Star," in *Building the Collective: Soviet Graphic Design 1917–1937*, ed. Leah Dickerman (New York: Princeton Architectural Press, 1996), 45.

19. Richard Stites, *Revolutionary Dreams: Utopian Vision and Experimental Life in the Russian Revolution* (Oxford: Oxford University Press, 1989), 184.

20. Quoted in Stites, *Revolutionary Dreams*, 160.

21. Velimir Khlebnikov, "The Radio of the Future" (1921), trans. Gary Kern, *Semiotext(e)* 16 (1993): 32.

22. Khlebnikov, "The Radio of the Future," 34–35.

23. Vladimir Mayakovsky, *The Bedbug and Selected Poetry*, ed. Patricia Blake and trans. Max Hayward and George Reavey (Bloomington: Indiana University Press, 1960), 271–277.

24. Stites, *Revolutionary Dreams*, 29, 34; Yevgeny Zamayatin, *We*, trans. Clarence Brown (New York: Penguin Books, 1993).

25. Aleksander Beliayev, *The Struggle in Space*, trans. Albert Parry (1928; repr., Washington, DC: Arfor, 1965).

26. For a description of the currently only partially existing newsreel, see Yuri Tsivian's notes on *Kino-Pravda 23 (Radio Pravda)* (Kultkino, USSR 1925) in the program of Le Giornate del Cinema Muto (2004), http://www.cinetecadelfriuli.org/gcm/ed_precedenti/edizione2004/Vertov6_10.html#p8.

27. Dziga Vertov, "Kino-Pravda," *Kinofot* 6 (1923), translated and reprinted in *Kino-Eye*, 34.

28. Vertov, "Kino-Pravda and Radio-Pravda," 52, emphasis added.

29. Dziga Vertov, "An Answer to Five Questions," *Kino* 21 (October 1924), translated and reprinted in *Lines of Resistance*, 94–95.

30. Vertov, "Kino-Pravda and Radio-Pravda," 56, emphasis added.

31. See "Dziga Vertov on Kino-Eye," a lecture given in Paris in 1929, published in *Filmfront* 2, no. 7 (January 1935): 6–8, translated and reprinted in *Lines of Resistance*, 354.

32. Aleksander Fevralsky, "Tendentsii ikusstva i radio-glaz," *Molodaya gvardija* 7 (July 1925): 166–168. The English translation is from "Currents in Art and the Radio-Eye," trans. Andrey Gordienko, *Historical Journal of Film Radio and Television* 28, no. 1 (March 2008): 68–69.

33. Vertov, "From Kino-Eye to Radio-Eye" (1929), translated and reprinted in *Kino-Eye*, 91, emphasis in the original.

34. Dziga Vertov, "Replies to Questions" (1930), translated and reprinted in *Kino-Eye*, 105.

35. See, for example, Vertov's claim that distributors had boycotted his newsreels, in his 1923 public talk "On the Significance of the Newsreel," translated and reprinted in *Kino-Eye*, 32.

36. Dziga Vertov, "From Kino-Eye to Radio-Eye," 91; "Kino-Pravda and Radio-Pravda," 56, emphasis added.

37. Bertolt Brecht, "The Radio as an Apparatus of Communication" (1932), trans. John Willett, *Semiotext(e)* 16 (1993): 15.

38. Siegfried Zielinski, *Audiovisions: Cinema and Television as Entr'actes in History*, trans. Gloria Custance (Amsterdam: Amsterdam University Press, 1999), 120.

39. Vertov, "From Kino-Eye to Radio-Eye," 91–92, emphasis in the original.

40. Vertov, "*The Man with a Movie Camera*: A Visual Symphony" (1928), translated and reprinted in *Kino-Eye*, 283.

41. Vertov, "*Man with the Movie Camera*, Absolute Kinography and Radio-Eye," 319.

42. André Bazin, "The Myth of Total Cinema," in *What Is Cinema?*, vol. 1, trans. Hugh Gray (Berkeley: University of California Press, 1967), 20–21.

43. Malcolm Turvey, "Can the Camera See? Mimesis in *Man with a Movie Camera*," *October* 89 (Summer 1999): 34.

44. Dziga Vertov, "Kinoks: A Revolution," *LEF*, no. 3 (1923), translated and reprinted in *Kino-Eye*, 15, emphasis added.

45. Dziga Vertov, "Kino-Eye," *Na putika iskusstva* (Moscow: Proletkul't, 1926), translated and reprinted in *Kino-Eye*, 67.

46. Vertov, "Kino-Eye," translated and reprinted in Tsivian, *Lines of Resistance*, 119.

47. Vertov, "Replies to Questions," 104.

48. Dziga Vertov, "On the Significance of Nonacted Cinema," translated and reprinted in *Kino-Eye*, 35, emphasis added.

49. An important work that addresses Vertov within the tradition of modernist medium-specificity concern is Annette Michelson, "From Magician to *Epistemologist*: Vertov's *The Man with a Movie Camera*," *Artforum* 10, no. 7 (February 1971): 60–72.

50. Dziga Vertov, "On the Newsreel—A Speech at ARK" (March 19, 1926), translated and reprinted in *Lines of Resistance*, 133.

51. The different ways Eisenstein and Vertov commemorated a decade of the revolution in 1927 are telling: whereas Eisenstein directed *October*, which reenacts the first days of the 1917 uprising, Vertov (lagging one year behind), focused in his film on the current events of *The Eleventh Year*—for a historical representation simply could not offer its spectators a better comprehension of their reality.

52. See Vertov's references to film archives and to nonacted film vaults in "The Same Thing from Different Angles" and in "The Factory of Facts" (both 1926), in *Kino-Eye*, 57, 59.

53. Dziga Vertov, "On the Organization of a Film Experiment Station" (1923), translated and reprinted in *Kino-Eye*, 22, emphasis added.

54. Dziga Vertov, "Kino-Eye on *Strike*" (originally published in *Kino*, February 3, 1925), translated and reprinted in *Lines of Resistance*, 126.

55. Dziga Vertov, "Kino-Eye" (1926), translated and reprinted in *Kino-Eye*, 75; David Tomas, *Vertov, Snow, Farocki: Machine Vision and the Posthuman* (New York: Bloomsbury, 2013), 61.

56. Vertov, "On the Organization of a Film Experiment Station," 21.

57. Elizabeth Astrid Papazian, *Manufacturing Truth: The Documentary Moment in Early Soviet Culture* (DeKalb: Northern Illinois University Press, 2009), 74.

58. Papazian, *Manufacturing Truth*, 79.

59. As Hans Magnus Enzensberger writes, *Kino-Pravda* "were no 'newsreels' but political television-magazine programs *avant l'écran*." See Enzensberger, *Critical Essays*, ed. Reinhold Grimm and Bruce Armstrong (New York: Continuum, 1982), 64. See also Graham Roberts, *Forward Soviet! History and Non-fiction Film in the USSR* (London: I. B. Tauris, 1999), 26; Jeremy Hicks, *Dziga Vertov: Defining Documentary Film* (London: I. B. Tauris, 1999), 18, 34.

60. Dziga Vertov, "Speech to the First All Union Conference on Sound Cinema"

(1930), in *The Film Factory: Russian and Soviet Cinema in Documents*, ed. Richard Taylor and Ian Christie (Cambridge, MA: Harvard University Press, 1988), 303.

61. Dziga Vertov, "The Essence of Kino-Eye" (1925), translated and reprinted in *Kino-Eye*, 49.

62. Vertov, "Kino-Pravda and Radio-Pravda," 56.

63. Vertov, "From Kino-Eye to Radio-Eye," 92.

64. Vertov, *"Man with the Movie Camera*, Absolute Kinography and Radio-Eye," 319, spelling modified.

65. Rosalind Krauss, "Two Moments from the Post-medium Condition," *October* 116 (Spring 2006): 56.

66. Vertov, *"Man with the Movie Camera*, Absolute Kinography and Radio-Eye," 319.

67. See Jean-Paul Fargier, "Le cinéma plus l'électricité," *Cahiers du Cinéma* 406 (April 1988): 56–57, and Gilles Delavaud, "Dziga Vertov ou le cinéma comme anticipation de la television," *Dossiers de l'audiovisuel* 112 (November–December 2003): 23–25.

68. Tom Gunning, "Weaving a Narrative: Style and Economic Background in Griffith's Biograph Films," in *Early Cinema: Space, Frame, Narrative*, ed. Thomas Elsaesser and Adam Barker (London: BFI, 1990), 340–341.

69. Dziga Vertov, "Three Songs of Lenin and Kino-Eye" (1934), translated and reprinted in *Kino-Eye*, 125.

70. Vertov, *"Man with a Movie Camera*: A Visual Symphony," 289.

71. Walter Benjamin, "The Work of Art in the Age of Its Technological Reproducibility," in *Walter Benjamin: Selected Writings*, vol. 2, ed. Michael W. Jennings, Howard Eiland, and Gary Smith (Cambridge, MA: Belknap Press of Harvard University Press, 2003), 118.

72. Vertov, "Speech to the First All Union Conference on Sound Cinema," 305.

73. Vertov, "Speech to the First All Union Conference on Sound Cinema," 305.

74. Letter from the Technical-Scientific Administration of the People's Commissariat of Post and Telegraph to Jenkins Television Corporation, May 25, 1930. George H. Clark Collection, National Museum of American History, series 5, box 43, folder 6.

75. Paul Shmakov, "Television in the USSR," *Journal of the Television Society* (March 1932): 126–130.

76. Paul Shmakov, "The Development of Television in the USSR," *Journal of the Television Society* (March 1936): 97–105; Russell W. Burns, *Television: An International History of the Formative Years* (London: Institution of Electrical Engineers, 1998), 538.

77. Joseph H. Udelson, *The Great Television Race: A History of the American Television Industry, 1925–1941* (Tuscaloosa: University of Alabama Press, 1982), 20–21.

78. Enzensberger, *Critical Essays*, 48.

79. Michael Shamberg and Raindance Corporation, *Guerrilla Television* (New York: Holt, Rinehart and Winston, 1971), 57.

80. See, for example, Henry Jenkins, *Convergence Culture: Where Old and New Media Collide* (New York: New York University Press, 2006).

6. Thinking across Media

An earlier version of chapter 6 was published as "Television from Afar: Arnheim's Understanding of Media," in *Arnheim for Film and Media Studies*, ed. Scott Higgins (New York: Routledge, 2011).

1. D. N. Rodowick, *Elegy for Theory* (Cambridge, MA: Harvard University Press, 2014). For a canonical consideration of key texts in classical film theory see Noël Carroll, *Philosophical Problems of Classical Film Theory* (Princeton, NJ: Princeton University Press, 1988).

2. D. N. Rodowick, *The Virtual Life of Film* (Cambridge, MA: Harvard University Press, 2007), 28, emphasis in the original.

3. Rodowick, *The Virtual Life of Film,* 28–29.

4. Mary Ann Doane, "The Object of Theory," in *Rites of Realism: Essays on Corporeal Cinema*, ed. Ivone Margulies (Durham, NC: Duke University Press, 2003), 85.

5. See, for instance, Mary Ann Doane, "Indexicality and the Concept of Medium Specificity," *Differences* 18, no. 1 (Spring 2007): 128–152; Laura Mulvey, *Death 24x a Second: Stillness and the Moving Image* (London: Reaktion Books, 2006); and Garrett Stewart, *Framed Time: Towards Postfilmic Cinema* (Chicago: University of Chicago Press, 2007).

6. Bazin's writings on television are collected and commented on in Dudley Andrew, ed., *André Bazin's New Media* (Berkeley: University of California Press, 2014).

7. Thomas Elsaesser, "Siegfried Kracauer's Affinities," NECSUS (Spring 2014), http://www.necsus-ejms.org/siegfried-kracauers-affinities/.

8. Siegfried Kracauer, *Theory of Film: The Redemption of Physical Reality* (Princeton, NJ: Princeton University Press, 1960), 166–167.

9. Walter Benjamin, "Moonlit Nights on the Rue La Boétie," in *Walter Benjamin: Selected Writings*, vol. 1, part 2, *1927–30*, ed. Michael W. Jennings, Howard Eiland, and Gary Smith (Cambridge, MA: Belknap Press of Harvard University Press, 2005), 108. See also Miriam Bratu Hansen, *Cinema and Experience: Siegfried Kracauer, Walter Benjamin, and Theodor W. Adorno* (Berkeley: University of California Press, 2012), 338n28.

10. Walter Benjamin, "Vorstufen zum Erzahler-Essay," in *Gesammelte Schriften* 2, ed. Rolf Tiedemann and Hermann Schweppenhauser (Frankfurt am Main: Suhrkamp, 1991), 1282–1283. See also Wolfgang Ernst, "Between Real Time and Memory on Demand: Reflections on/of Television," *South Atlantic Quarterly* 101, no. 3 (Summer 2002): 626.

11. Antonio Somaini, "Cinema as 'Dynamic Mummification,' History as Montage: Eisenstein's Media Archaeology," in *Sergei Eisenstein: Notes for a General History of Cinema*, ed. Naum Kleiman and Somaini (Amsterdam: Amsterdam University Press, 2016), 100–105. According to Kleiman and Somaini (456n17), Eisenstein also addressed American experiments in television in his unpublished Mexican diaries of the early 1930s.

12. See Sergej [*sic*] M. Eisenstein, *Schriften 3. Oktober* (Munich: Hanser, 1975), 350–351. For an English translation of this passage, see Sergei Eisenstein, *Film Essays and a Lecture*, ed. and trans. Jay Leyda (Princeton, NJ: Princeton University Press, 1968), 45. For a reason unknown to me, Leyda translates the word *Fernsehens* to "telescope." The same passage, quoted in a slightly different translation which uses the

word "television," appears in Léon Moussinac, "From Georges Méliès to S. M. Eisenstein," *Experimental Cinema* 1, no. 2 (June 1930): 22.

13. See Rudolf Arnheim, *Film* (London: Faber & Faber, 1933), 294; *Radio* (London: Faber & Faber, 1936), 286; and "Televisione, domani sarà così," *Cinema* 20 (April 1937): 337–338 (unpublished translation by Bobby Baird).

14. Arnheim, *Radio*, 277–280.

15. Arnheim, *Radio*, 278, emphasis added.

16. Arnheim, *Radio*, 278.

17. Arnheim, *Radio*, 235.

18. Arnheim, *Film*, 294.

19. Arnheim, "The Sad Future of Film," in *Film Essays and Criticism*, trans. Brenda Benthien (Madison: University of Wisconsin Press, 1997), 11.

20. Arnheim, *Radio*, 276, 16.

21. Arnheim, *Film*, 295.

22. Arnheim, *Film*, 296.

23. For a history of the institute, its studies, and the methodologies it promoted, see Jürgen Wilke, "Cinematography as a Medium of Communication: The Promotion of Research by the League of Nations and the Role of Rudolf Arnheim," *European Journal of Communication* 6 (1991): 337–353. A tentative outline of the encyclopedia appears in *Intercine* 7, no. 3 (March 1935): 130. For a bibliography of Arnheim's writings on cinema from his Italian era and extensive commentary, see Adriano D'Aloia's website, https://rudolfarnheim.net/.

24. Zoë Druick, "The International Educational Cinematograph Institute, Reactionary Modernism, and the Formation of Film Studies," *Canadian Journal of Film Studies* 16, no. 1 (Spring 2007): 83.

25. Rudolf Arnheim, "Seeing Afar Off," *Intercine* 7, no. 2 (February 1935): 80.

26. Arnheim, "Seeing Afar Off," 82, translation modified.

27. Arnheim, "Seeing Afar Off," 77.

28. Arnheim, "Seeing Afar Off," 77.

29. Rudolf Arnheim, *Film as Art* (Berkeley: University of California Press, 1957), 195, and "Seeing Afar Off," 77.

30. Arnheim, "Seeing Afar Off," 78.

31. Siegfried Kracauer, "Photography," in *The Mass Ornament: Weimar Essays*, ed. and trans. Thomas Levin (Cambridge, MA: Harvard University Press, 1995), 59; Arnheim, *Radio*, 281.

32. Arnheim, *Radio*, 282.

33. Arnheim, "Seeing Afar Off," 78.

34. Arnheim, "Seeing Afar Off," 81.

35. Arnheim, "Seeing Afar Off," 81.

36. Arnheim, "A Forecast of Television," in *Film as Art*, 195.

37. Ara Merjian, "Middlebrow Modernism: Rudolf Arnheim at the Crossroads of Film Theory and the Psychology of Art," in *The Visual Turn: Classical Film Theory and Art History*, ed. Angela Dalle Vacche (New Brunswick, NJ: Rutgers University Press, 2003), 162. See also Dudley Andrew, *The Major Film Theories: An Introduction* (London: Oxford University Press, 1976), 35–41.

38. Rudolf Arnheim, introduction to *Film Essays and Criticism*, 5.

39. Walter Benjamin, "On Some Motifs in Baudelaire," in *Walter Benjamin: Selected Writings*, vol. 4, ed. Howard Eiland and Michael W. Jennings (Cambridge, MA: Belknap Press of Harvard University Press, 2003), 314–355. For commentaries that foreground and illuminate the sense of anaesthetics in Benjamin's thought, see Susan Buck-Morss, "Aesthetics and Anaesthetics: Walter Benjamin's Artwork Essay Reconsidered," *October* 62 (Autumn 1992): 3–41; Hansen, *Cinema and Experience*.

40. Marshall McLuhan, *Understanding Media: The Extensions of Man* (Cambridge, MA: MIT Press, 1994), esp. 41–48.

41. Rudolf Arnheim, "Disciplining the Gramophone, Radio, Telephone, and Television," trans. Christy Wampole, *Modernism/Modernity* 16, no. 2 (April 2009): 422.

42. Arnheim, "Disciplining the Gramophone, Radio, Telephone, and Television," 426.

43. See the discussions of Arnheim's work in Carroll, *Philosophical Problems of Classical Film Theory*.

44. Arnheim, *Radio*, 277. It should be noted that in the German original, Arnheim uses the word *Rundfunk*, which is translated here to "broadcasting" but also means "radio" (indeed, up to the mid-1930 the two words were effectively synonymous). My argument about the medium not being bound to a certain material basis, however, brings the two optional translations to a similar conclusion.

45. Gotthold Ephraim Lessing, *Laocoön: An Essay on the Limits of Poetry and Painting* (Boston: Roberts Brothers, 1887), 110.

46. Arnheim, *Film*, 209.

47. See Arnheim, *Film*, esp. 24–29.

48. Arnheim, "Televisione, domani sarà così."

49. Arnheim, *Radio*, 277.

50. See the special volume "A Return to Classical Film Theory?," *October* 148 (Spring 2014), and the dossier "What's New in Classical Film Theory?," *Screen* 55, no. 3 (September 2014).

Conclusion

1. On the end of television, see Lynn Spigel and Jan Olsson, eds., *Television after TV: Essays on a Medium in Transition* (Durham, NC: Duke University Press, 2004); special issue, "The End of Television? Its Impact on the World (So Far)," *Annals of the American Academy of Political and Social Science* 625 (September 2009). On the end of cinema and the postcinema condition, see Paolo Cherchi Usai, *The Death of Cinema: History, Cultural Memory, and the Digital Dark Age* (London: BFI, 2001), and Shane Denson and Julia Leyda, eds., *Post-cinema: Theorizing 21st-Century Film* (Falmer, UK: Reframe Books, 2016).

2. Peter Bart, "Film Academy Reviewing Netflix's Eligibility Amid Angst over Streaming Services," *Deadline Hollywood*, October 2, 2017, deadline.com/2017/10/oscars-academy-netflix-eligibility-in-question-membership-meeting-1202180576/.

3. For a critique of the debates on photographic and digital image, see Philip

Rosen, *Change Mummified: Cinema, Historicity, Theory* (Minneapolis: University of Minnesota Press, 2001), 301–349.

4. Thomas Elsaesser, "Digital Cinema: Delivery, Event, Time," in *Cinema Futures: Cain, Abel or Cable?*, ed. Elsaesser and Kay Hoffmann (Amsterdam: Amsterdam University Press, 1998), 209.

5. Elsaesser, "Digital Cinema," 209, spelling altered.

6. Erkki Huhtamo, "From Kaleidoscomaniac to Cybernerd: Towards an Archeology of the Media," in *ISEA '94*, ed. Minna Tarkka (Helsinki: University of Art and Design, 1994), 130–135.

7. See, for example, Amanda Lotz, *The Television Will Be Revolutionized* (New York: NYU Press, 2007).

8. Jane Feuer, "The Concept of Live Television: Ontology as Ideology," in *Regarding Television*, ed. E. Ann Kaplan (Frederick, MD: University Publications of America, 1983), 12–22; Raymond Williams, *Television: Technology and Cultural Form* (London: Routledge, 1990), 77–120; John Ellis, *Visible Fictions: Cinema, Television, Video* (London: Routledge and Kegan Paul, 1982).

9. Manuel Castells, "Informationalism, Networks, and the Network Society: A Theoretical Blueprint," in *The Network Society: A Cross-Cultural Perspective*, ed. Castells (Cheltenham, UK: Edward Elgar, 2004), 24.

BIBLIOGRAPHY

Web Sources

British Newspaper Archive, https://www.britishnewspaperarchive
.co.uk/.
D'Aloia, Adriano. Arnheim, Cinema, Italy website, https://rudolf
arnheim.net/.
Lange, André. Histoire de la télévision website, https://www.histv
.net/.
Library of Congress, Chronicling America, https://chronicling
america.loc.gov/.
Media History Digital Library, Lantern search platform, http://
lantern.mediahist.org/.

Books and Articles

Abel, Richard, ed. *The Encyclopedia of Early Cinema.* New York:
Routledge, 2004.
Abramson, Albert. *The History of Television, 1880 to 1941.* Jefferson,
NC: McFarland, 1987.
Albera, François. "First Discourses on Film and the Construction
of a 'Cinematic Episteme.'" In *A Companion to Early Cinema,* ed-
ited by André Gaudreault, Nicolas Dulac, and Santiago Hidalgo,
121–140. Malden, MA: Wiley-Blackwell, 2012.
Anderson, Christopher. "Television and Hollywood in the 1940s." In
Boom and Bust: American Cinema in the 1940s, edited by Thomas
Schatz, 422–444. Berkeley: University of California Press, 1997.
Andrew, Dudley, ed. *André Bazin's New Media.* Berkeley: University
of California Press, 2014.
Andrew, Dudley. *The Major Film Theories: An Introduction.* London:
Oxford University Press, 1976.

Andriopoulos, Stefan. "Psychic Television." *Critical Inquiry* 31 (Spring 2005): 618–637.

Arnheim, Rudolf. "Disciplina del grammofono, della radio, del telefono e della televisione." *Sapere* 6, no. 71 (December 15, 1937): 415–417.

Arnheim, Rudolf. "Disciplining the Gramophone, Radio, Telephone, and Television." Translated by Christy Wampole. *Modernism/Modernity* 16, no. 2 (April 2009): 421–426.

Arnheim, Rudolf. *Film*. London: Faber & Faber, 1933.

Arnheim, Rudolf. *Film as Art*. Berkeley: University of California Press, 1957.

Arnheim, Rudolf. *Film Essays and Criticism*. Translated by Brenda Benthien. Madison: University of Wisconsin Press, 1997.

Arnheim, Rudolf. *Radio*. London: Faber & Faber, 1936.

Arnheim, Rudolf. "Seeing Afar Off." *Intercine* 7, no. 2 (February 1935): 71–82.

Arnheim, Rudolf. "Televisione, domani sarà così." *Cinema* 20 (April 1937): 337–338.

Arnheim, Rudolf. "Die Zukunft des Tonfilms" (1934). *Montage A/V* 9, no. 2 (2000): 19–32.

Auerbach, Jonathan. *Body Shots: Early Cinema's Incarnations*. Berkeley: University of California Press, 2007.

Bailey, James Osler. *Pilgrims through Space and Time: Trends and Patterns in Scientific and Utopian Fiction*. New York: Argus Books, 1947.

Baird, John Logie. *Television and Me: The Memoirs of John Logie Baird*. Edited by Malcolm Baird. Edinburgh: Mercat, 2004.

Batchen, Geoffrey. *Burning with Desire: The Conception of Photography*. Cambridge, MA: MIT Press, 1999.

Bazin, André. *What Is Cinema?* Vol. 1. Translated by Hugh Gray. Berkeley: University of California Press, 1967.

Beer, Gillian. *Open Fields: Science in Cultural Encounter*. New York: Oxford University Press, 1996.

Beliayev, Aleksander. *The Struggle in Space*. Translated by Albert Parry. 1928; repr., Washington, DC: Arfor, 1965.

Bellamy, Edward. *Equality*. New York: Appleton and Co., 1913.

Belton, John. "If Film Is Dead, What Is Cinema?" *Screen* 55, no. 4 (Winter 2014): 460–470.

Benjamin, Walter. "Moonlit Nights on the Rue La Boétie." In *Walter Benjamin: Selected Writings*, vol. 1, part 2, *1927–30*, edited by Michael W. Jennings, Howard Eiland, and Gary Smith, 107–109. Cambridge, MA: Belknap Press of Harvard University Press, 2005.

Benjamin, Walter. "On Some Motifs in Baudelaire." In *Walter Benjamin: Selected Writings*, vol. 4, edited by Howard Eiland and Michael W. Jennings, 314–355. Cambridge, MA: Belknap Press of Harvard University Press, 2003.

Benjamin, Walter. "Vorstufen zum Erzahler-Essay." In *Gesammelte Schriften 2*, edited by Rolf Tiedemann and Hermann Schweppenhauser, 1282–1283. Frankfurt am Main: Suhrkamp, 1991.

Benjamin, Walter. "The Work of Art in the Age of Its Technological Reproducibility." In *Walter Benjamin: Selected Writings*, vol. 2, edited by Michael W. Jennings,

Howard Eiland, and Gary Smith, 101–133. Cambridge, MA: Belknap Press of Harvard University Press, 2003.

Berton, Mireille, and Anne-Katrin Weber, eds. *La télévision du téléphonoscope à Youtube: Pour une archéologie de l'audiovision*. Lausanne: Antipodes, 2009.

Bleiler, Everett F., and Richard J. Bleiler. *Science-Fiction, the Early Years*. Kent, Ohio: Kent State University Press, 1990.

Boddy, William. *Fifties Television: The Industry and Its Critics*. Urbana: University of Illinois Press, 1992.

Bolter, Jay David, and Richard Grusin. *Remediation: Understanding New Media*. Cambridge, MA: MIT Press, 1999.

Bordwell, David. *The Way Hollywood Tells It: Story and Style in Modern Movies*. Berkeley: University of California Press, 2006.

Bottomore, Stephen. "'Devant le cinématographe': The Cinema in French Fiction 1896–1914." *KINtop* 13 (2005): 92–110.

Brecht, Bertolt. "The Radio as an Apparatus of Communication" (1932). Translated by John Willett. *Semiotext(e)* 16 (1993): 15–17.

Brown, Richard. Introduction to "Seeing by Wire." *Early Popular Visual Culture* 6, no. 3 (November 2008): 305.

Buck-Morss, Susan. "Aesthetics and Anaesthetics: Walter Benjamin's Artwork Essay Reconsidered." *October* 62 (Autumn 1992): 3–41.

Burns, Russell W. *British Television: The Formative Years*. London: Peregrinus, 1986.

Burns, Russell W. *John Logie Baird: Television Pioneer*. London: Institution of Engineering and Technology, 2000.

Burns, Russell W. *Television: An International History of the Formative Years*. London: Institution of Electrical Engineers, 1998.

Cantril, Hadley. *The Invasion from Mars: A Study in the Psychology of Panic*. New Brunswick, NJ: Transaction, 2005.

Carey, James. "Technology and Ideology: The Case of the Telegraph." In *Communication as Culture: Essays on Media and Society*, 155–177. New York: Routledge, 2009.

Carey, James W., and John J. Quirk. "The Mythos of the Electronic Revolution: Part II." *American Scholar* 39, no. 3 (Summer 1970): 395–424.

Carroll, Noël. *Philosophical Problems of Classical Film Theory*. Princeton, NJ: Princeton University Press, 1988.

Carter, Huntly. *The New Spirit in the Russian Theatre, 1917–28*. New York: Brentano's, 1929.

Casetti, Francesco. *The Lumière Galaxy: Seven Keywords for the Cinema to Come*. New York: Columbia University Press, 2015.

Castells, Manuel. "Informationalism, Networks, and the Network Society: A Theoretical Blueprint." In *The Network Society: A Cross-Cultural Perspective*, edited by Manuel Castells, 3–45. Cheltenham, UK: Edward Elgar, 2004.

Castells, Manuel. *The Internet Galaxy: Reflections on the Internet, Business, and Society*. New York: Oxford University Press, 2001.

Castells, Manuel. "An Introduction to the Information Age." *City* 2, no. 7 (1997): 7–16.

Ceram, C. W. *Archaeology of the Cinema*. London: Thames and Hudson, 1965.

Charney, Leo, and Vanessa R. Schwartz, eds. *Cinema and the Invention of Modern Life*. Berkeley: University of California Press, 1995.

Cherchi Usai, Paolo. *The Death of Cinema: History, Cultural Memory, and the Digital Dark Age*. London: BFI, 2001.

Chun, Wendy Hui Kyong. "Crisis, Crisis, Crisis, or Sovereignty and Network." *Theory, Culture, and Society* 28, no. 6 (2011): 91–112.

Clarke, Edwin, and L. S. Jacyna. *Nineteenth-Century Origins of Neuroscientific Concepts*. Berkeley: University of California Press, 1987.

Comolli, Jean-Louis. "Machines of the Visible." In *The Cinematic Apparatus*, edited by Teresa De Lauretis and Stephen Heath, 121–141. New York: St. Martin's, 1980.

Crafton, Donald. *The Talkies: American Cinema's Transition to Sound, 1926–1931*. New York: Charles Scribner's Sons, 1997.

Crary, Jonathan. *Techniques of the Observer: On Vision and Modernity in the Nineteenth Century*. Cambridge, MA: MIT Press, 1990.

Crary, Jonathan. *24/7: Late Capitalism and the Ends of Sleep*. London: Verso, 2013.

Czitrom, Daniel J. *Media and the American Mind: From Morse to McLuhan*. Chapel Hill: University of North Carolina Press, 1982.

Delavaud, Gilles. "Dziga Vertov ou le cinéma comme anticipation de la télévision." *Dossiers de l'audiovisuel* 112 (November–December 2003): 23–25.

Denson, Shane, and Julia Leyda, eds. *Post-cinema: Theorizing 21st-Century Film*. Falmer, UK: Reframe Books, 2016.

De Paiva, Adriano. *La télescopie électrique basée sur l'emploi du selenium*. Porto: José da Silva, 1880.

de Sola Pool, Ithiel. *Forecasting the Telephone: A Retrospective Technology Assessment of the Telephone*. Norwood, NJ: Ablex, 1983.

Dickson, W. K. L., and Antonia Dickson. *History of the Kinetograph, Kinetoscope and Kinetophonograph*. New York: Albert Bunn, 1895.

Dinsdale, Alfred. *Television: Seeing by Wireless*. London: W. S. Caines, 1926.

Doane, Mary Ann. *The Emergence of Cinematic Time: Modernity, Contingency, the Archive*. Cambridge, MA: Harvard University Press, 2002.

Doane, Mary Ann. "Indexicality and the Concept of Medium Specificity." *Differences* 18, no. 1 (Spring 2007): 128–152.

Doane, Mary Ann. "Information, Crisis, Catastrophe." In *New Media, Old Media: A History and Theory Reader*, edited by Wendy Hui Kyong Chun and Thomas Keenan, 251–264. New York: Routledge, 2006.

Doane, Mary Ann. "The Object of Theory." In *Rites of Realism: Essays on Corporeal Cinema*, edited by Ivone Margulies, 80–89. Durham, NC: Duke University Press, 2003.

Doane, Mary Ann. "Technology's Body: Cinematic Vision in Modernity." In *A Feminist Reader in Early Cinema*, edited by Jennifer Bean and Diane Negra, 530–551. Durham, NC: Duke University Press, 2002.

Donguy, Jacques. "Machine Head: Raoul Hausmann and the Optophone." *Leonardo* 34, no. 3 (June 2001): 217–220.

Douglas, Susan J. *Inventing American Broadcasting, 1899–1922*. Baltimore: Johns Hopkins University Press, 1987.

Druick, Zoë. "The International Educational Cinematograph Institute, Reactionary Modernism, and the Formation of Film Studies." *Canadian Journal of Film Studies* 16, no. 1 (Spring 2007): 80–97.

Edgerton, Gary R. *The Columbia History of American Television*. New York: Columbia University Press, 2009.

Eisenstein, Sergei. *Film Essays and a Lecture*. Edited and translated by Jay Leyda. Princeton, NJ: Princeton University Press, 1968.

Eisenstein, Sergej [*sic*] M. *Schriften 3. Oktober*. Munich: Hanser, 1975.

Ellis, John. *Visible Fictions: Cinema, Television, Video*. London: Routledge and Kegan Paul, 1982.

Elsaesser, Thomas. "Digital Cinema: Delivery, Event, Time." In *Cinema Futures: Cain, Abel or Cable?*, edited by Elsaesser and Kay Hoffmann, 201–222. Amsterdam: Amsterdam University Press, 1998.

Elsaesser, Thomas. "Early Film History and Multi-media: An Archaeology of Possible Futures?" In *New Media, Old Media: A History and Theory Reader*, edited by Wendy Hui Kyong Chun and Thomas Keenan, 13–26. New York: Routledge, 2006.

Elsaesser, Thomas. "Louis Lumière: The Cinema's First Virtualist." In *Cinema Futures: Cain, Abel or Cable?*, edited by Elsaesser and Kay Hoffmann, 45–62. Amsterdam: Amsterdam University Press, 1998.

Elsaesser, Thomas. "Siegfried Kracauer's Affinities." NECSUS (Spring 2014), http://www.necsus-ejms.org/siegfried-kracauers-affinities/.

Elsaesser, Thomas, and Adam Barker, eds. *Early Cinema: Space, Frame, Narrative*. London: BFI, 1990.

Elsaesser, Thomas, and Malte Hagener. *Film Theory: An Introduction through the Senses*. London: Routledge, 2009.

Elsner, Monika, Thomas Müller, and Peter M. Spangenberg. "The Early History of German Television: The Slow Development of a Fast Medium." *Historical Journal of Film, Radio and Television* 10, no. 2 (1990): 193–219.

Enns, Anthony, and Shelley Trower, eds. *Vibratory Modernism*. New York: Palgrave, 2013.

Enzensberger, Hans Magnus. *Critical Essays*. Edited by Reinhold Grimm and Bruce Armstrong. New York: Continuum, 1982.

Ernst, Wolfgang. "Between Real Time and Memory on Demand: Reflections on/of Television." *South Atlantic Quarterly* 101, no. 3 (Summer 2002): 621–637.

Ernst, Wolfgang. *Digital Memory and the Archive*. Edited by Jussi Parikka. Minneapolis: University of Minnesota Press, 2013.

Evans, Arthur B. "The 'New' Jules Verne." *Science Fiction Studies* 22, no. 1 (March 1995): 35–46.

Fanning, William J., Jr. "The Historical Death Ray and Science Fiction in the 1920s and 1930s." *Science Fiction Studies* 37 (2010): 253–274.

Fargier, Jean-Paul. "Le cinéma plus l'électricité." *Cahiers du Cinéma* 406 (April 1988): 56–58.

Felix, Edgar H. *Television: Its Methods and Uses.* New York: McGraw-Hill, 1931.

Feuer, Jane. "The Concept of Live Television: Ontology as Ideology." In *Regarding Television,* edited by E. Ann Kaplan, 12–22. Frederick, MD: University Publications of America, 1983.

Fevralsky, Aleksander. "Currents in Art and the Radio-Eye" (1925). Translated by Andrey Gordienko. *Historical Journal of Film Radio and Television* 28, no. 1 (March 2008): 65–70.

Flichy, Patrice. *Dynamics of Modern Communication: The Shaping and Impact of New Communication Technologies.* Translated by Liz Libbrecht. London: Sage, 1995.

Flichy, Patrice. *Understanding Technological Innovation: A Socio-Technical Approach.* Translated by Liz Carey-Libbrecht. Cheltenham, UK: Edward Elgar, 2007.

Forster, E. M. *The Machine Stops and Other Stories.* London: Andre Deutsch, 1997.

Foster, Hal. "Prosthetic Gods." *Modernism/Modernity* 4, no. 2 (1997): 5–38.

Foucault, Michel. *Discipline and Punish: The Birth of the Prison.* Translated by Alan Sheridan. New York: Vintage, 1977.

Fournier d'Albe, Edmund Edward. *The Moon Element: An Introduction to the Wonder of Selenium.* New York: D. Appleton and Co., 1924.

Freud, Sigmund. *Civilization and Its Discontents.* Translated by James Strachey. New York: Norton, 1961.

Friedberg, Ann. "The End of Cinema: Multimedia and Technological Change." In *Reinventing Film Studies,* edited by Christine Gledhill and Linda Williams, 438–452. London: Arnold, 2000.

Friedberg, Ann. *Window Shopping: Cinema and the Postmodern.* Berkeley: University of California Press, 1993.

Galili, Doron. Introduction to Aleksander Fevralsky, "Currents in Art and the Radio-Eye." *Historical Journal of Film Radio and Television* 28, no. 1 (March 2008): 61–65.

Galili, Doron. "Postmediales Wissen um 1900: Zur Medienarchäologie des Fernsehens." *Montage AV* 25, no. 2 (2016): 181–200.

Galloway, Alexander. *The Interface Effect.* Cambridge: Polity, 2012.

Garvey, Michael Angelo. *The Silent Revolution, or, The Future Effects of Steam and Electricity upon the Condition of Mankind.* London: William and Frederick G. Cash, 1852.

Gaudreault, André. "The Diversity of Cinematographic Connections in the Intermedial Context of the Turn of the 20th Century." In *Visual Delights: Essay on the Popular and Projected Image in the 19th Century,* edited by Simon Popple and Vanessa Toulmin, 8–15. Trowbridge, UK: Flicks Books, 2000.

Gaudreault, André. *Film and Attraction: From Kinematography to Cinema.* Translated by Timothy Barnard. Urbana: University of Illinois Press, 2011.

Gaudreault, André. *From Plato to Lumière: Narration and Monstration in Literature and Cinema.* Translated by Timothy Barnard. Toronto: University of Toronto Press, 2009.

Gaudreault, André. "Temporality and Narrativity in Early Cinema, 1895–1908." In

Film before Griffith, edited by John Fell, 311–329. Berkeley: University of California Press, 1983.

Gaudreault, André, and Philippe Marion. *The End of Cinema? A Medium in Crisis in the Digital Age.* Translated by Timothy Barnard. New York: Columbia University Press, 2015.

Gaudreault, André, and Philippe Marion. "A Medium Is Always Born Twice . . . " *Early Popular Visual Culture* 3, no. 1 (May 2005): 3–15.

Gitelman, Lisa. *Always Already New: Media, History, and the Data of Culture.* Cambridge, MA: MIT Press, 2006.

Gitelman, Lisa. "How Users Define New Media: A History of the Amusement Phonograph." In *Rethinking Media Change: The Aesthetics of Transition,* edited by David Thorburn and Henry Jenkins, 61–80. Cambridge, MA: MIT Press, 2003.

Gitelman, Lisa. *Scripts, Grooves, and Writing Machines: Representing Technology in the Edison Era.* Stanford, CA: Stanford University Press, 1999.

Gitelman, Lisa, and Geoffrey Pingree. "Introduction: What's New about New Media?" In *New Media 1740–1915,* edited by Gitelman and Pingree, xi–xxii. Cambridge, MA: MIT Press, 2003.

Godfrey, Donald G. *C. Francis Jenkins, Pioneer of Film and Television.* Urbana: University of Illinois Press, 2014.

Gomery, Douglas. "The Coming of Television and the 'Lost' Motion Picture Audience." *Journal of Film and Video* 37, no. 3 (1985): 5–11.

Gomery, Douglas. "Failed Opportunities: The Integration of the U.S. Motion Picture and Television Industries." *Quarterly Review of Film Studies* 9, no. 3 (1984): 219–228.

Gomery, Douglas. "Theatre Television: The Missing Link of Technological Change in the U.S. Motion Picture Industry." *Velvet Light Trap* 21 (1985): 54–61.

Gomery, Douglas, and Clara Pafort-Overduin. *Movie History: A Survey.* 2nd ed. New York: Routledge, 2011.

Gough, Maria. "Switched On: Notes on Radio, Automata, and the Bright Red Star." In *Building the Collective: Soviet Graphic Design 1917–1937,* edited by Leah Dickerman, 39–55. New York: Princeton Architectural Press, 1996.

Gregory, R. L. *Eye and Brain: The Psychology of Vision.* Princeton, NJ: Princeton University Press, 1997.

Gunning, Tom. "An Aesthetic of Astonishment: Early Film and the (In)Credulous Spectator." *Art and Text* 34 (1989): 31–45.

Gunning, Tom. "The Birth of Film out of the Spirit of Modernity." In *Masterpieces of Modernist Cinema,* edited by Ted Perry, 13–40. Bloomington: Indiana University Press, 2006.

Gunning, Tom. "Heard over the Phone: *The Lonely Villa* and the De Lorde Tradition of Terrified Communication." *Screen* 32, no. 2 (Summer 1991): 184–196.

Gunning, Tom. "Modernity and Cinema: A Culture of Shocks and Flows." In *Cinema and Modernity,* edited by Murray Pomerance, 297–315. New Brunswick, NJ: Rutgers University Press, 2006.

Gunning, Tom. "Systematizing the Electric Message: Narrative Form, Gender and Modernity in *The Lonedale Operator.*" In *American Cinema's Transitional Era,* edited by Charlie Keil and Shelley Stamp, 15–50. Berkeley: University of California Press, 2004.

Gunning, Tom. "Tracing the Individual Body: Photography, Detectives, and Early Cinema." In *Cinema and the Invention of Modern Life*, edited by Leo Charney and Vanessa R. Schwartz, 15–45. Berkeley: University of California Press, 1995.

Gunning, Tom. "Weaving a Narrative: Style and Economic Background in Griffith's Biograph Films." In *Early Cinema: Space, Frame, Narrative*, edited by Thomas Elsaesser and Adam Barker, 336–347. London: BFI, 1990.

Gunning, Tom. "The Whole Town's Gawking: Early Cinema and the Visual Experience of Modernity." *Yale Journal of Criticism* 7, no. 2 (1994): 189–201.

Hansen, Miriam Bratu. "America, Paris, the Alps: Kracauer (and Benjamin) on Cinema and Modernity." In *Cinema and the Invention of Modern Life*, edited by Leo Charney and Vanessa R. Schwartz, 362–402. Berkeley: University of California Press, 1995.

Hansen, Miriam. *Babel and Babylon: Spectatorship in American Silent Film*. Cambridge, MA: Harvard University Press, 1991.

Hansen, Miriam Bratu. *Cinema and Experience: Siegfried Kracauer, Walter Benjamin, and Theodor W. Adorno*. Berkeley: University of California Press, 2012.

Harben, William N. *The Land of Changing Sun*. 1894; repr., Middlesex, UK: Echo Library, 2007.

Harris, Neil. "Utopian Fiction and Its Discontents." In *Cultural Excursions: Marketing Appetites and Cultural Tastes in Modern America*, 150–173. Chicago: University of Chicago Press, 1990.

Hathaway, Kenneth. *Television: A Practical Treatise on the Principles upon Which the Development of Television Is Based*. Chicago: American Technical Society, 1933.

Hendricks, Gordon. *The Edison Motion Picture Myth*. Berkeley: University of California Press, 1961.

Hendy, David. "Television's Prehistory: Radio." In *The Television History Book*, edited by Michele Hilmes, 4–7. London: BFI, 2008.

Herbert, Stephen, ed. *A History of Early Television*. 3 vols. New York: Routledge, 2004.

Hicks, Jeremy. *Dziga Vertov: Defining Documentary Film*. London: I. B. Tauris, 1999.

Hilmes, Michele. *Hollywood and Broadcasting: From Radio to Cable*. Urbana: University of Illinois Press, 1990.

Hilmes, Michele. "NBC and the Network Idea: Defining the 'American System.'" In *NBC: America's Network*, edited by Michele Hilmes, 7–24. Berkeley: University of California Press, 2007.

Hong, Sungook. "Marconi and the Maxwellians: The Origins of Wireless Telegraphy Revisited." *Technology and Culture* 35, no. 4 (October 1994): 717–749.

Horkheimer, Max, and Theodor Adorno. *Dialectic of Enlightenment*. Translated by Edmund Jephcott. Stanford, CA: Stanford University Press, 2002.

Huhtamo, Erkki. "From Kaleidoscomaniac to Cybernerd: Towards an Archeology of the Media." In *ISEA '94*, edited by Minna Tarkka, 130–135. Helsinki: University of Art and Design, 1994.

Huhtamo, Erkki. "Seeing at a Distance: Towards an Archaeology of the Small

Screen." In *Art@Science*, edited by Christa Sommerer and Laurent Mignonneau, 262–278. Vienna: Springer, 1998.

Innis, Harold A. *Empire and Communications*. Edited by David Godfrey. Toronto: Press Porcépic, 1986.

Jacobs, Jason. *The Intimate Screen: Early British Television Drama*. Oxford: Oxford University Press, 2000.

Jenkins, Charles Francis. *Animated Pictures: An Exposition of the Historical Development of Chronophotography, Its Present Scientific Applications and Future Possibilities*. Washington, DC: Press of H. L. McQueen, 1898.

Jenkins, Charles Francis. *The Boyhood of an Inventor*. Washington, DC: National Capital Press, 1931.

Jenkins, Charles Francis. *Radiomovies, Radiovision, Television*. Washington, DC: National Capital Press, 1929.

Jenkins, Henry. "Convergence? I Diverge." *Technology Review*, June 2001, 93.

Jenkins, Henry. *Convergence Culture: Where Old and New Media Collide*. New York: New York University Press, 2006.

Jewell, Richard B. "Hollywood and Radio: Competition and Partnership in the 1930s." *Historical Journal of Film, Radio and Television* 4, no. 2 (1984): 125–141.

John, Richard R. *Network Nation: Inventing American Telecommunications*. Cambridge, MA: Belknap Press of Harvard University Press, 2010.

Jones, Samuel. *The New Right: A Plea for Fair Play through a More Just Social Order*. New York: Eastern Book Concern, 1899.

Jowett, Garth. "Dangling the Dream? The Presentation of Television to the American Public, 1928–1952." *Historical Journal of Film, Radio, and Television* 14, no. 2 (1994): 121–145.

Kac, Eduardo. *Telepresence and Bio-Art: Networking Humans, Rabbits, and Robots*. Ann Arbor: University of Michigan Press, 2005.

Kaes, Anton. "War—Film—Trauma." In *Modernität und Trauma: Beiträge zum Zeitenbruch des Ersten Weltkrieges*, edited by Inka Mülder-Bach, 121–130. Vienna: Edition Parabasen, 2000.

Keil, Charlie, and Shelley Stamp, eds. *American Cinema's Transitional Era: Audiences, Institutions, Practices*. Berkeley: University of California Press, 2004.

Kern, Stephen. *The Culture of Time and Space, 1880–1918*. Cambridge, MA: Harvard University Press, 1983.

Khlebnikov, Velimir. "The Radio of the Future" (1921). Translated by Gary Kern. *Semiotext(e)* 16 (1993): 32–35.

Kingsbury, John E. *The Telephone and Telephone Exchanges: Their Invention and Development*. London: Longmans Greens and Co., 1915.

Kirby, Lynn. *Parallel Tracks: The Railroad and Silent Cinema*. Durham, NC: Duke University Press, 1997.

Kittler, Friedrich A. *Discourse Networks 1800/1900*. Stanford, CA: Stanford University Press, 1990.

Kittler, Friedrich A. *Gramophone, Film, Typewriter*. Translated by Geoffrey Winthrop-Young and Michael Wutz. Stanford, CA: Stanford University Press, 1999.

Koszarski, Richard. "Coming Next Week: Images of Television in Pre-war Motion Pictures." *Film History* 10, no. 2 (1998): 128–140.

Koszarski, Richard. *Hollywood on the Hudson: Film and Television in New York from Griffith to Sarnoff.* New Brunswick, NJ: Rutgers University Press, 2008.

Koszarski, Richard, and Doron Galili. "Television in the Cinema before 1939: An International Annotated Database." *Journal of E-Media Studies* 5, no. 1 (2016), http://journals.dartmouth.edu/cgi-bin/WebObjects/Journals.woa/xmlpage/4/article/471.

Kracauer, Siegfried. *The Mass Ornament: Weimar Essays.* Edited and translated by Thomas Levin. Cambridge, MA: Harvard University Press, 1995.

Kracauer, Siegfried. *Theory of Film: The Redemption of Physical Reality.* Princeton, NJ: Princeton University Press, 1960.

Kramer, Peter. "The Lure of the Big Picture: Film, Television and Hollywood." In *Big Picture, Small Screen: The Relations between Film and Television,* edited by John Hill and Martin McLoone, 9–46. Luton, UK: John Libbey, 1996.

Krauss, Rosalind. "Photography's Discursive Spaces: Landscape/View." *Art Journal* 42, no. 4 (Winter 1982): 311–319.

Krauss, Rosalind. "Two Moments from the Post-medium Condition." *October* 116 (Spring 2006): 55–62.

Larner, Edgar Thomas. *Practical Television.* New York: D. Van Nostrand, 1928.

Lastra, James. *Sound Technology and American Cinema: Perception, Representation, Modernity.* New York: Columbia University Press, 2000.

Lenning, Arthur. *The Immortal Count: The Life and Films of Bela Lugosi.* Lexington: University Press of Kentucky, 2003.

Lenoir, Timothy. "Helmholtz and the Materialities of Communication." *Osiris* 9 (1994): 184–207.

Lessing, Gotthold Ephraim. *Laocoön: An Essay on the Limits of Poetry and Painting.* Boston: Roberts Brothers, 1887.

Levine, Elana. "Distinguishing Television: The Changing Meanings of Television Liveness." *Media, Culture and Society* 30, no. 3 (2008): 393–409.

Lodge, Oliver. *The Ether of Space.* New York: Harper and Brothers, 1909.

Lodge, Oliver. *Signaling across Space without Wires: Being a Description of the Works of Hertz and His Successors.* London: Electrician Printing and Publishing, 1900.

Lotz, Amanda. *The Television Will Be Revolutionized.* New York: NYU Press, 2007.

Mannoni, Laurent. "The Art of Deception." In *Eyes, Lies and Illusion: The Art of Deception,* edited by Mannoni, Werner Nekes, and Marina Warner, 41–52. London: Hayward Gallery, 2004.

Mannoni, Laurent. *The Great Art of Light and Shadow: Archaeology of the Cinema.* Translated by Richard Crangle. Exeter: University of Exeter Press, 2000.

Marinetti, F. T. *Critical Writings.* Edited by Gunter Berghaus, translated by Doug Thompson. New York: Farrar, Straus and Giroux, 2006.

Marvin, Carolyn. *When Old Technologies Were New.* New York: Oxford University Press, 1988.

Marx, Karl, and Friedrich Engels. *The Communist Manifesto: A Modern Edition.* Translated by Samuel Moore. London: Verso, 2012.

Matuszewski, Bolesław. "A New Source of History: The Creation of a Depository for Historical Cinematography" (1898). Translated by Laura U. Marks and Diane Koszarski. *Film History* 7, no. 3 (Autumn 1995): 322–324.

Mayakovsky, Vladimir. *The Bedbug and Selected Poetry.* Edited by Patricia Blake and translated by Max Hayward and George Reavey. Bloomington: Indiana University Press, 1960.

McChesney, Robert. *Telecommunications, Mass Media, and Democracy: The Battle for the Control of U.S. Broadcasting, 1928–1935.* Oxford: Oxford University Press, 1993.

McLuhan, Marshall. *Understanding Media: The Extensions of Man.* Cambridge, MA: MIT Press, 1994.

McNair, Brian. *Glasnost, Perestroika, and the Soviet Media.* London: Routledge, 1991.

Melnick, Ross. *American Showman: Samuel "Roxy" Rothafel and the Birth of the Entertainment Industry, 1908–1935.* New York: Columbia University Press, 2012.

Merjian, Ara. "Middlebrow Modernism: Rudolf Arnheim at the Crossroads of Film Theory and the Psychology of Art." In *The Visual Turn: Classical Film Theory and Art History,* edited by Angela Dalle Vacche, 154–192. New Brunswick, NJ: Rutgers University Press, 2003.

Michelson, Annette. "From Magician to Epistemologist: Vertov's *The Man with a Movie Camera.*" *Artforum* 10, no. 7 (February 1971): 60–72.

Miller, Toby. *Television Studies: The Basics.* London: Routledge, 2009.

Mills, John. *Through Electrical Eyes.* New York: Bell Telephone Laboratories, 1928.

Morus, Iwan Rhys. "The Measure of Man: Technologizing the Victorian Body." *History of Science* 37 (1999): 249–282.

Morus, Iwan Rhys. "The Nervous System of Britain: Space, Time and the Electric Telegraph in the Victorian Age." *British Journal for the History of Science* 3, no. 4 (December 2000): 455–475.

Moussinac, Léon. "From Georges Méliès to S. M. Eisenstein." *Experimental Cinema* 1, no. 2 (June 1930): 21–22.

Mulvey, Laura. *Death 24x a Second: Stillness and the Moving Image.* London: Reaktion Books, 2006.

Munro, John. *The Romance of Electricity.* London: Religious Tract Society, 1893.

Musser, Charles. *The Emergence of Cinema: The American Screen to 1907.* New York: Scribner's, 1990.

Musser, Charles. "Stereopticon and Cinema: Media Form or Platform?" In *Cine-Dispositives: Essays in Epistemology across Media,* edited by François Albera and Maria Tortajada, 129–159. Amsterdam: Amsterdam University Press, 2014.

Newman, Michael Z. *Video Revolutions: On the History of a Medium.* New York: Columbia University Press, 2014.

Noam, Eli. *Television in Europe.* Oxford: Oxford University Press, 1991.

Nowell-Smith, Geoffrey, ed. *The Oxford History of World Cinema.* Oxford: Oxford University Press, 1996.

Nye, David. *Electrifying America: Social Meanings of a New Technology.* Cambridge, MA: MIT Press, 1990.

Otis, Laura. "The Metaphoric Circuit: Organic and Technological Communication in the Nineteenth Century." *Journal of the History of Ideas* 63, no. 1 (2002): 105–128.

Otis, Laura. *Networking: Communicating with Bodies and Machines in the Nineteenth Century.* Ann Arbor: University of Michigan Press, 2001.

Otter, Chris. *The Victorian Eye: A Political History of Light and Vision in Britain, 1800–1910.* Chicago: University of Chicago Press, 2008.

Papazian, Elizabeth Astrid. *Manufacturing Truth: The Documentary Moment in Early Soviet Culture.* DeKalb: Northern Illinois University Press, 2009.

Parikka, Jussi. *What Is Media Archaeology?* Cambridge: Polity, 2012.

Passuth, Krisztina, ed. *Moholy-Nagy.* New York: Thames and Hudson, 1985.

Peters, John Durham. "Helmholtz, Edison, and Sound History." In *Memory Bytes: History, Technology, and Digital Culture,* edited by Lauren Rabinovitz and Abraham Geil, 177–198. Durham, NC: Duke University Press, 2004.

Peters, John Durham. *The Marvelous Clouds: Toward a Philosophy of Elemental Media.* Chicago: University of Chicago Press, 2015.

Peters, John Durham. "Technology and Ideology: The Case of the Telegraph Revisited." In *Thinking with James Carey: Essays on Communications, Transportation, History,* edited by Jeremy Packer and Craig Robertson, 137–155. New York: Peter Lang, 2006.

Pfaelzer, Jean. *The Utopian Novel in America, 1886–1896: The Politics of Form.* Pittsburgh: University of Pittsburgh Press, 1984.

Pierce, David. "'Senile Celluloid': Independent Exhibitors, the Major Studios and the Fight over Feature Films on Television, 1939–1956." *Film History* 10, no. 2 (1998): 141–164.

Pisano, Giusy. "The Théâtrophone, an Anachronistic Hybrid Experiment or One of the First Immobile Traveler Devices?" In *A Companion to Early Cinema,* edited by André Gaudreault, Nicolas Dulac, and Santiago Hidalgo, 80–98. Malden, MA: Wiley-Blackwell, 2012.

Plessner, Maximilian. *Ein Blick auf die grossen Erfindungen des zwanzigsten Jahrhunderts I: Die Zukunft des elektrischen Fernsehens.* Berlin: F. Dümmler, 1893.

Poggioli, Renato. *The Theory of the Avant-Garde.* Translated by Gerald Fitzgerald. New York: Harper and Row, 1968.

Prescott, George Bartlett. *The Speaking Telephone, Talking Phonograph, and Other Novelties.* New York: D. Appleton and Co., 1878.

Puyal, Alfonso. *Arte y radiovisión: Experiencias de los movimientos históricos de vanguardia con la televisión.* Madrid: Editorial Complutense, 2009.

Rabinbach, Anson. *The Human Motor: Energy, Fatigue, and the Origins of Modernity.* Berkeley: University of California Press, 1992.

Roberts, Adam. *The History of Science Fiction.* Basingstoke, UK: Palgrave Macmillan, 2006.

Roberts, Graham. *Forward Soviet! History and Non-fiction Film in the USSR.* London: I. B. Tauris, 1999.

Roberts, Ivy. "Edison's Telephonoscope: The Visual Telephone and the Satire of Electric Light Mania." *Early Popular Visual Culture* 15, no. 1 (2017): 1–25.

Robida, Albert. *The Twentieth Century.* Middletown, CT: Wesleyan University Press, 2004.

Robinson, Edward A., and George A. Wall. *The Disk: A Tale of Two Passions.* Boston: Cupples, Upham and Co., 1884.

Rodowick, D. N. *Elegy for Theory.* Cambridge, MA: Harvard University Press, 2014.

Rodowick, D. N. *The Virtual Life of Film.* Cambridge, MA: Harvard University Press, 2007.

Roemer, Kenneth M. *The Obsolete Necessity: America in Utopian Writings, 1888–1900.* Kent, Ohio: Kent State University Press, 1976.

Rosen, Philip. *Change Mummified: Cinema, Historicity, Theory.* Minneapolis: University of Minnesota Press, 2001.

Rossell, Deac. *Living Pictures: The Origins of the Movies.* Albany: State University of New York Press, 1998.

Rotha, Paul. *The Film till Now: A Survey of the Cinema.* New York: Jonathan Cape and Harrison Smith, 1930.

Russo, Alexander. "Defensive Transcriptions: Radio Networks, Sound-on-Disc Recording, and the Meaning of Live Broadcasting." *Velvet Light Trap* 54 (Fall 2004): 4–17.

Sarnoff, David. *Pioneering in Television: Prophecy and Fulfillment.* New York: Radio Corporation of America, 1946.

Schickore, Jutta. "Locating Rods and Cones: Microscopic Investigations of the Retina in Mid-Nineteenth-Century Berlin and Wurzburg." *Science in Context* 13, no. 1 (2000): 137–152.

Schivelbusch, Wolfgang. *The Railway Journey: The Industrialization of Time and Space in the Nineteenth Century.* Berkeley: University of California Press, 1986.

Schwoch, James. "Selling the Sight/Site of Sound: Broadcast Advertising and the Transition from Radio to Television." *Cinema Journal* 30, no. 1 (Fall 1990): 55–66.

Sconce, Jeffrey. *Haunted Media: Electronic Presence from Telegraphy to Television.* Durham, NC: Duke University Press, 2000.

Seldes, Gilbert. "The 'Errors' of Television." *Atlantic* 159, no. 5 (May 1937): 531–541.

Seldes, Gilbert. *Writing for Television.* New York: Doubleday, 1952.

Seltzer, Mark. *Bodies and Machines.* New York: Routledge, 1992.

Sewell, Philip. *Television in the Age of Radio: Modernity, Imagination, and the Making of a Medium.* New Brunswick, NJ: Rutgers University Press, 2014.

Shamberg, Michael, and Raindance Corporation. *Guerrilla Television.* New York: Holt, Rinehart and Winston, 1971.

Shaviro, Steven. *Connected, or What It Means to Live in the Network Society.* Minneapolis: University of Minnesota Press, 2003.

Shiers, George. *Early Television: A Bibliographic Guide to 1940.* New York: Garland, 1997.

Shiers, George. "Historical Notes on Television before 1900." *SMPTE Journal* 86, no. 3 (March 1977): 129–137.

Shmakov, Paul. "The Development of Television in the USSR." *Journal of the Television Society* (March 1936): 97–105.

Shmakov, Paul. "Television in the USSR." *Journal of the Television Society* (March 1932): 126–130.

Singer, Ben. "The Ambimodernity of Early Cinema." In *Film 1900: Technology, Perception, Culture,* edited by Annemone Ligensa and Klaus Kreimeier, 37–51. Eastleigh, UK: John Libbey, 2009.

Singer, Ben. *Melodrama and Modernity: Early Sensational Cinema and Its Contexts.* New York: Columbia University Press, 2001.

Smoodin, Eric. "Motion Pictures and Television, 1930–1945: A Pre-history of the Relations between the Two Media." *Journal of the University Film and Video Association* 34, no. 3 (Summer 1982): 3–8.

Somaini, Antonio. "Cinema as 'Dynamic Mummification,' History as Montage: Eisenstein's Media Archaeology." In *Sergei Eisenstein: Notes for a General History of Cinema,* edited by Naum Kleiman and Somaini, 19–105. Amsterdam: Amsterdam University Press, 2016.

Spehr, Paul. *The Man Who Made Movies: W. K. L. Dickson.* New Barnet, UK: John Libbey, 2008.

Spigel, Lynn. *Make Room for TV: Television and the Family Ideal in Postwar America.* Chicago: University of Chicago Press, 1992.

Spigel, Lynn, and Jan Olsson, eds. *Television after TV: Essays on a Medium in Transition.* Durham, NC: Duke University Press, 2004.

Stadel, Luke. "Television as a Sound Medium, 1922–1994." PhD diss., Northwestern University, 2015.

Standage, Tom. *The Victorian Internet.* New York: Walker and Co., 1998.

Stephens, Carlene. "'The Most Reliable Time': William Bond, the New England Railroads, and Time Awareness in 19th-Century America." *Technology and Culture* 30, no. 1 (January 1989): 1–24.

Stern, Robert H. "Regulatory Influences upon Television's Development: Early Years under the Federal Radio Commission." *American Journal of Economics and Sociology* 22 (April 1963): 347–362.

Sterne, Jonathan. *The Audible Past: Cultural Origins of Sound Reproduction.* Durham, NC: Duke University Press, 2003.

Sterne, Jonathan. "Television under Construction: American Television and the Problem of Distribution, 1926–62." *Media, Culture and Society* 21 (1992): 503–530.

Stewart, Garrett. *Framed Time: Towards Postfilmic Cinema.* Chicago: University of Chicago Press, 2007.

Stites, Richard. *Revolutionary Dreams: Utopian Vision and Experimental Life in the Russian Revolution.* Oxford: Oxford University Press, 1989.

Stokes, Jane. *On Screen Rivals: Cinema and Television in the United States and Britain.* New York: St. Martin's, 2000.

Strauven, Wanda. "The Imagination of Wireless Distribution." In *Networks of Entertainment: Early Film Distribution 1895–1915,* edited by Frank Kessler and Nanna Verhoeff, 295–303. Eastleigh, UK: John Libbey, 2007.

Streeter, Thomas. *Selling the Air: A Critique of the Policy of Commercial Broadcasting in the United States.* Chicago: University of Chicago Press, 1996.

Swift, John. *Adventure in Vision: The First Twenty-Five Years of Television*. London: John Lehmann, 1950.

Taylor, Richard, and Ian Christie, eds. *The Film Factory: Russian and Soviet Cinema in Documents*. Cambridge, MA: Harvard University Press, 1988.

Terpak, Frances, and Barbara Stafford, eds. *Devices of Wonder: From the World in a Box to Images on a Screen*. Los Angeles: Getty Publications, 2001.

Tomas, David. *Vertov, Snow, Farocki: Machine Vision and the Posthuman*. New York: Bloomsbury, 2013.

Trotsky, Leon. "Radio, Science, Technology and Society" (1926). *Semiotext(e)* 16 (1993): 241–252.

Tsivian, Yuri, ed. *Lines of Resistance: Dziga Vertov and the 1920s*. Pordenone, Italy: Le Giornate del Cinema Muto, 2004.

Turvey, Malcolm. "Can the Camera See? Mimesis in *Man with a Movie Camera*." *October* 89 (Summer 1999): 25–50.

Twain, Mark. "From the London Times of 1904." In *The Writings of Mark Twain*, vol. 22, 276–292. New York: Harper and Brothers, 1899.

Udelson, Joseph H. *The Great Television Race: A History of the American Television Industry, 1925–1941*. Tuscaloosa: University of Alabama Press, 1982.

Uricchio, William. "Cinema as Detour? Towards a Reconsideration of Moving Image Technology in the Late 19th Century." In *Der Film in der Geschichte*, edited by Knut Hickethier, Eggo Müller, and Rainer Rother, 19–25. Berlin: Edition Sigma, 1997.

Uricchio, William. "Contextualizing the Broadcast Era: Nation, Commerce, and Constraint." *Annals of the American Academy of Political and Social Science* 625 (September 2009): 60–73.

Uricchio, William. "Storage, Simultaneity and the Media Technologies of Modernity." In *Allegories of Communication: Intermedial Concerns from Cinema to the Digital*, edited by John Fullerton and Jan Olsson, 123–138. Eastleigh, UK: John Libbey, 2004.

Uricchio, William. "Television as History: Representations of German Television Broadcasting, 1935–1944." In *Framing the Past: The Historiography of German Cinema and Television*, edited by Bruce A. Murray and Christopher J. Wickham, 167–197. Carbondale: Southern Illinois University Press, 1992.

Uricchio, William. "Television's First Seventy-Five Years: The Interpretive Flexibility of a Medium in Transition." In *The Oxford Handbook of Film and Media Studies*, edited Robert Kolker, 286–305. Oxford: Oxford University Press, 2008.

Uricchio, William. "Ways of Seeing: The New Vision of Early Non-fiction Film." In *Uncharted Territory: Essays on Nonfiction Film*, edited by Daan Hertogs and Nico de Klerk, 119–131. Amsterdam: Stichting Nederlands Filmmuseum, 1997.

Verdegiglio, Diego. *La TV di Mussolini: Sperimentazioni televisive nel ventennio fascista*. Rome: Cooper & Castelvecchi, 2003.

Verne, Jules. "In the Year 2889." In *Collected Works of Jules Verne*, 69–84. Charleston, SC: Bibliobazaar, 2007.

Vertov, Dziga. *Kino-Eye: The Writings of Dziga Vertov*. Edited by Annette Michelson. Berkeley: University of California Press, 1984.

Vianello, Robert. "The Power Politics of 'Live' Television." *Journal of Film and Video* 38 (Summer 1985): 26–40.

von Helmholtz, Hermann. *Popular Lectures on Scientific Subjects*. New York: D. Appleton and Co., 1897.

von Schilling, James. *The Magic Window: American Television 1939–1953*. New York: Haworth, 2003.

Weber, Anne-Katrin. "Audio-Visionen um 1880: Zum Beispiel George Du Mauriers Edison's Telephonoscope." In *Medien in Raum und Zeit: Maßverhältnisse des Medialen*, edited by Ingo Köster and Kai Schubert, 293–312. Bielefeld, Germany: Transcript, 2009.

Weber, Anne-Katrin. "Recording on Film, Transmitting by Signals: The Intermediate Film System and Television's Hybridity in the Interwar Period." *Grey Room* 56 (Summer 2014): 6–33.

Weber, Anne-Katrin. "Television before TV: A Transnational History of an Experimental Medium on Display, 1928–1939." PhD diss., Université de Lausanne, 2014.

Wees, William C. *Light Moving in Time: Studies in the Visual Aesthetics of Avant-Garde Film*. Berkeley: University of California Press, 1992.

Welch, Walter L., and Leah Brodbeck Stenzel Burt. *From Tinfoil to Stereo: The Acoustic Years of the Recording Industry, 1877–1929*. Gainesville: University Press of Florida, 1994.

Wells, H. G. *Thirty Strange Stories*. New York: Harper and Brothers, 1898.

Wells, H. G. *When the Sleeper Wakes*. London: Harper and Brothers, 1899.

Wenzlhuemer, Roland. *Connecting the Nineteenth-Century World: The Telegraph and Globalization*. Cambridge: Cambridge University Press, 2013.

Whissel, Kristen. *Picturing American Modernity: Traffic, Technology, and the Silent Cinema*. Durham, NC: Duke University Press, 2008.

White, Mimi. "The Attractions of Television: Reconsidering Liveness." In *Mediaspace: Place, Scale, and Culture in a Media*, edited by Nick Couldry and Anna McCarthy, 75–91. London: Routledge, 2004.

Wilke, Jürgen. "Cinematography as a Medium of Communication: The Promotion of Research by the League of Nations and the Role of Rudolf Arnheim." *European Journal of Communication* 6 (1991): 337–353.

Willaert, Tom. "How Literature Imagined Television, 1880–1950." *Orbis Litterarum* 72, no. 6 (2017): 591–610.

Williams, Mark. "History in a Flash: Notes on the Myth of TV Liveness." In *Collecting Visible Evidence*, edited by Jane Gaines and Michael Renov, 292–312. Minneapolis: University of Minnesota Press, 1999.

Williams, Raymond. *Television: Technology and Cultural Form*. London: Routledge, 1990.

Winker, Klaus. *Fernsehen unterm Hakenkreuz: Organisation, Programm, Personal*. Cologne: Böhlau, 1994.

Winston, Brian. *Media Technology and Society: A History. From the Telegraph to the Internet*. New York: Routledge, 1998.

Young, Paul. *The Cinema Dreams Its Rivals: Media Fantasy Films from Radio to the Internet*. Minneapolis: University of Minnesota Press, 2005.

Young, Paul. "Media on Display: A Telegraphic History of Early American Cinema." In *New Media 1740–1915*, edited by Lisa Gitelman and Geoffrey B. Pingree, 229–264. Cambridge, MA: MIT Press, 2003.

Zamayatin, Yevgeny. *We*. Translated by Clarence Brown. New York: Penguin Books, 1993.

Zielinski, Siegfried. *Audiovisions: Cinema and Television as Entr'actes in History*. Translated by Gloria Custance. Amsterdam: Amsterdam University Press, 1999.

Zielinski, Siegfried. *Deep Time of the Media: Toward an Archaeology of Hearing and Seeing by Technical Means*. Translated by Gloria Custance. Cambridge, MA: MIT Press, 2006.

INDEX

Page numbers in italics refer to illustrations.

body, human: the brain, 55, 62, 68; disembodiment and transport, 69–71; fatigue and, 58–59; limbs, 67, 72; the mind, 177–78; self-preservation strategy, 71–72; technologized, 53–54, 73. *See also* eye, human; nervous system
Bolter, Jay David, 95, 128
Bordwell, David, 134
Bottomore, Stephen, 99, 139
bourgeoisie, 30, 36, 37, 152, 160
Brecht, Bertolt, 153
broadcasting model, 12, 109, 120, 187, 188. *See also* radio broadcasting; television broadcasting

camera, motion picture, 84, 139; crosscutting sequences, 162; human eye association, 67–68, 154; point-of-view shots, 97, 182; television, 123, 125; as a witness trope, 99–101. *See also* montage
Cameraman's Revenge, The (1913), 99, 100
camera obscura, 18, 23, 73; human eye association, 57, 59, 62–63, 65
capital, 28, 41, 118
capitalism, 29, 41, 42, 58, 120, 159
Carey, James, 26, 29
Casetti, Francesco, 128–29
Castells, Manuel, 33, 41, 188
catastrophes, 100, 123, 143–44
chromolithograph illustration, 75, 76
Chun, Wendy, 41
cinema of attractions, 46, 47, 48
cinema-television relationship: artistic potential, 171–73; convergence and divergence, 25, 74–75, 92–93, 128–29, 183; development trajectories, 42–43, 114–15, 154–55, 185; film theory, 168–70; intermedial connection/clash, 18, 127–28, 134–35, 136, 140, 169; liveness ontology and, 90, 127, 143, 168, 203n50; media identity, 121–22; modes of representation, 45–48; recording and transmission distinction, 6–8, 11, 43–45, 75–76, 88–89; rivalry, 12, 126–27; spectatorship, 129–34, 143–44; temporal differences, 43–45, 155–57
cinematic image, 88–89
cinematic medium, 7, 8, 12, 44, 107, 154, 168; artistic potential, 171, 172–73; emergence of digital media and, 185–86; specificity, 128, 129, 160, 167; visual experience of, 128–29
cinematic representation, 45–46, 76, 89, 90, 97–98, 144, 171
cinematograph, 1, 27, 86, 88
Clark, Florence, 123
classical film theory: Arnheim's, 13, 171–83; definition, 167–68; engagement with television, 168–70; "return to," 183
collectivization, 157, 175
colonialism, 30–32
Columbia Broadcasting Services (CBS): Paramount partnership, 116–117; radio broadcasting, 110; television broadcasting, 121, 123–25
communism, 147, 148, 151–52, 157, 158
Cosmic Voyage, The (1936), 150
Crary, Jonathan, 41–42, 52, 63
culture industry, 10, 37, 120, 166

Daguerre, Louis, 57
Delavaud, Gilles, 161
De Paiva, Adriano, 18, 35, 59
Dickson, W. K. L., and Antonia, 27
digital media, 83, 166, 168, 185–86, 187
discontinuities, 46, 47–48
Disk: A Tale of Two Passions, The (Robinson and Wall), 39–42
distances, 20, 28–32, 59; seeing at, 37, 69–72, 77, 97–102, 100
Doane, Mary Ann, 44–45, 58, 89, 94, 100, 143, 168
documentary films, 156, 157–58
domestic media, 5, 73, 110, 129, 136
Don Lee Broadcasting, 130–31
Dr. Ams Tram Grams Kikkert (1915), 94–95, 96, 98, 204n61
Druick, Zoë, 174
dystopias. *See* utopias/dystopias

Hollywood: classical system, 5, 132; studios, 116–17; television broadcasting and, 114–16, 118–19, 126–27, 131, 134
Horkheimer, Max, 107, 120

identity. *See* media identity
image transmission devices. *See* moving image transmission technologies; optical devices; television apparatus
imaginary, 20, 47, 95, 154, 187; technological, 10, 26–27, 32, 36, 92; televisual, 7, 184, 210n110
infidelity narratives, 99–101
Innis, Harold, 6
inscription, 4, 44–45, 79, 80, 83, 89
instantaneity: of communication, 28–29, 31–32, 187; modernity's obsession with, 44–45, 196n90; televisual, 7, 70, 100, 122, 146, 162; transmission, 17, 43–44, 54, 89, 102
institutionalization, 107, 108, 140, 174–75, 204n58
intermediality, 2, 13, 18, 169; Arnheim on, 171, 182–83; Gaudreault on, 8–9, 24
International Institute of Educational Cinematography, 1, 174
intertitles, 145, 161
"In the Year 2889" (Verne), 36
Italy, 12, 146, 173–74

Jenkins, Charles Francis: image transmission scheme, *61*, 105; prismatic rings, 105, 129; radio-vision apparatus, 105–7; studio and broadcasting, 121, 122–23, *123*, 130; television apparatus, 11, 22, 110, 115, 118, 128, 151, 164, 199n43

Kaes, Anton, 101
Kashnitsky, V., 149
Khlebnikov, Velimir, 149
kinetograph, 81, 82
kinetoscope: invention, 9, 27, 77–79, 80; public response, 80–82; telectroscope association, 85–86

Kino-Eye: concept, 146, 151–53, 160; moving image transmission media and, 157–58. *See also* Radio-Eye
Kinoks, 151, 153, 156–58, 160
Kino-Pravda (Vertov), 152, 156, 160, 214n59; *Radio-Pravda* (1925), 150, 212n15
Kirby, Lynne, 29
Kittler, Friedrich, 44, 67, 168, 201n15
Knudsen, Hans, 95
Korn, Arthur, 90, 92, 94–95
Koszarski, Richard, 117, 130
Kracauer, Siegfried, 169, 176–77
Krauss, Rosalind, 160

labels, 142, *143*
Land of the Changing Sun, The (Harben), 38
Lastra, James, 67
Lenin, V. I., 147, 148, 152, 156
Lenoir, Timothy, 55
Lessing, Gotthold Ephraim, 181
Lichtspiel (1930), 147
light: camera obscura and, 62; eye's sensitivity to, 50, 53, 58, 61, 62–63, 68; selenium and, 56, 58, 59–60; television devices and, 84; transmission of, 40–42; waves, 21, 60
Lodge, Oliver, 53
long-distance communication, 20, 30–32, 36, 50, 149. *See also* telegraph; telephone
Long Distance Wireless Photography (1908), 94–95, *96*, *97*
Love and Science (1912), 98–102, *100*
Lugosi, Bela, 136, 138
Lumière, Louis, 1–2, 4, 35, 84

magic lantern, 22, 43, 82, 131, 163, 193n21, 205n6
manufacturers, 110, 113, 116, 119, 120, 128
Man with a Movie Camera (1929), 145–46, 159, 160–62, *163*, 164, 212n15
Marinetti, F. T., 72, 146
Marion, Philippe, 8–9, 92, 107